THE ALMOND BLOSSOM APPRECIATION SOCIETY

A SORT OF SEQUEL TO

DRIVING OVER LEMONS

AND

A PARROT IN A PEPPER TREE

ANNIVERSARY EDITION

WITH AUTHOR INTERVIEW

THE ALMOND BLOSSOM
APPRECIATION SOCIETY

Chris Stewart

Published in June 2006 (and in this new edition 2009) by
SORT OF BOOKS,
PO Box 18678, London NW3 2FL
www.sortof.co.uk

Distributed by the Profile/Independent Alliance and TBS in all territories excluding the
United States and Canada.

Typeset in Iowan Old Style BT , THE Sans and Vitrina to a design by Henry Iles.
Printed in the UK by CPI Bookmarque, Croydon, CR0 4TD,
on Forest Stewardship Council (mixed sources) certified paper.

304pp
A catalogue record for this book is available from the British Library.
ISBN 978-0-9560038-2-9

Mixed Sources
Product group from well-managed
forests and other controlled sources
www.fsc.org Cert no. TT-COC-002227
© 1996 Forest Stewardship Council
FSC

Thanks

The longer I live the more I realise how much we depend upon one another to do everything. All the usual suspects know who they are, and I hope they are aware of my gratitude, but just in case... 1001 thanks to Nat Jansz, my miraculously understanding and skilful editor, without whom this book would not have been possible, and to Mark Ellingham, publisher and long-time friend. MOROCCO wouldn't be half as nice without the hospitality and generosity of Mohammed Benghrib. In SPAIN, José Guerrero remains a constant source of inspiration and fun; Matias Morales and Manolo del Molinillo keep me rooted, and continue to show me how to get things done; Fernando and Jesús of Nevadensis (*www.nevadensis.com*) have got me out of more tricky situations than they've got me into; Michael Jacobs makes me laugh and think; Paco Sánchez and José Pela have been the finest *tertúlia* companions; my sisters Carole and Fiona have been sterling supporters; and above all I owe everything to Ana and Chloë, who live these books with me, and are always there when I need a little comfort and joy.

In addition, CHRIS STEWART AND SORT OF BOOKS thank our invaluable design and production team: Peter Dyer, Henry Iles, Nikky Twyman, Miranda Davies, and to Paul Nobbs at Clays.

BLACK AND WHITE PHOTOS by David Aspinall, Chloë Stewart, John Mullen, Mark Ellingham, Nevadensis, Pepe Vílchez, James McConnachie, Carl Sandeman and Chris Stewart.

The Almond Blossom Appreciation Society

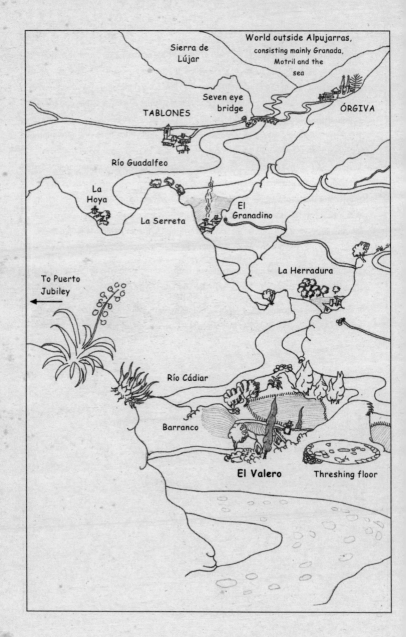

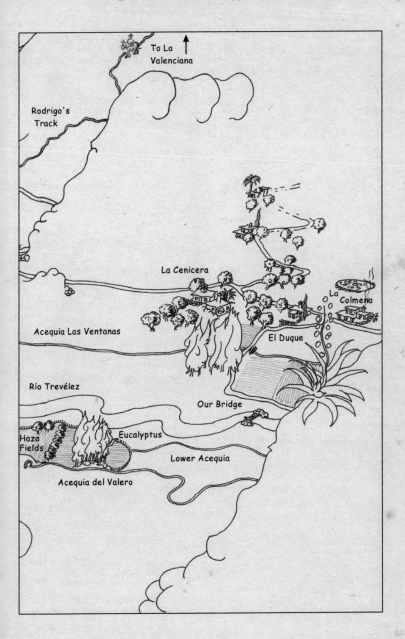

CONTENTS

PROLOGUE

On Closer Examination of a Dung Beetle

AT THE BEGINNING OF THIS YEAR, my daughter Chloë and I decided that we had to get fit, and that the best way to do this would be to create a running track in the riverbed. We go there every evening now and our pounding feet have marked out a fairly clear circuit.

The grass is long and makes a pleasant thripping noise as you race along, and in spring the ground is sprinkled with dandelions and daisies which grow so dense that, through half-shut eyes, you might be running through a field of cream. The track, however, remains just a bit too rustic for a good sprint. You have to be careful to hop over the thistles, skip to avoid an ankle-cracker of a stone, and cut in close to the *gayomba*, or Spanish broom, on the third turn, while ducking your head to avoid a poke in the eye. The second turn is between the third and fourth euphorbia bush and the start and finish is at the tamarisk tree where we hang our sweaters, and afterwards, if it's sunny, rest in the wispy shade. The going is soft sandy turf and sheep turds.

As we returned from our run the other night Chloë called me excitedly to the gate: 'Quick, Dad! Come and have a look at this!' I turned back and looked where she was pointing. There, battling its way across the track was a dung beetle doing what dung beetles do, rolling a ball of dung. I was instantly captivated: a dung beetle is one of the great sights of the insect world, the determination and purpose of its Sisyphean labour putting you in mind of the crazed industry of ants, except that *Scarabaeus semipunctatus* operates in pairs or alone.

This particular beetle had lost its jet-black shine under a thick covering of dust. It was steering the ball with its back legs, while it scrabbled for purchase with its horny front legs. Progress was unthinkably difficult as the ground was rough, and, of course, it was quite unable to see where it was going, head down, facing away from the desired direction of travel, with a huge ball of shit in the way. The ball kept going out of control and rolling over the poor creature, yet without so much as a moment to dust itself down, the beetle picked itself up and patiently resumed rolling on its intended course. Chloë and I marvelled at its dogged persistence, and felt sorry for it, and tried to suppress our giggles when the dung ball rolled over it time and again.

Now the presence of a dung beetle in our valley is a matter of some symbolic importance, being a direct result of our policy not to worm the sheep more than absolutely necessary. The sheep are fine; they have a few intestinal parasites – all such organisms do – but they live with them in a reasonably harmonious symbiotic state and as a result produce dung that's safe enough for the humble beetle to deposit its eggs in.

I know about this because I once had the privilege of chatting with a world expert on dung beetles – Jan Krikken, a Dutch entomologist whom I happened to bump into one afternoon in the valley while he was staying in our neighbour's cottage. He had been creeping along on all fours by the edge of our *acequia*, the irrigation channel, stopping from time to time to suck on his pooter – a strange device like a jamjar with two tubes sticking out of it, one with gauze at the end which you put in your mouth, and the other an open tube which you place above an insect under study. By giving the first a spirited suck, the specimen is whooshed painlessly and undamaged (if a little surprised) into the jamjar to be examined at leisure. Suck on the second, however, and the surprise is all yours.

Dr Krikken had been employed some years earlier by the Australian government to reintroduce dung beetles after decades of excessive sheep worming had all but eradicated them. There was a fear that without the beetles' help in rolling and burying the dung, it would fail to decompose and the continent would become caked in a mat of excrement. Fortunately, he had been able to save the Antipodeans from this fate. 'If you ever doubt the importance of organic farming,' he suggested to me, 'just spend some time looking at dung beetles.'

It seemed good advice, and I follow it as often as I can – and, indeed, here I was, head down and deep in contemplation. Yet, the longer I looked at our specimen, the more it seemed that something wasn't quite right. I thought about it for a bit and then the full, astonishing truth dawned on me. 'You know what, Chloë?' I announced. 'That ball is not a ball of dung at all. It's a squash ball.' I paused to let this dramatic revelation sink in.

'What's a squash ball?' she asked.

'Well, it's a ball you play squash with.'

'Yes, but what's squash?' she persisted, as any Spanish schoolgirl might.

'It's a game, where you hit a ball... with a racket... in a court... and it bounces off these three walls...'

It was at this point that I started to realise the utter fatuousness of my conjecture. The nearest squash court would probably be two hundred miles away in Marbella or Sotogrande. How, then, did a squash ball come to be rolling around in our valley propelled by a dung beetle? It made no sense. However, I'd got started on this tack now, and I wasn't about to stop. I dug down deeper into my hole.

'You see, Chloë,' I continued, 'this particular ball is just too perfect to be the work of a beetle. Look, it's absolutely spherical and perfectly uniform in colour and texture. How is a creature as ungainly as that going to create a thing so perfect from a heap of sheep shit? You tell me that. It's a rubber ball.'

Chloë looked closely at the beetle and its ball.

'It's dung, Dad. I'm sure it is. I know dung when I see it.'

'No, it's a rubber ball, child. And the awful thing is that, when this poor benighted *bicho* gets its ball home, after all that terrible effort, it's going to find that it's made of rubber and not dung, so it will neither be able to form it into a pear shape, scoop out a hollow and lay its eggs in it, which is what they do, nor eat it. It's going to break its little heart.'

'It'll be alright, Dad. It's dung, really,' Chloë reassured me. 'It's not what you think it is. Its little heart will be fine.'

I had to differ. 'No, Chloë, I know I'm right and I'm not just going to sit here and watch the poor thing being deceived like this. I'm going to take its ball away. At least then it will still have the time and energy to make itself a proper ball and get the job finished.'

Chloë was appalled. 'Don't do that, you can't do that. The poor thing will be devastated if you take it.'

'It'll be a lot less so now than after all that futile effort of rolling the cussed thing home,' I insisted.

'Dad – don't!' cried Chloë, as I crouched down next to the insect and its ball.

But I, with my fifty years of experience of the world, was adamant. I reached out a hand to pick up the dusty squash ball... and my fingers sank into the soft dung.

'Oh God, it *is* dung.'

'I told you so. Now look what you've done! You've gone and ruined it.'

I looked at the once-perfect dung ball. It was split right open, the moist dung in the centre temptingly displayed. It looked like one of those delicious chocolate-dusted truffles, with a moist greenish filling. I tried to mould it back to its earlier shape, to emulate the beetle's perfect craftsmanship, but to no avail.

'Put it back, Dad. You're only making it worse.'

I was filled with a terrible remorse. The tiny creature looked up at me disconsolately from way down on the ground. Chloë stared at me as if I were some sort of half-wit.

Gingerly I returned the squidged mound of dung to the beetle and straightened up. There was an awkward silence.

'Why?' I asked, falling back on a little wordplay to try and defuse the tension. 'Why is a beetle called *escarabajo* in Spanish?'

'What do you mean?'

'Why is an *escarabajo* called *escarabajo*?'

'I don't know. I thought "scarab" was a really old name for beetles. Why do you ask?'

'Because it's *es cara bajo* – it's face down.'

My daughter considered me thoughtfully for a moment, shook her head and set off up the hill to the house, no doubt to tell her mother.

THE BOSTONIANS

ONE OF THE GREAT CULTURAL CONTRIBUTIONS of Spain to the world is the *carmen*. Now a true carmen is an enclosed patio garden on the hill of the Albaicín in Granada, and to qualify for the name it must have a view of the Alhambra and the peaks of the Sierra Nevada beyond. Apart from that, a number of essential elements can be deployed more or less at random: these include grapevines, tall slender cypresses, orange and lemon trees, a persimmon or two, perhaps a pomegranate, and myrtle – whose scent was believed by the Moors to embody the very essence of love.

The surface of a carmen should be cobbled in the style known as *el empedrado Granadino* – a grey and white pattern, again devised by the Moors, using the river stones that occur in abundance throughout the province. There should also be a fountain and a pool and preferably a number of runnels and rills leading the water hither and thither in a fashion perfectly conceived to make you feel cool and contemplative on a hot summer's day. If the thing has been done right, the interplay between light and shade, the mingling scents of the flowers and the chuckling of the water in its channels will induce a profound contentment and sense of peace as you wander the cobbled paths, perhaps hand in hand with a good friend, musing playfully, the pair of you, upon the mysteries of the universe.

If you are really fortunate, a nightingale will come and nest in your cypress tree and then the pleasure becomes sublime. But that can't be counted on, so most *carmen* owners make do with a canary in a cage. I personally rather like the sound of caged canaries – it is one of the essentials of a Spanish street – but it hardly compares to the nightingales and, besides, the song of the caged bird should be more a source of distress than pleasure to sensitive, modern man.

Halfway up the Cuesta del Chápiz, between Sacromonte and the Albaicín, is the Carmen de la Victoria. Owned by the university, it is one of the prettiest *carmenes* in the city. I pushed open the gate and stood for a minute adjusting to the deep shade after the brightness of the street with its glaring white walls. I was passing through the city on the way home from a trip to Málaga, and had come here partly to visit the *carmen* – but mainly to see my friend Michael.

Michael Jacobs is an art historian, a writer, a traveller and a scholar and a formidable cook, as well as being one of the most entertaining people I know. Somewhere within the confines of the *carmen* he was holding court to a group of English tourists who had paid good money to be guided around the cultural monuments of Andalucía. Michael had doubtless dazzled them that morning with his erudition and somewhat unorthodox views on the Alhambra: he likes to point out that, given how much of the Moorish palace was rebuilt after a fire at the end of the nineteenth century, it is about as authentic as the Alhambra Palace Hotel down the hill. Now there would be a slack period while they wandered among the delights of the *carmen*, sinking a drink or two before lunch.

I came upon Michael pacing to and fro along a rose arbour, talking agitatedly on his mobile phone. He was gesticulating wildly and occasionally clapping his free hand to his head. Some catastrophe was clearly assailing him, as it tends to do, for he is a person who hovers happily on the very verge of chaos. An ordinary mortal's carefully laid plans, meticulous organisation and unsurprising results would be hell for him – even if he were able to aspire to such a mode of existence.

I waited, sat on a bench and watched as two tiny white butterflies wove in and out of a trellis of dusty pink roses. At last Michael was finished. We embraced in a sort of manly Mediterranean bear hug – a gesture by which we seek to confound the stiffness of our Anglo-Saxon upbringings. 'Ah yes, Chris... That's w-wonderful... Just the man... It's good you're here, actually, because... W-would you like a beer, yes you must have a beer...'

We moved to the bar where I ordered a wine; I've never much liked Spanish beer. 'Well, actually,' resumed Michael, 'what I was thinking w-was... have you ever been on one of those... it's just that... I know there are people who... w-why don't you?' He was saved from having to commit himself to anything more substantial by the ringing of his phone. 'Excuse me, Chris' – he looked at the screen – 'Ah, it's Jeremy again. Ah... H-hallo, Jeremy... Yes Jeremy...' There followed a conversation if possible even more inconclusive than the one I had just been involved in.

Michael has the energy, proportionate to his size, of an insect, and races about at great speed on unpredictable courses full of hesitations and volte-faces, but somehow manages to achieve a great deal, in much the same way, I suppose, as the insect does. He has published, I think, twenty-six books, and never more than three, he says happily, with the same publisher. And all these books are the sort of books for which you need to do immense quantities of research and have reams of arcane knowledge at your disposal. He forever has some new project on the boil. As well as his copious output he has the most terrifying capacity for drinking and socialising that I have ever encountered. He will stay out carousing in bars and knocking back gargantuan quantities of wine until four or five in the morning and then wake at seven to hurl himself into the next day with not the faintest trace of a hang-over. One imagines that an organism that receives such constant and merciless battering would soon fall to bits, but no – at fifty, Michael is as vital and lively as ever.

'Ah yes... Chris, I've got a bit of a problem with this group... or not so much this group as another one. You see I'm... erm... double-booked... well, not exactly double-booked but I was supposed to stay available in case the itinerary changed and it... erm... has, and I'm... erm... not...' He looked decidedly sheepish. 'I'm booked in to lecture to a whole load of college students instead. Jeremy's having a nervous breakdown over it.'

'Who's Jeremy?'

'Ah, Jeremy... you'd like Jeremy... Well, actually he's quite a strange sort of person... Very... erm... organised.'

'Yes, but who is he?'

'Ah yes, well, Jeremy runs these tours for well-heeled Americans...'

'Oh, I see now,' I said, although in fact I didn't.

'As a matter of fact...' said Michael, studying me with an odd intensity. 'Yes, you could be. I mean, w-why not...?'

I returned the stare, as the meaning of Michael's look and meandering words began to dawn on me. It was maybe a not very striking coincidence that we both happened to be wearing black jeans, white collarless shirts and black leather jackets that had seen better days. But the resemblance went beyond that. We both wore round glasses, both had thinning curly grey hair and rather rubicund complexions, and although Michael loomed half a head taller, we were of similar build.

Michael was by now smiling complacently, with the look of one who has resolved a mathematical conundrum. 'You d-don't by any chance fancy spending a few days in Seville do you, Chris?' he asked, in a tone that seemed deliberately casual.

'You mean, impersonating you – and taking round one of your groups?!'

'Er... yes, that's more or less what I had in mind.'

'They'd rumble us. I mean I may look a bit like you and even dress a bit like you, but I know bugger all about art!'

'Oh, that doesn't matter a bit. I've got some books you can borrow right here in my bag and you've got all of the ones I've written on Andalucía. And there's some pamphlets about the group, too – they're inside the b-books.'

Michael's head almost completely disappeared into an ancient, scuffed leather briefcase. He emerged clutching a couple of books, and a few nondescript twigs which he stared at in amazement and then tossed aside. 'You'll be fine,' he assured me, handing over the haul. 'You're used to giving talks and you read Spanish, don't you? So at the worst you can just translate the gallery's captions.'

There's something immensely encouraging about Michael, which makes a madcap scheme, coupled with the offer of an all-perks-included midweek break in Seville, seem oddly attractive. 'Okay,' I said. 'I'm on.'

'Well, of course you are,' he clapped me on the shoulder. 'That's w-wonderful. They'll be meeting me... um... you in the foyer at the Hotel Alfonso XIII at 10am on Monday and the first trip's to...' He rummaged among the papers. 'Ah yes, the Giralda, quite exquisite and easy to explain. You just turn up and talk about the Moors. I'll square it all with Jeremy, who'll go with you.'

And so it was that I found myself launched on a new career path, as lecturer on Andalucían art and architecture, shepherd to wealthy American art lovers, and Michael Jacobs impersonator. I strolled down the hill to the city and turned in at the doorway of the Librería Urbana to pick up the tools of my new trade.

A slight feeling of nausea crept over me there, confronted by a shelf full of art history books, but I forced myself to get a grip and limit the search to the buildings we would be visiting in Seville. I would bone up on each subject the night before – a tried and tested measure that had got me through school (though admittedly not through any actual exams). Still, I had a whole four days ahead of me to get up to speed. It would be fine. These wealthy Americans were bound to have more money than erudition. And thus I comforted myself as I drove out of Granada towards the provincial town of Órgiva and the remote patch of mountainside that I call home.

●

'Who are these people, then, Chris?' asked my wife Ana, leaning over my shoulder as I pored over the brochures that had spilled from Michael's book. Porca, our parakeet and Ana's familiar, seemed to echo the question in squawks from a new perch he'd made on the top of my art history pile.

'Um, well, they're all Americans and...' I scanned the printed sheet again as if unwilling to take in the import of the words. 'Well, it seems that they're the Trustees of the Boston Museum of Fine Arts. Hell's teeth! And they're not just ordinary trustees either... They're a sort of elite – they all cared enough about fine art to donate over a million dollars to the museum, which is what seems to have qualified them for a place on this jaunt.'

Ana fixed me with one of her steady looks. 'You can't do it, Chris. It won't work. You'll just have to phone Michael and tell him it's impossible. You could offer to help out a bit, but you surely can't go through with this stunt!'

She was right, of course. I needed to talk to Michael, and soon. But then again, I hate to let a friend down and I really do believe that most things will work out in the end if you sit back and let them. So I put the phone call off, got on with other chores and leafed casually through the odd art book while waiting for the kettle to boil or for Chloë to get ready for school. And before I knew it Sunday night had hurtled along, leaving me with no other choice but to do some last minute homework and present myself to the good Bostonians.

Now, I pride myself that I can absorb books as well as the next literate being. But I am constitutionally unable to swot. As soon as I have to glean information for any real purpose, my eyes glaze over or rake the room for a distraction, and before I know it I'm either asleep with my head on the book cover or replacing the strings on my guitar and tuning them up. That night it was sleep that got me and at ten o'clock Chloë took pity and woke me with tea and an offer to test me on the differences between Almoravid and Almohad motifs. However, we soon gave it up for a bad job and went out to lock up the sheep and chickens instead.

It was a beautiful night. Bumble and Big, our dogs, rocketed down to the river, barking the trail of a wild boar. The air was light and balmy and suffused with the summer scent of jasmine and wild lavender. It was a night for having not a care in the world and yet I was bowed down with foreboding. A feeling that returned with double intensity when I rose the next morning, slipped on my one respectable outfit and set off to Seville.

●

The Hotel Alfonso XIII, I portentously explained to my car windscreen, is a somewhat overblown nineteenth-century building in the neo-Mauresque style – as evidenced by the blue tilework juxtaposed with the fancy bricks. It is also one of the most expensive hotels in Spain, and as I pulled into the forecourt, and stated my purpose, I began to feel sweaty, sticky and distinctly out of place. All the more so as I walked around to the imposing front entrance, where a group of hoods in shades and dark suits milled around a fleet of black Mercedes with smoked windows, waiting for a meeting of Andalucían captains of industry to end.

There seemed an edginess to this gathering – a visible hint of the murky underworld that supports the super-rich. Shuffling through them I was nearly at the steps when something small and white caught my eye. There on the ground, between two gleaming black Mercedes, lay a tiny white pigeon. Some of the hoods were peering down at the bird, not at all sure what to make of it. One of them fidgeted beneath his sharp suit jacket, perhaps itching to whip out his revolver and take a pot shot.

Somehow the plight of the creature resonated with my own predicament, so I muscled my way nonchalantly in amongst the heavies and demanded to know what was going on.

'It's a baby. Fallen off a roof. Can't fly.'

'Well… what are you going to do about it?' I asked, fixing the nearest hood with a stern eye.

'Nothing,' he said. 'The cats can get it, or Tonio can run it over for us when he pulls out.' He sniggered nastily.

'Oh, come on now!' I expostulated. 'Have you no hearts? Look at the poor little thing shivering with fear.'

The hood looked nervously at his colleagues and shrugged, nonplussed perhaps as much by hearing a foreigner speak with a strong country accent as by my championing of the bird. I stooped to gather up the terrified creature in my cupped hands.

'You really don't want to do that,' suggested one of the suits, who had crowded around, eager to see what was going on.

'And why not?' I proferred pugnaciously, holding up the bird so everyone could see. I felt pretty good – sort of heroic – amid this assembly of gangsters.

'They got diseases – and fleas. Aerial rats they are, pigeons. And the little babies are just as bad.'

'Nonsense,' I said, but looked cautiously down at the tiny creature in my hands, all the same. Sure enough, on each wrist was an army of the most infinitesimal insects imaginable, swarming in their thousands up my wrists, heading for my shirt cuffs and the warmer parts of my body. I suppose they had figured that their previous host's number was up and now would be a good time to jump ship. I yelped and ran over to the garden, where I dumped the pigeon in a flowerbed. Sure as hell the cats would get it there, but it was, after all, only an aerial rat, and I needed to get something done about these lice, and quick.

I barged through the throng of sniggering hoods and raced up the marble stairs three at a time. The lice were moving faster now. I shot past the top-hatted flunky, spun through the revolving door, and hurtled across the vestibule. There, arrayed before me like a wedding line, exquisitely groomed and composed and shining with expensive unguents, were my Bostonians. I stopped in mid-flight, raised my seething hands and opened my mouth, but the right words eluded me. With a strangled croak, I continued my headlong dash to the cloakroom.

Once inside I tried to calm myself down by focusing on the task at hand. The first thing was to try and scrub myself down, then make some attempt to dry shirtsleeves that were actually dripping. And finally, I needed to psych myself into the infinitely knowledgeable, professorial persona of Michael Jacobs.

I managed the scrubbing part, at least, and emerged from the cloakroom more or less devoid of insect life. I smiled at the assembled Bostonians, who had turned towards me with a look of surprised but good-natured enquiry. I decided not to offer an explanation of my unorthodox entrance and sopping cuffs. 'And you must be…?' – the tall lady at the front of the group asked with a slight tilt of her well-coiffured head.

'Erm, I'm, erm…' I had rehearsed this part of the proceedings hundreds of times but instead of answering I just stood there mouthing silently like a dying cod. It was the sight of a tall, curly-haired, bespectacled man striding towards me across the lobby that had provoked this apparent identity crisis. He bore an uncanny resemblance to Michael Jacobs.

'Ah – Chris,' Michael shouted across the remaining expanse of carpet. 'This is Chris Stewart, everyone!' he announced. 'That's w-wonderful, you've come early. Chris is leading the group this afternoon and I'm going to join you all at dinner at the Torre del Oro – sumptuous fare.' There were pleasant smiles of approbation all round. 'Just one word, Chris.' And he neatly spun me to one side just out of view.

I felt my body sag with relief. 'You haven't introduced yourself to anyone yet, have you?' Michael whispered. 'Thank God for that! Jeremy threw an absolute f-fit when I told him our plan, but he's squared it with everyone now, and the great news is that you can guide them around as yourself. They've all been most w-wonderfully sympathetic, and curious – I've been handing out that book of your's to them.'

'You mean I do the tour of the Giralda and Museo de Bellas Artes as me?' I asked, amazed that they'd actually want such a dilettante at the helm.

'Er… no. Jeremy managed a change of schedule. You're taking them to the carriage museum. You can do carts and horses, can't you?' he asked, suddenly anxious again. I could – but perverse as this might sound, I was rather deflated by the idea.

We rejoined the reception. It seemed as if there were Bostonians everywhere: a murmur of cultured American tones filled the room along with the rustle of expensive clothes and the clink of ice in glasses. Throughout that day, the Bostonians were continuing to gather; private jets touched down at Seville's airport; long limousines sped into the city.

A luxury bus, the size of a smallish aeroplane, pulled up at twelve to herd us all to the carriage museum. I don't think I'd ever been in such a plush, well-upholstered vehicle before, or one with such ferocious air-conditioning. Cardigans, if not fleeces, were essential rig for travelling round Seville on that summer's day.

Jeremy joined the group just before we set off. He waited a respectful step or two to one side before springing up, checking surreptitiously that no one had been kidnapped on the walk from the kerb, and sat beside me. A suntanned man with impeccable white hair, he wore a dark blazer, quiet silk tie and smiled with great ease. But you could tell he was nervous.

'Things have to be got right,' he muttered to me as the bus moved gently into the flow of traffic. 'Just one call to a lawyer and we'd be done for. Can you imagine if they heard about that stunt Michael was planning to pull!' And he leaned forward with eyes closed and rubbed his temples. Apparently it helps with the frown lines.

At the museum the idea was to drink fizzy wine, eat tapas, get addressed by local dignitaries and, time permitting, look at some of the exhibits before departing again for lunch. 'All you have to do, Chris,' explained Jeremy, 'is keep things pleasant, and if they want to know anything about Spain and the Spanish, you tell them. Okay? And, oh-dear-lord, can you do anything about those shirt cuffs?'

Apart from the cuffs it was an easy enough task. These were people groomed in the well-bred, polished manners of Boston's patrician class and keeping them pleasant was a bit like asking a group of teenagers to be moody. They even smiled graciously while I paraphrased and embellished captions they had already just translated perfectly competently for themselves. To be honest, I couldn't work up too much enthusiasm for the horse-drawn coaches; it was nice that somebody was keeping them polished, but the truth is that Americans do that sort of thing much better than anybody else.

Later that evening the luxury bus was again purring outside the hotel, waiting to drive us a half-dozen blocks to our destination for dinner. I suggested we left it where it was and made use of the beautiful night to work up an appetite. Everybody enthusiastically agreed and we set off, in one of the most improbable crocodiles I've ever been part of, along the palm-lined river bank of the

Guadalquivir, marvelling at the luminous glow of leaves in the light of the streetlamps. 'Now this is a worry,' whispered Jeremy, through the corner of his mouth. 'If someone so much as loses a heel or steps in donkey shit, we could be in serious trouble, you know!' But I could tell that even *he* was starting to relax a bit, swinging his blazer over his shoulder.

Michael managed to join us for the tail-end of our dinner in the courtyard of a fabulously furnished sixteenth-century *palacete* or mansion. Just as the waiters were circulating with plates of *petits fours*, he burst in and, hovering around the tables with the trajectory of a bee in a lavender bush, plonked himself on a chair beside me.

'Ah, Chris,' he intoned, craning his neck to study the beautifully carved marble fountains and scan the aftermath of the feast, 'what a sybarite you've become!'

It turned out that he had hot-footed it from dinner with the university students. In fact, he had been on a binge of double booking all day: two large meals and as many pre- and post-prandial drinks as could mathematically be accommodated. A lesser man would have gone under, but Michael was in his element. Indeed, as the Bostonians were seen safely back to the Alfonso XIII, he clearly felt the night was young. 'W-what we need, Chris, is to w-wind d-down a bit. An extra glass or two would do us good.'

Michael knew Seville well: he'd lived for years in the city and had many friends. We drank with most of them that night, in the sort of bars you'd never normally find – let alone go into. Returning to the Alfonso XIII at five in the morning, I stood in the bathroom, swaying slightly and trying to focus on the haggard face staring back at me through rheumy eyes. It looked sorely in need of some plain country living.

Next morning Michael seemed, if anything, rejuvenated, and as we arrived at the Bellas Artes museum, slipped back into the persona of art expert. In we trooped, about twenty of us, our rubbery trainers squeaking on the marble floors, as he hurried us at great speed through room after room – 'You don't want to b-bother with any of this stuff – constipated, sycophantic, depressingly conventional' – until at last we reached a sculpture or painting he thought worthy of our attention.

It was a figure of a kneeling Saint Jerome, carved by Torrigiani. Michael then launched into a virtuoso display of art lore and gossip ('...and to think that the man who sculpted these delicate features should have broken the nose of Michelangelo and been hounded from Florence!') before whisking us upstairs to admire Zurbaran's panel of Saint Hugo presenting a joint of lamb to Carthusian monks. 'The world's first icon of vegetarianism,' Michael declared, pointing out how the lamb had spontaneously combusted to prevent the monks breaking their vow to eschew the eating of meat.

It was a real tour de force and I felt privileged to be a part of it. But it was the evening's visit to Seville's massive cathedral that most strongly encapsulated the trip. The cathedral's builders boasted that successive generations would regard them as mad, in their ambition of scale. But they could not have imagined the true strangeness of the scene that was to unfold. As we arrived at the northwest gate, where a stuffed crocodile known as the Apothecary's Lizard hangs from the rafters, it took a while to grasp that uniformed security guards were actually clearing the public from the building. Shortly, one of the guards came over and addressed us in deferential English: 'If you'd like to come this way, please...' The cathedral authorities had emptied the building, the largest church in Europe after St Peter's in Rome, for less than two dozen visitors. I wondered just what sort of donation Jeremy must have put in the poor-box.

The emptiness was all the more disorientating when we were assembled in the choir stalls, and the cathedral organist, dressed impeccably in a grey suit, stepped across the marble tiles to put his instrument through its paces. 'This is the highest note – that little pipe up there,' he told us, pointing to a tiny pipe nestling miles above among at least four thousand others. He pressed the key and from the tiny pipe came a peep so high and thin that you'd imagine only the keenest-eared bat could appreciate it. 'And this is the lowest...' It seemed that the very chasms of the earth were being sundered open somewhere deep in the crypt.

Then he played a few pieces, doubtless full of nuance and emotion, though I couldn't really enjoy them. Organ recitals remind me inescapably of school: first they depress me a little, then send me into an uneasy doze. The Bostonians, too, began dropping off in ones and twos, and it was a relief to be suddenly jarred awake by the organ's last shuddering bass notes and to be ushered out again into the fresh air and light, by our secret entrance. Looking back I noticed the congregation reforming to take up their private devotions again, while tourists streamed along the main aisles. It was good to be back amid the bustle of the Sevillian throng ourselves, off in search of an evening's pleasure.

Against my fears and expectations, my role as tour guide had been an easy one – Michael had miraculously appeared for all the big numbers and had managed to appear at all the dinners. However, the final evening set a challenge even he could not defy. We were to be treated to the best seats in the house for the Seville Opera, to see *La Traviata*. But the musicians had gone on strike. They did so at the last minute, so there we were, the Bostonians in their evening wear, all dressed up, with nowhere to go.

'W-well, this is an opportunity,' declared Michael to everyone. 'We can't have opera, but we can have litera-ture. Chris has most kindly agreed to read to you from his m-marvellous book.' It was hardly on a par with Verdi, I felt, and nor did it seem right, somehow, to be offering this black-leg labour. But we headed to a bar in the Barrio Santa Cruz, ordered a dozen bottles of house wine, and had a genuinely jolly evening of it.

We read the next morning, however, that the conductor at the Opera, exasperated by the intransigence of the musi-cians, had walked onto the stage, swished his tails over the edge of the piano stool and played the entire work of *La Traviata* as a solo piano recital. The crowd were ecstatic and the press proclaimed it one of the city's greatest ever cultural events. I don't think I was the only one who felt a bit short-changed.

FENCING FOR BEGINNERS

Not long after I returned from Seville, I was standing beside the cooker, gathering the nerve to flip a frying pan full of *tortilla de patatas* onto a plate, when the phone rang.

'Telephone...' Chloë called out.

'Well it won't be for me, so I'm not getting it,' said Ana.

'Nor am I – I'm busy,' I muttered, pushing some bits of potato back into the amorphous mound.

'Well, it won't be for me, as everyone calls me on my mobile,' Chloë noted smugly.

'Well it'll just have to ring, that's all,' I insisted. And so it did, bleating from its place in the draughty corner by the door.

'Look,' argued Ana, 'if it's really important, then whoever it is will ring back, won't they?'

The phone finally stopped ringing, and with a simultaneous sigh we turned our attention to the neat round disc of egg and potatoes that I had plonked on the table. Then it rang again. Everybody looked at one another accusingly. At last, Chloë broke the silence: 'It must be important; they've called back.'

'Aha, but how can you be sure it's the same person? It might be someone else,' I suggested.

It was Ana who finally snapped. Glaring at us she pushed back her chair and went over to the telephone.

'*Hola, dígame,*' she growled in the grumpy tone she uses to intimidate time-wasters. Then, turning towards the phone with a surprised smile, she relaxed and her voice took on a new note of warmth. From this subtle shift in tone, Chloë and I deduced that it was Antonia.

'That was Antonia,' she announced when she finally rejoined us. 'She was ringing from Holland to say that Yacko has escaped…' Antonia was the Dutch sculptor who had been living for the last six years with our neighbour Domingo, in the farm across the river. Yacko was her parrot.

'How could he, though?' I asked. 'I thought she clipped his feathers.'

'They grow back. You have to keep doing it regularly. Anyway, she's desperate. Domingo, apparently, has spent all day trying to capture the bird, but whenever he gets close Yacko just flits away to the next tree. It was partly his idea that she phoned. They think I'll be more successful.'

It was hard to imagine Domingo abandoning his flock of sheep for a day to wander about the hillside looking for his girlfriend's parrot; and from what I'd gathered, he had never been very keen on Antonia's parrots in the first place. But it was his fault that Yacko had escaped, and Antonia was frantic, saying that she would have to fly back early from Holland if the bird wasn't recaptured. Antonia had gone back to visit the foundry she uses, near Utrecht, to have some models cast in bronze – one of them a rather fine centaur that Domingo had posed for (the top half, of course).

'She must be crazy,' I hazarded. 'For the cost of a plane ticket she could buy herself half a dozen African Greys and much finer specimens than that one.'

'That's hardly the point, though, Chris,' Ana replied frostily. And, as if to echo her words, Porca, who had been sitting on my shoulder, leaned forward to take a pull from my wineglass. (Those who have read before of my abysmal relationship with Ana's parakeet will note that we have reached an uneasy truce – he is willing to tolerate me in order to enjoy my facilities, such as broader shoulders for a perch and a more readily available glass of wine (I top mine up more frequently than Ana.)

'I promised I'd give it a try,' said Ana, 'but how I'm going to find a grey parrot amongst the olive groves of El Duque, let alone catch it, is anybody's guess.'

She had a point. A grey parrot amongst all those silvery leaves would be pretty well camouflaged.

'Oh, well. We'd better turn in early and start at first light before he gets restless,' she concluded, with a note of resignation.

It didn't seem worth commenting on, but I couldn't actually recall having volunteered for the expedition.

●

At a quarter past nine, which is as close to first light as Ana gets, we shut the dogs in the house and set off across the valley. I wasn't quite sure what my role was supposed to be; I'm blind as a plaster cat, as the Spanish would have it, and thus was hardly likely to spot the errant bird. But Ana seemed to think that an extra pair of hands and eyes, however short-sighted, might turn out to be useful.

As we crossed the river I looked up at the great expanse of terraced hillside that rises from El Duque up to Cerro Negro, at what must be a couple of thousand silver-grey olive trees, growing amongst the greyish rock and stone and the dusty grey vegetation. It seemed impossible that we'd find a small grey parrot in all that lot. He could be anywhere by now.

'I can't see how we're going to find Domingo,' I mused as we left the path and struck up the hill. 'Let alone the parrot.'

'Don't be so feeble... There's Domingo anyway.'

And there he was, wandering amongst Bernardo's olive groves, a muscular figure, in old jeans and a threadbare shirt, scanning the horizon with one hand shading his eyes. He saw us and beckoned us over, a brief smile of relief flitting across his features.

'*Hola*, Domingo. How's it going? Any luck?'

'*Nada, nada*... Every time I get near him he ups and hops off into the next tree. I was trying to catch him all of yesterday, and today I've not caught sight of him. Trouble is, he doesn't like me much – but then, I don't like him so much, either. I tell you, I've had it with parrots. Maybe you'll have more luck, Ana,' he said turning towards her. 'Your voice is similar – if you call him, maybe he'll fly to you.'

So we split up and ambled to and fro amongst the olive trees, Domingo and I keeping quiet, and Ana calling every now and then 'Yacko, Yacko', in imitation of that peculiar way the Dutch have of speaking with the tongue cloven to the roof of the mouth and the lips not moving. It sounded quite authentic.

After ten minutes or so, we regrouped.

'Tell me some words in Dutch, Chris,' Ana demanded.

I'd lived in Amsterdam during a mis-spent period of my youth and could still summon up something of the language. I reeled off obediently one of the few phrases that had somehow stuck in my mind.

'So what does all that mean?'

'Not too much mayonnaise on the chips, please,' I confessed.

Ana raised an eyebrow. 'Chris,' she said with an exasperated look, 'can you just try and take this seriously?'

The morning drew on with the sun moving high over the hills of the Contraviesa, casting deep shadows among the olive trees and glinting off the Cádiar River as it snaked along the gorge below. I sat in the shade, drowsily following my wife's voice calling in a slightly stagey accent from the terraces below. '*Yacko, Yacko, kom hier, Yacko. Kom hier, alsjij-blieft*' (Yacko, Yacko, come here, if you please), she cried – a dull but courteous admonishment which suited the bird rather well.

Antonia actually has two African Greys. One is an ancient bird who has been in her family for over thirty years, and who can't fly at all as he has lost most of his feathers. He seems content to scuttle about behind the fridge, imitating the radio, which he does uncannily well, and muttering the word 'Yacko' to himself – Yacko being his name. Then there's the younger one, the escapee we were looking for; his name is Yacko, too. *Yacko*, apparently, means 'African Grey' in Dutch. Luckily this was unlikely to cause any confusion here, as Yacko was probably the only Dutch-speaking African Grey loose in our valley at the time.

It struck me, as I waited for the bird to respond to his lacklustre tag, that the Dutch approach to choosing a name was not so very far removed from that of the rural Spanish. People here take a similarly literal approach: 'Mulo', for example, is the name of choice for a mule, and 'Burro' (meaning 'donkey') for a donkey. And if those names are taken, then there is always the colour of the beast to fall back on: 'Pardo' ('brown') or 'Negro' ('black'), for instance.

At least that is how it has been for generations, although changes are creeping in. I know an Irish architect who lives in a village in the high Alpujarras and keeps a mule called 'Preciosa'. He told me that his neighbours were so taken with this name for a mule that they'd followed suit and given more imaginative names to their own dogs, mules and even (in one instance) goats. And then there was Manolo, who helps out with the farm work at El Valero. He told me that he was thinking of buying a mule from an English couple in the town: 'It's called Pinfloy,' he confided, looking baffled, wondering if I could shed some light on the matter. I couldn't, though some time later I met the couple, who asked fondly after their mule, 'Pink Floyd'. Manolo had by then renamed the animal 'Tordo', which is the traditional name for white mules. 'It's a lot easier to shout than "Pinfloy",' he explained.

My reverie at this point was suddenly interrupted by an urgent call from Ana. She had spotted Yacko. He was sitting contemplating the fruits of freedom from the branch of an olive tree not a stone's throw from where I was sitting.

We all crept silently towards the tree from our respective places. There he was, grey as dust with a flash of bright red tail... Now to catch the bugger. I was told to stand stock still, being the likeliest to balls up the operation, while Ana took up position below the tree and began to coax the wretched bird down in her faux-Dutch.

The dim-witted creature seemed to be fooled, and edged closer to Ana to get a better look. Meanwhile Domingo, in accordance with our prearranged plan, crept out along the branch towards the parrot. Beneath his weight the branch lowered towards Ana, who held out the special stick that Antonia uses for training parrots (not to hit them with, but as a portable perch). Yacko stepped meekly onto the stick and thence to Ana's shoulder, where he stared at her fixedly for a bit, wondering if he might not have made a mistake. But, too late – at that instant Domingo leapt and flung his jacket over the foolish bird.

We'd done it. The mission had been a success. With the infuriated creature squawking and screeching from inside the jacket, we walked down towards La Colmena, Domingo's house. We were all feeling rather pleased with ourselves, and the usually phlegmatic Domingo seemed almost light-headed with relief. Suddenly he could look forward with pleasure, rather than dread, to his partner's return. I could sense, too, that Ana, a person of normally modest demeanour, was rather proud of her own part in the adventure.

'We should celebrate,' I declared, although my own part in the triumph was slightly harder to discern. 'A glass of wine is just what we need.'

'I really should be taking the sheep out. I don't like to leave them penned in too long,' Domingo demurred. Then in an entirely uncharacteristic change of heart: 'Well, a glass or two first won't do any harm.'

●

Domingo spends most of his time walking in the valley and hills with his sheep. That's what you have to do when your flock grows too large to graze on your farm, and at getting on for three-hundred-and-fifty sheep, he has built up one of the largest flocks in the area. On rare occasions – when he needs to drive to Málaga to pick up Antonia or drop off a sculpture at a gallery, for instance – he will let the sheep loose for a few hours in a field of sorghum and forage maize that he's fenced off specially for those occasions. But he has simply too many sheep to leave grazing in the same place for long.

Now, there's a certain romance in ranging the hills all day with one's flock, getting to know intimately every rock and tree, and Domingo takes a real pleasure in the beauty of the landscape. He loves to amble amongst the cliffs at the top of Campuzano, and on summer nights, when Antonia can join him, to sleep beneath the stars high in the wild meadows of El Picacho. But there are also serious drawbacks to having to graze sheep in this way. When you're out walking with the flock, that's more or less all you can do; you can't linger at home with your partner, or read, or finish a piece of sculpting, or mend your tractor. And although Domingo and Antonia rarely complain about their lot, I know that there are days – especially when Antonia is about to leave for Holland – when they long to spend more time together.

Antonia also worries that Domingo is neglecting his considerable artistic talent. She's convinced that he is a gifted sculptor in his own right – he is certainly the only shepherd we know who exhibits bronzes in prestigious galleries in Granada and on the coast, but he insists that the flock must come first. 'We don't own this piece of land we live on; these sheep are the only security we have,' he explains in his gentle but firm manner. 'Maybe people want bronze sculptures, and maybe they won't, but they'll always need lamb.'

And there is an end of it.

Although I was the one who introduced sheep into our valley, I had always assumed that I would keep a modest flock and fence them in. There are, after all, only so many sheep a farm can sustain without being turned into a dusty desert and I knew I couldn't take them grazing – I don't have the sort of fortitude to stick with it and ignore all other temptations. Had I known, though, what a Herculean task the fencing of El Valero would become, I might well have shelved my pastoral plans altogether.

Our farm sits on a steep fold of mountainside that slopes down from a lower peak of the Sierra Nevada, through wild scrubland and almond groves; from there it drops into a river valley on one side and a sheer gorge on the other. This is an awful lot of perimeter to cover, so I limited myself to fencing the riverbed edge to stop the sheep from paddling across the ford and tucking into the orchards and vegetable crops of our neighbours. Few at the time would have bothered with fences other than to keep the wild boar out of their maize or alfalfa. The land at the bottom of the farm is flat, with a decent track running alongside to transport wire and poles, so in just a few days I managed to string together a more or less serviceable fence and position some appropriately Alpujarran bedsteads as gates.

To my great surprise the sheep seemed impressed by the barrier and kept away from it. Too far away, in fact, because they upped and disappeared instead over the topmost part of our land to roam across the wild scrubland at the foothills of the Sierra Nevada. Time and again I'd have to slog all the way up to the lower peaks, aptly known as Los Peñones Tristes – The Sad Rocks – to try and coax them down. Eventually, I resigned myself to the fact that I would have to fence the hillside as well.

Now, the hillside above our farm is not just steep, but is made up of uneven and broken rock covered with barely an inch and a half of topsoil. It would be hard to imagine a worse place to try hammering in fence posts. But I was younger then, and full of enthusiasm about creating the first sheep enclosures in the Alpujarras. So I plunged myself into the work with a will, loading five thick steel rods onto my shoulder, trudging up the projected fence-line, and dropping a post off every half dozen paces.

It was heavy, back-breaking work that became significantly harder with each load. By the end of the third day I was scrabbling up an almost perpendicular quarter-mile with the rods before I could even begin to pace out the land and drop them off. At the end of the week both my shoulders were bleeding and raw, and my thigh muscles were as hard as bones.

Next there was the business of making holes and hammering in the posts, more often than not into solid rock. That took me a good day, and a bit of the next morning. Then I decided I deserved a day off, before I got started with setting up the strainers and stringing the wires.

Including the day off, it took me two full weeks to fence from the slope by the house up to the top and then along the upper border of our land. On the fifteenth day, in order to admire my handiwork, I walked up the completed side and along the top and sat down in the scrub to contemplate the long run down to the river on the south side of the farm. It was the roughest, most tormented piece of hillside I had ever seen; it made the part I had already done seem like fencing a children's playground. I looked at it long and hard, thought about it for a bit... and decided to have nothing further to do with the job. Maybe the sheep wouldn't like the look of the land, either, and steer away from that side of the farm.

When Ana found out that I had fenced just two sides of the farm and left the third side to chance, she gave me a withering look. 'Surely', she had the temerity to suggest, 'an unfinished ring-fence is no fence at all?' She did have a point, but when I suggested that perhaps she herself might like to get up there and finish it off, she backed down.

The very next day the sheep ambled up the hill, keeping close to the fenceline, which they regarded with some curiosity. When they got to the top they turned around the last fence post and continued their inspection, this time ambling downhill on the other side. Then, after fifty metres or so, they dropped straight down into a steep *barranco*, and left the farm, spending the day ranging to and fro on the heights above the Trevélez River. Of course, when they returned in the evening they couldn't find their way back in. I had succeeded in fencing them out.

So that was the reward for my labours: a hard day rounding up the flock and marching them back up the mountainside in order to guide them back around the fence. However, over the next few weeks and months, the sheep gradually got the measure of the farm's limits and a contentment to stay within it. These days, they very rarely take it into their heads to make a sortie far into the hills, and when they do they usually find the right way back, using the now rather slack pieces of wire as a half-hearted visual prompt. They have developed what hill farmers call 'heft', a flock's communal knowledge of its grazing boundaries.

●

A couple of days after Antonia returned from Holland I met her on the road walking back from town. You can tell her from a distance by her slight frame crowned by a large floppy hat. She waved me down for a chat and asked with her eyes crinkled into a smile, 'Have you seen Domingo?'

'No, not today,' I answered. Then, glancing across the river, 'Isn't that him on the rock beneath the canebreak, talking with Jesús?' For the last two decades Jesús Carrasco has walked his three hundred goats down through the olive groves to graze in our valley, and on the odd occasion when their paths coincide, he and Domingo stop to fill one another in on local gossip.

'Yes,' she replied. 'He's got something to show you, a present I brought him from Holland. I've been plotting it for ages.'

'I'll go and inspect it right away,' I promised, smiling back; not that I had a clue what Antonia was talking about, but she seemed so pleased with herself it was infectious.

By the time I reached Domingo, Jesús and his flock had begun to move up the hillside, the goats daintily skipping from rock to rock. Domingo's horse, tethered to a clump of coarse grass, was contentedly munching on a bramble, and its master was sitting on a rock gazing at the hill above. He was listening to the sound of the bells of his flock, and picking it out from the orchestral bongling of Jesús's departing goats; once you're used to them, each set of bells is as clear and as subtly different as birdsong.

I sat down beside Domingo to pass the time of day. 'Want to see something good?' he asked, watching the hill.

'I don't mind,' I responded, in the phlegmatic way of locals hereabouts. 'Always nice to see something good. What did you have in mind?'

Domingo ignored this bit of playful banter and pointed up. The hill is steep and rocky and overgrown with the sort of maquis that grows in this part of Andalucía – low bushes of *genista* and *anthyllis* and tall wispy-fronded *retama*. It was quite hard to make out amongst this scrub Domingo's enormous flock of sheep, spread far and high across the hillside. But I could hear the bells, busy with some concerted movement, and occasionally I could glimpse a gaggle of sheep, bobbing like rocking-horses as they scuttled down the serpentine path that led to the bridge. Soon the first few of them showed up, galloping down in a cloud of dust, then another sheep and then some more, until little by little the whole flock was gathered around us, smelling sweetly of hot wool and rosemary, coughing and farting copiously. Finally there came a few stragglers, followed by Domingo's scurvy pack of dogs: mad-eyed Mora, three-legged Curro, and several curs without names... and then, something I'd never expected to see amongst Domingo's menagerie, a beautiful, shiny black-and-white Border collie. The dog moved low and slow through the flock and came to a halt by our rock, where she looked up at Domingo.

'This is what I meant,' he said, tousling the dog's head. 'This is Chica.'

I was amazed, partly by the way he was showing affection towards the dog – Domingo had always seen his pack of dogs as more of a necessary evil than as potential pets – and partly because of the fact that, years before, unimpressed with the way his motley assortment of curs worked the sheep, I had offered to get him a proper sheepdog from Britain. But Domingo, as always fiercely independent, had declined the offer, saying that he could manage perfectly well with the existing pack. I resisted the temptation to remind him of this, and confined myself to asking where he had got his new dog from.

'Antonia brought her from Holland,' he explained. 'She'd been planning to get her since meeting the mother the year before, but had kept it as a surprise.' Chica put her forepaws on his knee and looked up at him adoringly. 'I'm going to train her,' he continued. 'I've never seen a dog as intelligent and willing to work as this one. She'll be wonderful with the sheep.'

'Well, Domingo,' I said. '*Enhorabuena* – congratulations – she's a real little beauty.'

From then on I hardly saw Domingo without Chica trotting by his side. And around three months later, when I returned after a trip to London, I came across the pair of them, surrounded by sheep, sitting by the bridge. Domingo had seen my car and was waiting for me. He beckoned me over. 'It's still early days, and she hasn't practised this much, but watch,' he demanded.

Some of the flock were heading across the bridge, probably with the idea of having a crack at Juan Barquero's olive trees while Domingo wasn't looking. He gave a low whistle and a click of the tongue and nodded his head in the direction of the recalcitrant sheep. Like a flash Chica was gone, round the edge of the flock, down the bank and across the river – which needed a bit of swimming. Then she slipped up the steps on the far side of the bridge and confronted the offenders. The sheep took one look and doubled back to the flock. Chica crept quietly over the bridge and lay down on it, and there she stayed, her head between her paws, eyeing the sheep with an occasional glance at Domingo for approval.

I was staggered – as much by Domingo's skill as a trainer as by the dog herself. It also made me feel a little nostalgic for my previous life as a shepherd in England. To enter a huge field rolling across the downs, and with a quiet command send your dog racing low across to a distant flock of sheep and return, driving them before her, is a truly wonderful experience. Our own dogs, Big and Bumble, are both good and loyal pets, but they're not worth a light when it comes to sheep work. There's a lack of professionalism about them, an excitability that gets in the way. It's not their fault: they weren't designed for the job, and besides, with a little flock that's used to going in and out of the stable morning and night, there's not much call for the virtuoso stuff.

A TEENAGE FROG HUNT

MY DAUGHTER CHLOË IS A TEENAGER now, and this brings with it a whole new bag of puzzles and conundrums. My brain is constantly exercised thinking of ways to keep the lines of communication open. I don't read to her any more, which is a thing I miss a lot. Neither do I make up stories. Made-up stories were what she once liked best – and she'd probably like them still, but it's not easy to create a story for a teenager. It would, of course, be too much to expect her to like the same music as me, although there are odd bands we agree upon. Every now and then, though, something crops up in which I think we may be able to share an interest. I asked her very tentatively one summer morning what she thought of the idea of going on a frog hunt.

'A what?' she asked, looking up from the fantasy trilogy she had her nose in.

'A frog hunt – you know, go down to the river and catch some frogs.'

'Why would we want to do that?' She frowned at me. After all, it was a hot morning and a trip down to the river meant that we would later have to climb back up from the river – and in the heat of the day.

'We're going to see John and Giuliana today and they need some frogs for their pond.'

'And where are we going to find these frogs?'

'Down in the lagoon behind the dam. It looks like a great place for a frog hunt.'

'Okay, then,' she said brightly. 'I'll just go and change.'

My heart swelled a little as I set about gathering appropriate equipment – a bucket and a pair of nets, a hat to keep the sun off, a bag to put some figs in – while Chloë improvised a frog-hunting outfit.

She led the way, and with Big doing excited pirouettes in the dust, we headed down to the river. It hadn't rained for months and the Rio Trevélez was reduced to a red dribble: what little snow that had fallen in the mountains had melted long ago, so the river was running on deep aquifer-fed springs. But just below our farm the Trevélez River joins the Cádiar, and the Cádiar, curling along at the foot of the Contraviesa, still had a fair flow of clear water. We stood on a spit looking at the two streams, which run separate for a while, the red water of the high mountain river keeping aloof from the lowlier Cádiar, until eventually the rocks and rapids succeed in mingling their waters.

It put me in mind of a photo I'd seen in a National Geographic magazine showing the Yangtze merging with the Min River at Chongqing. Reviving my paternal role I looked to share this knowledge. 'This looks like a miniature version of the rivers at Chongqing, when the Min flows into the Yangtze,' I announced. 'The dam there is one of the biggest engine...'

'Dad, there's a frog! Quick, get it!' cried Chloë. I lunged with my net, and missed.

I could tell that Chloë was not inspired by the rather nebulous connection I was making to Chinese hydro engineering, so I threw myself instead into the task at hand. The place was alive with our quarry, hopping and plopping and diving deep into the fast-moving water to escape the attention of us hunters. On land, you feel sorry for the poor things, with their laughably inadequate means of locomotion – imagine what it must be like, your every pace being an arc of about thirty feet in the air with an unpredictable outcome. Fortunately for the poor frog, though, he comes to his own in the water; they are amphibians, after all.

We continued walking down the river until we arrived at the curious plains of silt that the rivers have carried down from the mountains to deposit behind the dam. I recalled how bitterly we had opposed the building of this dam a few years before, convinced that it would result in the loss of our home and farm. Our fear had been fuelled by a diagram of an enormous construction, forty-five metres high, which would have buried our house, along with much of the valley, beneath the silt. Despite a groundswell of opposition, people power did not prevail, and the *confederación* went ahead and built the thing anyway. Fortunately for us, they only built it fifteen metres high and we, and our home and farm, remain on dry land; and to cap things off, they faced the dam tastefully in stone.

The big surprise, though, is the pleasure we now get from the wetland ecosystem that is developing above the dam. There's a lot of dead vegetation – drowned dry-land plants sticking sadly out of the mud, sand and shingle – but, little by little, flood-resistant plants are moving in. Curious lagoons, green and red, coloured by their respective water-weeds, have formed, and have drawn a rich diversity of creatures: frogs and toads of various persuasions, the tiniest of turtles, schools of minnows, ferocious dragonflies of many hues, water-boatmen, pondskaters. And down the scale, I'm sure a jam jar and microscope would yield hosts of daphne, hydra, paramecium and the other microscopic monsters that people a healthy aquatic environment. As time passes, transient birds, too, are finding out about the place, and each year there are more herons and ducks – and a curious creature that nobody has ever seen, and which we only hear as night falls, when down in the riverbed it honks to itself in a humorous sort of a way.

But back to the frog hunt. We waded on down through the river until we arrived at the lagoons. Big and Bumble were clearly not going to be much help, as they got hysterically excited at a sniff of even the most infinitesimal creature and leapt, barking into the water, stirring up great clouds of evil-smelling black mud. This made it tricky to see the frogs, so we left the dogs to work one lagoon while Chloë and I concentrated on the other.

They are odd creatures, frogs. They sit on warm rocks beside the water, seemingly inscrutable because it's hard to see which way their eyes are looking. They seem to ignore you, and then at the last moment leap into the water and scuttle down to lurk in the mud at the bottom. It's difficult to catch them once they've made it down to the mud, so we hit on a method of creeping along the bank, fixing on a frog and lunging with the net just as he jumped, to catch him in mid-air. This was sport indeed, and soon we were shrieking with wild excitement and, as we both got our eye in, plopping frog after frog into the bucket.

Easier to catch are the tadpoles, and probably better, as they would be more likely to adapt to the high mountain environment where we were taking them. So we fished about in the frogspawn and soon we had dozens of eager young tadpoles in the bucket, too. It was hard to stop once the bloodlust was up. Not that we were killing the frogs, of course, but I think I got some understanding of what drives the hunter on to his gruesome excesses.

With reluctance, Chloë and I eventually tore ourselves away and splashed home up the river, catching minnows as we went, and then throwing them back, just for the fun of the thing. We had a whole bucket of frogs and tadpoles, which would gladden the nights of John and Giuliana with their croaking. But the real joy of it had been in sharing an hour of foolish exuberance.

As kids enter the teens, you can't help but feel keenly the gentle but firm pressure with which the offspring shoves away from the nest in order to take off with their peers. Before we'd even dried the mud of the river from our shoes, Chloë was on the phone to her two best friends inviting them to join her in a frog-hunting expedition while the river was still low. Usually Chloë's circle just send text messages to each other, but I'm not sure you could convey the full appeal of such an expedition in that particular format.

●

There was a time, an increasingly hard one to recall, when my daughter used to look up to me as something of an intellectual – or, at least, someone worth having in her corner when it came to tackling the homework. Not so any more; Chloë's work has moved into a formidable dimension where I scarcely dare to tread. I know it sounds feeble, but not only am I unable to help my daughter out with *matemática*, *física* and *química* but I've learned to distrust the very questions they pose.

'Dad?,' Chloë asked the other night, 'D'you know what X is?' From her tone I deduced that she was testing my credentials rather than just seeking the answer. It sounded simple but I've learnt that the simple ones are, in fact, the most fiendish, and not just in Maths. I'm routinely called upon to tackle apparently innocent queries like 'What happens when we cough?' or 'Why do we see reflections in colour?' or 'Why is the sea so salty?': those clever-dick conundrums that you never quite master enough to retain into adulthood.

I tried to front it out. 'Well, for a start it's the twenty-fourth letter of the alphabet... and it sounds like "ks"...' I could tell straight away that this wasn't going to do.

'No Dad, I mean the mathematical absolute. You can find its value by this equation,' and off she went, tripping along with her pencil, filling the squared paper with a succession of numbers and letters to the square and to the root of whatnot that all seemed to slot neatly into place on either side of an equals sign. I watched in dumbfounded admiration.

'Ah, I see,' I said, when she finally came to a halt.

'You don't really understand it, do you, Dad?'

'Er... no, I suppose not,' I confessed, feeling nostalgic for the last time that I was of real use with the homework. I remembered it with absolute clarity, as it had been such fun. Supposedly, then too it had been *matemática*, but it had seemed more like art.

The task had been to draw a series of contiguous heptagons – seven-pointed stars – and then colour them in. But when Chloë got started on the project, she realised that there were about six hours of work involved. 'Dad,' she had commanded, 'you've got to help me with my homework.'

'"Got to" isn't good,' I said absently. 'I'm busy.'

But I am nothing if not biddable, and so before I knew it I found myself with compass and pencil sitting beside my daughter as she explained the technique. It wasn't long before I was captivated by the beauty of the task, so just in case you don't know and fancy having a crack at it, I'm going to tell you how to draw an accurate seven-pointed star. You'll need a decent compass, a pencil and a sheet of paper, at least A4 size. All equipped, then? Well, here goes.

First you draw a circle with your compass, nice and wide and note where the centre pin-prick is. That's *O*. Then draw a line straight through *O* that cuts the circle in half, and call the intersections *A* and *B*. Next, set your compass to a little more than half the distance between *O* and *A* and, with the point at *A*, draw an arc inside the circle. Then move your compass point to *O* and draw the same size arc. The two arcs should intersect at two points, one on either side of the line *A*–*B*. Now draw a line connecting these two intersections (be very precise) and you'll note that it crosses the line *A*–*B* at right angles exactly halfway between *O* and *A*: we'll call that point *R*. Continue this line until it crosses the circumference at a point we'll call *C*.

This last part is crucial, as the measure you've been trying to discover all along is the distance from *R* to *C* (or the distance from mid-point on the radius to its corresponding point on the circumference). Set your compass to this measure and mark it off at intervals around the circumference... and, miracle of miracles, it goes exactly seven times, if you've been accurate with your drawing. Now join each dot on the circumference to its two opposites and, like magic before your eyes, that most elusive and exquisite form, the seven-pointed star, will appear. If it looks more like a pig's ear, start again.

Seven, according to the science of numerology, is the perfect number – but how on earth do you accurately divide a thing into seven? Now I know, and so do you. And if you, like me, have ever wondered why on earth people love mathematics, then this simple task might help you understand. For the business of producing these lovely stars was entrancing. Ana came and joined us, and for an hour or so we sat together, our tongues between our teeth, lost in rapt concentration on the pattern that was forming. Chloë, for whom it was homework rather than pleasure, was engaged on the colouring in on the far edge of the page.

Suddenly I realised what it was that was taking shape before us: it was a polychrome wooden ceiling that could have come from the Alhambra – except that those craftsmen had created their heptagons and stars nearly a thousand years ago, from accurately cut wood. The thought of doing what we'd been doing, but in wood, was quite staggering.

As I drove through Órgiva a couple of days later, the school was disgorging its mob of fledgling citizens, the future and hope of mankind, onto the street. Gangs of sloppily dressed, slack-jawed youths with fags hanging out of their mouths, slouched nihilistically around the gates.

'God,' I thought, as I slowed down to avoid mowing down those who, for a dare, dashed in front of the car. 'To think that these people not only know the value of *X* but have mastered the secret of the heptagon.'

I saluted them with respect as I crawled past.

Despite this gloomy vision of parental redundancy, there remains one area of expertise and experience that we keep in our armoury, and – having a flattish piece of farm track leading from the bridge – can dispense at whim. I offered to teach Chloë to drive.

This was a new scheme of mine designed to make good use of the journey back from the school bus. Chloë may have only just turned thirteen but she was long enough to reach the pedals, and dead keen to embark on this next step towards independence. If she were a little drained from the long school morning, then so much the better: the driving would clear her mind.

I embarked on our first lesson in deliberately casual manner. Having strolled down from the bridge I climbed into the passenger seat of the old Land-Rover we keep on the near side of the river and tossed her the keys. 'Right, Chloë,' I said, pretending to be more relaxed than I really felt. 'Foot on the clutch, turn the ignition halfway…'

'What's ignition?'

'The key. Turn it until the lights come on the dashboard, then wait for the yellow light to go out. Now, clutch in…'

'What's clutch?'

'*Embrague,* the pedal on the left. Press it down and turn the key all the way.'

Chloë jumped as the engine started. The starter motor graunched and screamed...

'What do I do now?'

'Let the key slip back on the spring... Good. Now, foot hard on the clutch and slip it into first.'

Chloë fumbled with the gearstick and finally pushed it in. Big and Bumble, sitting in the back, looked disapproving; it didn't normally take as long as this to get the car on the move.

'Now what?' She turned to me uneasily, gripping the steering wheel hard.

'Well, now it's time to get home for lunch. Give it a touch of throttle, let the clutch out and steer it along the track. Okay?' I turned to quell the early signs of mutiny among the worried dogs in the back.

'Give it a little more throttle and away you go...'

Chloë jumped the clutch, a burst of throttle. The car bucked hard and stalled. The dogs fell off the back seat.

'What did I do wrong?' she said with a slight quake in her voice.

'Too brutish, too impetuous. A little more throttle and a little gentler with the clutch. Feel the contact...'

When you teach somebody to drive, you realise what an incredibly complicated business it is. And yet it has become so much second nature that you perform each action quite automatically... Ah, what a piece of work is man.

Finally, to the relief of the poor baffled dogs, Chloë succeeded in getting the dilapidated old Land-Rover in motion.

'STEER IT! Look out, you've got to keep in the middle of the track... There, there you go...' And we headed off along the rough track for home, Chloë gripping the wheel tightly with a look of grim determination while I, feigning nonchalance, put my feet on the dusty dashboard and looked out of the window.

The idea is that one's apparent nonchalance infects and relaxes the pupil: a trick I picked up while learning to fly, many years ago in Texas, under the instruction of Gary, a deranged and unpredictable Hawaiian. Now, in general terms there's nothing dangerous about aeroplanes so long as they're up in the air. There's an awful lot of air up there, and the likelihood of hitting any of the few objects that are capable of getting up there in it, is extremely thin. No, your problems only really start when you decide to return to earth. It's when your aeroplane actually regains contact with the ground that the – well – that the shit really can hit the fan.

Anyway, there I was, sitting in the pilot's seat, next to Gary, who was looking out of the window, thinking impure thoughts, as we were coming in to land at Red Bird Airport, Dallas. It was the very first time I had ever attempted to land a plane and I was scared. My knuckles were white on the wheel and my attention darted desperately between the altimeter, air-speed indicator, turn and bank indicator, and the windscreen – through which I could see the planet's surface hurtling perilously towards us. My whole body was tensed and quivering in an anguish of anxiety to get this right. Gary, however, continued picking his teeth and looking out of the side window. Then suddenly he looked up, assessed the situation, opened the door and made to leap out. 'Shit, man!' he yelled, over his shoulder. 'You're too nervous. You going to fuck it all up! I'm getting out!'

'Hey, Gary! What d'you mean?' I screamed in blind

panic. 'You can't leave me all alone in here... I don't even know how to drive this thing!'

He shut the door and howled with laughter. 'Just testin' you, man... Just testin' you. Loosen up for fuck's sake, loosen up!'

I loosened up. I hooted with laughter, more from relief than anything. Then suddenly the bastard had his hands around my throat – he'd turned into a homicidal maniac seconds before our plane hit the ground. 'Hey, man... Never laugh when you landin' a plane. You'll fuck it up for all of us!'

We both rocked with mad laughter. I was laughing so much I couldn't grip the wheel at all, let alone with white knuckles. I looked out of the window. In less than a second we'd be plastered like a cowpat on the runway. I eased back, tears of laughter in my eyes, and cut the throttle. The plane flared and, eased by the cushion of wind, touched the ground with a gentle thump and a rumble of wheels. Gary's unorthodox technique had worked well; the mad distraction had killed my nervousness, and without the nervousness I had performed smoothly and well.

'I don't pull that stunt with just anybody, boy,' he said. 'I figure you got to be least as crazy as me to use that treatment.'

That was more than twenty years ago, when I had blown my life savings on an incredibly cheap and unethically short three-week flying course in Dallas, Texas. As it happened, I was the only one of the over-stressed pupils who actually earned my wings at the end of the stint – not because of any prowess on my part, but because my flying examiner couldn't seem to get over the fact that he had a sheep shearer at the controls.

'That's a mighty hard job,' he commented after I had ballsed up the figure-of-eight manoeuvre and overshot the airport, then looked at me thoughtfully, and added, 'I think I'm gonna pass you, boy.'

In fact I was as hopeless as the rest – and far too poor to keep up the flying hours necessary to take it further as either a hobby or career, so it wasn't the handiest qualification I've ever earned. But to return to our farm track...

Chloë by now had burst out from a tunnel of pomegranate and brambles, through which she'd managed to steer us and was suddenly faced with a sheep on the track, hysterical and mad-eyed, watching the inexorable approach of the car and wondering which way to go.

'Dad! Dad! What shall I do? There's a sheep in the way!'

'Well, stop of course...'

'HOW DO I STOP?!!' By now the whole of Domingo's three- hundred-and-fifty-strong flock had been apprised of the danger and were leaping in dim-witted terror from the terrace above the track right into the path of the car.

'Left foot on the clutch, right foot on the brake.' Chloë did as I said, and the car, bogged in a cloud of dust and an amorphous mob of panicking sheep, obediently stopped.

'Dad, I don't think I can do this. It's too dangerous...'

'Just stick with it, kid, and you'll be alright. Don't worry about it. And besides, how are we going to get home? I'm leaving the driving to you now.'

Behind this bravado there was a note of seriousness. Within a very few years I knew Chloë would be spending a lot of time being transported by young machos keen to show her just how fast you can go on a 49cc moto (at age sixteen in Spain you're allowed to ride a motorcycle with a capacity less than 50cc), and likely as not nobody would be wearing crash helmets. We live a long way from town, out along a rough and precipitous mountain track and I reckoned that if Chloë knew better how to drive a car and ride a motorbike than all the beastly testosterone-charged hoodlums, whom I could already see muscling in on the periphery of her hitherto exclusively female coterie of friends, then she would stand a better chance of coming through these dangerous years unscathed.

As the sheep dissipated toward the river, leaving a cloud of sweet-smelling dust behind, Chloë seemed to regain her spirit.

'Okay, they've gone,' she allowed. 'What do I do now?'

'Bit of throttle, clutch out and don't forget to steer.'

This time she got it better, and in a dignified fashion, in first gear, we continued towards home. More by luck than judgement she negotiated the narrow gap between the gateposts, smacked across the lower *acequia* with a great graunch of the sump, and ground on up the hill past the stable. With some foresight I had left open the gate that normally bars the track up to the house and acts as a fence for the horse.

'Now, once you hit the hill I want you to put your foot down on the accelerator and keep going until you get to the house. You should lift your foot slightly just before speeding up round the bend, but on no account stop. Have you got that?'

'Yes, but why?' she asked, not unreasonably.

'It's steep. You'll need a good steady pace to get to the top.'

What I didn't tell her was that the car had no handbrake to speak of and if she let her speed drop the car would inexorably grind to a halt and start rolling backwards – not quite what you want to happen on your very first lesson. Ana and I have developed an incredibly complicated way of stopping midway, to close the gate or the doors to the sheep shed, say, or pick up a bag of oranges left beneath a tree, but it involves backing the car into the shed wall with just the right circular motion so that it comes naturally to rest. It was a manoeuvre best left till later.

Finally we came to a halt outside the house, Chloë having skilfully contrived to butt the front wheel up against a stone cunningly placed to catch the back wheel.

'Okay, how do I stop it now?'

'Turn the key the other way.'

This she did, but the engine kept on grumbling away. This was another of the more eccentric deficiencies of the farm car: it starts like a dream, but it's often reluctant to stop.

'Well, put it into neutral and get out and I'll stop it.'

With some relief, Chloë clambered out. She'd done pretty well, I thought, and I told her so.

A couple of days later I was cutting some sheaves of alfalfa for the sheep and collecting together some bundles that had been drying in the field. The dogs, having heard a car arrive on the other side of the valley, came hurtling down the hill barking. It was our old friend Cathy and her teenage son Juanito, who were giving Chloë a lift back from school. I bent to the work again with my sickle and cut a few big bundles, gathered them together and tied them with a rope. Then, turning to hoist them onto my shoulder, I found

Manolo standing at the gate looking rather pleased about something. He had been walking up to the house for a beer after clearing the lower *acequia*.

'You'll never lift that, Cristóbal. Here, let me help you,' he said, as he took the great bundle of leaves and stalks from me, shouldered them effortlessly and turned towards the stable. That was the great thing about Manolo: he was always popping up just when you could do with a hand. I wondered, though, what was amusing him so much. Manolo is one of the most good-humoured people I know, but even he needs a reason to grin.

'Chloë's full of surprises, isn't she,' he commented, nodding down the track from where I could hear the sound of an engine gunning along in first gear. 'Better watch out or she'll be wanting that car for herself.'

I stopped and squinted in the direction of the sound. The Land-Rover burst into view, with Chloë peering anxiously over the top of the wheel. Cathy, I later discovered, had been a bit surprised when my daughter hopped onto the front seat and announced she was going to drive them up to the house, but thought she probably knew what she was up to. Cathy is one of those old-school feminists who would rather bite her tongue in two and swallow the other half than discourage a girl from showing a bit of initiative. Her son Juanito was simply impressed.

I panicked. The gate halfway up the hill was shut and Chloë wouldn't have the slightest clue about the complicated parking manoeuvre required, and would either slam into the horizontal pole or slide off the terraces. I dropped the alfalfa and raced to get there first. Chloë hardly noticed me holding the fence open as she gunned past, eyes glued to the track ahead, teeth set in grim determination. At the house Cathy and Juanito were climbing out of the car looking slightly aquiver. Chloë was still sitting in the driving seat, the engine running, her foot hard down on the brake pedal. I think she was just getting to grips with the enormity of what she had done.

'Dad, the engine's playing up again, and every time I take my foot off the pedal the car rolls backwards... what shall I do?'

I helped her sort out the problems and she clambered unsteadily out. 'I think I might have had enough driving for now,' she whispered, handing me the keys.

GUESTS WITHOUT PAPERS

UNLIKE MY SHEEP-SHEARING PARTNER, José Guerrero, who makes his living travelling from flock to flock throughout the Alpujarras, my becoming a writer means that I can, these days, afford to be choosy about the work I take on. I'd hate to give up shearing entirely, and if a flock or its farmer or its patch of mountain appeals I'll be off like a shot, but it must be said there is some pleasure in saying no to jobs you know will be nothing but drudgery. Which made it all the odder that there I was hauling myself out of the connubial bed at the crack of dawn to help José shear Paco López's sheep.

Paco López is a notorious drunk who lives on a ramshackle farm high up in the Ilex forest above the Trevélez river valley. Frequently he would disappear for days, abandoning his sheep to whatever grazing they could find beneath the holm-oaks, and leaving them prey to the packs of wild dogs that are such a disagreeable feature of the Spanish countryside. It had been almost two years since José and I had last sheared his flock and I remembered that we had made a solemn pact never, ever, to accept another job from him again.

'Remind me just once more why we're doing this,' I bleated as we hurtled round the mountain bends in José's little tin van, deafened by the Led Zeppelin tape that he insisted on playing at full volume through his tinny radio speakers.

'*Parné, pasta, dinero!*' José shouted with a bristly grin. 'I need the money and I can't do it on my own! Also, it'll help you shake off those disgraceful rolls of flab! All that sitting on your arse with a pen in your mouth is doing you no good, Cristóbal.'

I supposed he had a point, and it is always hard to turn down work with José, who in spite of – or, perhaps, because of – his recent battle with cancer, remains one of the most cheerful and energetic people I have ever met. In the event, however, the job was worse than either of us could have anticipated. The past months had weighed heavily on poor Paco, who, ground down by the loneliness and the harshness of a mountain shepherd's life, had been hitting the bottle hard. He had that pinched and distracted look of the serious imbiber, coupled with an evident querulousness about money. His sheep were no bundles of fun, either. They were bonier and thinner-skinned than ever and each one hosted a thriving colony of parasitical arachnids (ticks have eight legs so don't qualify as insects).

We pitched in to the job with all the good humour we could muster, but it was a stretch even for José's natural cheer. The air in Paco's asbestos-roofed shed was baking, and stagnant with the putrid stench of dung, and the ticks were making it almost impossible to get the wool off. Each stroke of the clippers left a livid trail of blood as it hacked through thirty or forty engorged bodies, and the cutters kept sticking, so we had to push and pull and tug and jab, while taking as much care as we could of the sheep's protruding bones and thin skin. Time and again we nearly gave up, took down the machinery and went home. But something kept us going – perhaps the money, perhaps some imbued work ethic, or maybe just sympathy for a shepherd and his sheep. So we stuck it out and at last our constancy was rewarded. The end of the job was in sight.

Paco didn't seem to share our relief, though, and was moving morosely around the flock, counting anxiously under his breath, as he appeared from the pen with another creature for me to shear. I grabbed hold of it, flexed my shearing arm ready to make the first blow and then stopped. 'Bloody hell! Paco,' I called above the buzzing of my partner's shears, 'I can't shear this one. Take it away!'

'Why, what's the matter with it?' he muttered,

'It's a goat, man. I'm not going to shear your goat!'

Paco looked – and there is no other word here – sheepish, then rallied. 'No, Cristóbal, that's no goat,' he insisted, fixing me with a bloodshot look. 'That's a sheep.'

It wasn't, of course. Goats *can* look a bit like sheep and some even have a certain ovine demeanour, a sheepish gait that at a distance – say, peering from one mountainside across to another – can lead to confusion. But there was no confusion at all about the particular specimen that was standing right before me. This wasn't just your run-of-the-mill, undistinguished goat; it was a goat's goat, with horns and a beard and all.

Paco reluctantly led the goat away and returned with another animal.

'Paco, what the hell are you up to? I'm not shearing that!'

'Why not?' asked Paco sulkily. 'It's a sheep, isn't it? Even you've got to admit that.'

'Yes, it is a sheep, Paco – but it hasn't a stitch of wool on it. I sheared this one half an hour ago!' We examined the naked sheep, with trail marks from the shears on its flanks, standing forlornly in front of me, and I cast a glance at José, who had let his last sheep wander off and was rocking helpless with laughter. 'It's the numbers, Cristóbal,' he gasped. 'Haven't you been counting?'

Of course: once you get beyond two-hundred-and-fifty sheep the price per animal goes down by a small percentage which has quite a significant effect on the whole day's pay. One or two short and the shepherd misses out on the price drop, while one or two over means that the shearers take the hit. It might seem a rough way to cost things, but that's how it's always been. Astute shepherds often borrow extra sheep to take them over the threshold, but poor Paco, who was almost a dozen sheep short of a discount, probably hadn't a clue that he'd lost so many of his charges until he brought them out for shearing.

In fairness, it is tricky to know where you are, numerically speaking, with sheep. Cows are easy to count, but not so sheep. With all that wool you get an impression of a numberless mass, and then, although I hesitate to say this within earshot of the animal, they are somewhat...

dispensable. If you have a big flock you can lose half a dozen without even knowing it. Sheep are very prone to dying of one thing or another – *The Diseases of Sheep* is by some way the thickest book in our library – as well as getting lost or straying into another flock. Of course, the converse is also true, and if you're lucky you may actually benefit from strays who unwittingly – and unwitting is the way of sheep – swell the numbers of your flock. Or you may get prodigal sheep that return to the flock: a ewe may lamb alone out on the hill somewhere, and trot back to the flock months later with her lamb in tow. All of which is to say that counting sheep is far from being an exact science.

I placed my shears back on the board and turned to face Paco. 'Look, let's split the difference,' I said. I might on another day have offered the full discount, but the heat and exhaustion and the farce of the goats and shorn sheep had got to me. And, for this day, at least, I had had more than enough.

Normally, at the end of a run of shearing, you can throw yourself down in the pile of wool and there subside limp and drained, contemplating a job well done. But we couldn't do that here, not in the tick-infested wool we had just shorn, so instead we had to sit on a stone in the hot evening sun. Paco begrudgingly handed each of us a tin of warm beer, which we sipped while watching him count, with trembling hands, the notes he owed us.

With a beer inside us, I revived enough to dismantle the machinery and pack up, while José cleaned off the combs and cutters and set up the grinding wheel. At which moment a tough, dapper little man with short grey hair appeared panting through the woods, followed by a couple of beautiful and very woolly Pyrenean mountain dogs. 'Are you... the shearers?' he gasped, wiping his face with a crisp, white cloth.

I could see what was coming. Goats, shorn sheep, dogs: it was becoming a theme of the day.

'Yes,' we said noncommittally.

'I... I'm... so glad I caught you,' he continued, still panting. 'Could you... take the wool off these... dogs for me?'

'I'm sorry,' said José, 'but we've taken down all the gear and...'

'But look here, I've just climbed all the way up here from the village to get these dogs sheared...'

'We don't do dogs,' I said matter-of-factly.

'What do you mean, you don't do dogs?' He was getting heated and a little aggressive. 'You're the shearers, aren't you? These dogs need shearing and I've just busted a gut getting all the way up here. How dare you tell me you don't do dogs!'

José had his head in his box, packing his gear.

'Look, it's simple,' I repeated. 'I'm sorry for your trouble but it's hardly any fault of ours and, as I said, we don't do dogs. This gear isn't designed for...'

'Hey, you,' he snarled, looking at me with narrowed eyes. 'You're not one of us. Where are you from? What are you doing here?'

'I'm from England but I live here,' I answered blithely, unscrewing the head of my machine.

'Oh, so you're one of those bloody foreigners then, are you?'

'Well,' I said brightly, 'I've lived here for a long time but I wasn't born here so I guess that makes me a foreigner, but my daughter was born here so she's a native...'

'You foreigners – you come here and pollute our culture – what you ought to be doing is do your job then fuck off back where you came from. We don't need you here taking the homes and land away from honest farmers!'

This was irresistible and I leapt gleefully into the fray. 'Pollute your culture? If you know anything about your culture at all, you'd know it's been enriched by foreigners for centuries and would be a shrivelled and half-arsed thing without them.'

Our new friend's eyes nearly burst out of their sockets at this, and he seemed almost to hop with rage. He turned towards José, who kept his head down, bent over the sharpening wheel. 'Who is this... this... person?' he spluttered.

'Oh,' said José, still intent upon the fast spinning wheel. 'I shear with him, he's a friend of mine.'

The little man stood between us, breathing deeply, looking from me, sitting in the sun cradling my shears, to José crouched over the grinding wheel. Finally he calmed down a bit and said with just a touch of a whine: 'Look, I really need to get these dogs clipped, and...'

'I already said' – I interrupted – 'we don't do dogs.'

'I'm not talking to you!' he snapped.

'I'm sorry,' said José standing up and stretching. 'But the foreigner's the boss. I do what he tells me, and it looks like he doesn't want us to shear your dogs.' He smiled pleasantly, trying to bring the argument down a gear.

'Right,' snarled the little man as he thumped back down the track into the woods. 'I'll not forget this. You'll be hearing from me.' And, so saying, he disappeared amongst the trees.

'He was a laugh, wasn't he?' I said to José, as we watched him out of sight.

'No, he wasn't – he was serious. I know that man a little bit, and I certainly know the type. He's one of those *hijo de puta* ham barons from Trevélez. People like that expect to get what they want; and when they don't get it, they get nasty.'

'Lord, I thought he was just messing about...'

'No, not a bit of it; that's the way those people are. Up here, they run things. They do exactly as they like and they don't let people stand in their way, especially not foreigners. They're the bastards who tip their used salt into the river instead of loading it up and taking it down to the sea.'

'Well, a bit of salt in the water's not too much of a threat. I'm not going to be shaking in my boots about that.'

'I would be – they tip dozens of tons in, and the water of the Trevélez River is high in salts anyway. My father lost a whole orchard of apricot trees because these bastards tipped their waste salt into the river. A small trick like that could lay your farm to waste.'

All in all, it hadn't been the best of days.

The heat of July grew more and more intense, the short nights barely giving respite to the burning air, as one long stultifying day rolled into another. July and August are the hardest months to bear in the Alpujarras, as the swelling heat is given voice by the ceaseless screaming of the cicadas, and even the smallest task drains you of all your energy. It's a time when all right-minded people cave in after lunch and take a long, deep siesta.

However, this simple pleasure is not always as easy to achieve as you might think, because the heart of summer is also the time that visitors start arriving. For some reason people from the northern hemisphere like nothing better than to stalk across mountains in the fierce midday heat, arrive on the terrace of a complete stranger and blast their hopes of waking naturally from a siesta. In the past month I had been dragged from my slumbers by, amongst others, a Danish hiker, a German ornithologist, and a man from Dorset who told me that he had borrowed my last book from the library and read most of it, and would I mind signing his map and posing for a photograph?

So it was that one August afternoon, replete with *gazpacho*, *tortilla* and salad, and pleasantly lulled by wine, I retreated to my bed, in the hope of sleeping undisturbed. I was lying on my back in bed – that being the best way of dissipating heat (and why dogs in summer lie with their bellies in the air) – and was peering lazily behind closed eyelids at the thoughts ambling through my mind. This is a trick I've discovered to slip more quickly into a light doze. You try not to follow any thoughts in a conscious way but just watch as they go by. Little by little, as you lie bathed in sweat, the thoughts become more disjointed, their rationality dissolves, rogue elements appear, and you find yourself skimming the upper hills of dreaming before descending into the valleys. This is a delicious moment, the moment before you dip into sleep. You say to yourself, 'I must be asleep because that last thought didn't make sense,' and then all of a sudden you've overcome the curse of the heat, and you're deep down in the veils of Morpheus, cloaked in mindless sleep.

At this point, often as not, a fly will attempt to dart up one of your nostrils, jarring you straight back to irritable wakefulness. You get up and shut the shutters – houseflies don't fly in the dark – but once disturbed it is not easy to regain that sweet oblivion. You manage at last and, ah, such pleasure, and then all of a sudden there impinges on your consciousness a shuffling, as human noises are heard moving forward on the terrace – perhaps a 'Hello, there!' or a whispered 'Do you think anyone's in?' A visitor has arrived.

Grumbling to myself, I ratch about for something to cover my ghastly nakedness and stumble out into the glaring light to face my uninvited guest. 'Oh-h,' they greet me, a slightly falling note if it's someone who is clutching my book, as they register an older and less amiable-looking version of the author than the man on the book jacket. I usually offer a cup of tea, which is what people unaccountably seem to want on a blistering summer afternoon, especially if they're English.

Yet this time things seemed different. The visitors didn't call out at all and their silence unnerved me. Then I picked out whispers, very quiet and urgent, and it occurred to me that this could be the ham baron's henchmen come to teach me a lesson.

I nudged Ana awake, raising a finger to my lips. Then I pulled on a pair of shorts and crept carefully to the front door. I peered out... Nothing. Then I caught sight of some figures at the bottom of the steps to the house. With relief, I realised that they weren't marauding heavies at all, but four young men, all of them just as nervous as I was. A thin youth with dark features and curly, matted hair seemed to be the spokesman. He stepped up to the edge of the terrace and hesitantly, in a hoarse voice, asked for some water. The others waited in the shade of the pomegranate tree to see how I reacted.

'Of course. Come up and I'll get you some,' I said, smiling in a manner that I hoped might put them at ease, and beckoned to them to come and sit on the patio. The youth stepped back and seemed to be conducting a mimed conference with the others, with the result that they stepped tentatively up behind him. If it wasn't already obvious from their features that they were Moroccan immigrants ('without papers,' as they say in Spanish) the shabby sports bags they clutched gave them away. I dredged up the tiny bit of Arabic I knew.

'*Salaam alekum,*' I said – welcome; '*Alekum Salaam,*' they answered uncertainly. It helped to galvanise the other three who, dusty and dishevelled like the first, moved closer to the table and chairs in the shade of the vine.

I went into the house to fetch a jug of water. When I returned, they were still standing around uneasily, holding on to their bags. 'Go on, sit down,' I said in Spanish, and placed the tray and jug and glasses on the table. Warily they moved to the chairs, perching on the edge as if still unsure.

The exhausted look on their faces told of a long and arduous journey, doubtless lasting many days. And they were clearly terrified of being reported to the authorities and deported. As well they might be, for, by sitting these destitute young men down and giving them water, I was breaking the law.

'You speak Spanish?' I asked, anxious to reassure my wary guests. Three of them looked in bafflement at the first, who shrugged apologetically.

'*Aah, parlez vous français?*' I tried.

'*Oui, un peu…*' he said as he gulped the water. I refilled their glasses.

'*Je m'appelle Christophe,*' I said, holding out my hand to the French speaker.

He bowed a little and shook my hand, afterwards placing it over his heart in that warm Moroccan way. 'I am Hamid, and these are my friends Mustapha, Aziz, and also Hamid.'

We each shook hands, bowing and touching our respective hearts. Ana emerged then from the darkness of the house. They all stood up and repeated the hand-shaking process. It appeared that it was only the first Hamid who spoke anything but Arabic or Berber, so we communicated in French through him.

'We have come from Algeciras,' he said.

'How are you travelling?'

'On foot, through the mountains. It is safer from the police.'

'On foot, all the way from Algeciras! That's halfway across the country! How long have you been walking?'

Hamid turned to his friends and they exchanged opinions on this in Arabic.

'We have walked for ten days, I think. We are going to El Ejido, monsieur. We know people who work there.'

'That is a hard place,' I replied. I knew a little of El Ejido and its hothouse fruit and vegetable industry, and wondered if it really would provide a better life than the one they were escaping. And yet it was impossible not to admire these determined youths. They were clearly exhausted, hungry, thirsty and destitute, and here they were wandering through a land whose language they didn't speak, ever at risk of being caught by police patrols. They were seeking hope and opportunity – a future with the dignity of work.

'Are you hungry?' asked Ana.

'We are a little hungry,' replied Hamid.

Ana got up to go to the kitchen. As she did, she noticed that they were all eyeing the packet of cigarettes she had left on the table. She smiled and pushed it across to Hamid. They fell hungrily upon the packet, and somehow the tiny act of generosity, the ritual and the sweet smoke of freshly lit tobacco worked a magical effect. The fear seemed to fall away, there was a tangible feeling of relief, as they pulled the calming smoke deep into their lungs. (I suppose that's the way it is with snouts; I've never managed to smoke one, so I don't know.)

Soon Ana had a meal on the table for them. There was a tureen of thick *gazpacho*, a buttery, yellow omelette made with our own farm eggs, thick slabs of bread and butter and honey. It was a bit short on the meat, but all we had in the house was bacon and ham and sausages of pig. Still, the four of them set to the food like thin wolves. Pausing briefly, Hamid told us that they had not eaten a thing for two days. They had no food, no money and, worst of all, no tobacco.

We watched them as they ate. They were painfully thin and, from what I could gather from Hamid, were village boys from the desert border area in the south, where unemployment is endemic and secondary education rare. Quite probably each of these boys represented the investments of a whole village, or at least of an extended family. People would have scraped together their assets and given them to these ill-prepared young men so that they could find work in the distant fastness of Fortress Europe, and send home what money they were able to put aside. They didn't look much – who of us *would* after ten days in the mountains with barely a thing to eat? – and yet these boys bore upon their shoulders huge burdens of hope, and were risking their lives to bring these dreams to fruition.

It was shocking to reflect, given their appearance, that things were going well for Hamid and his party, thus far. They had survived the appallingly treacherous sea journey, on some barely seaworthy boat; they had travelled east for ten days without being caught by the Guardia Civil patrols; and now they had fallen in with us. The tobacco and food were visibly reviving the group, but still their eyes darted narrowly about, casting glances around at the farm, and us, and searching for warning signs. I wanted to say something to convince Hamid of our good intentions, but it wasn't that easy, particularly in French. You can't say: 'We mean you no harm.' It sounds silly. 'Don't worry; you're safe with us.' Not much better.

As the group finished their meal and talked among themselves in Berber, Ana and I discussed what to do. El Ejido is a wretched place: acres and acres of greenhouses, where Moroccan and other illegal migrants work in dire conditions, for pitiful wages. It was awful to think of them ending up there, but they seemed determined and we had no other plan we could offer in its place. Reaching El Ejido, however, would be no simple matter. There remained a good four days' walk over some pretty rough and broken countryside. Ana looked thoughtful.

'We can at least take the trauma out of the journey,' she said. 'We could drive them there – or you could. You could wait for nightfall and then go the back way, via Cádiar.' Ana's caution was as much for my sake as for the Moroccans. Helping illegal immigrants is against the law, and carries the possibilities of a prison sentence and confiscation of one's car. It seemed unlikely that I'd be caught, but nonetheless it would be best not to be too obvious about it.

Getting this plan across to Hamid and his friends was by no means easy. I could sense that they still did not trust us – and why should they? Okay, we had shown them some kindness, but the water, the meal, it could all be some kind of trap. Eventually, though, we managed to persuade them that they should go and rest for a few hours in the *cámara*, an annexe where I work, up above the house, and where there are beds and couches for visitors. I would come up and fetch them when it got dark, then drive them to El Ejido or wherever they wanted to go next. Grabbing their bags, the Moroccans followed me up along the path that skirted the border of succulents surrounding the house. They kept their guard up and, at a bend in the path, where the view opens up to reveal the river bed, a strange and quiet commotion broke out.

Hamid stopped in his tracks, one hand shooting out to prevent the others moving forward and whispered, nodding his head towards the track. The others crouched back, frowning hard at me. I stood rooted to the spot unable to work out what the hell was going on and then it dawned on me. They'd seen our scarecrow: a deceptively life-like hunter that a sculptor friend had erected in the field, as a folly and a deterrent to wild boar. He'd shaped the body on a wire frame, covered it with acrylic painted plaster, and to add an authentic touch had positioned a wooden shotgun in the cradle of his arms and a painted cigarette dangling from his lips. The clothes were my own cast-offs and, to keep the wild boar on its toes, our model hunter's neckscarf was soaked from time to time in *Zotal*, which, refreshed by dew, purportedly smells like BO.

As soon as they understood their mistake, Hamid and his friends broke into smiles, but they were the brittle, hesitant smiles of people who still had much to fear and can't give anything unusual the benefit of the doubt. 'Try and sleep for a few hours if you can,' I said, handing Hamid another pack of cigarettes Ana had provided. 'We'll leave at eleven.' And I unlocked the door of the *cámara* and handed them the key.

The Moroccans looked around the room in open-mouthed amazement, exclaiming at the number of books and beds and then, delightedly, as if finding a long-lost cherished item, picked up the *djelaba* and *babouches* – the traditional Moroccan cloak and slippers – that I had hanging on the back of the door. The impression that we were an alien people might have diminished a tiny bit. Once again we shook hands and bowed. '*Merci, monsieur. Merci,*' said Hamid, holding on to my hand.

I returned to Ana at the table and we talked over the plan. I felt deeply uneasy about El Ejido. 'The gangs who run some of those farms are hardly better than the Mafia,' I worried. 'I don't know if it's enough that there are other Moroccans there. If only we could employ them here, and pay them decently and house them like human beings.'

'We couldn't sustain it, Chris,' Ana replied. 'We don't have enough work for them, or the money to keep on paying them properly, and we're just too exposed. Someone would be bound to denounce them sooner or later.' But she hated the thought of El Ejido even more than I did. We had both heard stories of the farms' brutal treatment of Moroccan and Eastern Europeans, who, without legal status, were worked like slaves and casually subjected to fearful levels of toxic chemicals. Such is the price paid for Europe's out-of-season fruit and vegetables. However, we couldn't think of a better alternative, despite talking the subject round and round until late in the evening, so at ten-thirty I wiped the grime off the car windscreen and went up to the *cámara* to gather my passengers.

The room was empty. Our guests had already gone. I shouted into the gathering night – 'Hamid! Hamid!' – but nothing. It seemed that, when it came to it, they had decided not to trust us. I hoped that they would maintain the same wariness in their dealings with the agricultural mob at the other end.

●

The next morning I woke early and, seeing Jesús Carrasco with his goats in the valley, went down to join him. He hadn't noticed any Moroccans passing but listened with interest to my account of their stay. 'They're young. What can they know of all these things they'll have to face?' he said, in an unusually compassionate tone. He told me that many of the farmers in the remote *cortijos* will do what they can to relieve the misery of migrants who come their way – not much, of course, for they haven't much to give, but they will give them bread and olives and a safe place to rest. 'Some of the old people have seen their children walk away to find work,' he explained. 'Maybe not quite so desperate – but people here know about poverty and what it drives you to.'

It was strange to be talking with such seriousness with Jesús. It threw me back to a conversation I'd had once with Domingo, where he mentioned that he'd gone to Barcelona as a young man to work in a bottle factory. It was *muy mal*, he had said, and then sharply changed the subject as if unwilling to linger. I realised that, although he often speaks of Catalunya, he'd never again made the slightest reference to having lived there himself. But my musing was interrupted. Jesús nudged me and pointed to the bend at the top of the cliff. 'Guardia Civil,' he muttered. 'I wonder what they want.'

Jesús's skill in picking out moving objects on the horizon has been honed by years of watching goats. It took another few minutes before I could make out the distant car and then the tell tale police light, but I watched with dismay as it drew closer, forded the river and came bumping up the track to arrive by the side of the fence between the alfalfa and the eucalyptus grove. Now, the Guardia don't like to get their cars wet and would only ford our river for the most serious of purposes. They had come to make an arrest.

Manolo, who had arrived on his motorbike just a few minutes earlier, ambled towards the car in his usual open manner – he had no knowledge of the Moroccans' visit and was treating the arrival of the police as a slice of daily soap opera. The officers were indeed following a tip-off – though this denunciation, it transpired, had nothing to do with our guests of last night. No, they were seeking a 'furtive hunter' (I translate literally here) who had been seen staking out the alfalfa fields down by the river, waiting to pot a *jabali*, or wild boar.

Now, it's illegal to hunt the *jabali* unless you have a licence for *caza mayor* – big game – and, besides, the policemen had heard that this character was acting suspiciously. Perhaps the most suspicious aspect of his behaviour was the fact that he had remained in exactly the same position for eleven months and stank of *Zotal*.

Manolo found the *civiles* shuffling around beside the car looking embarrassed. 'Come to arrest our scarecrow?' he asked.

The worthy officials muttered to each other and cast around for something with which to lambast Manolo and save face.

'We hear there have been hunters on your land. Is that true?' they demanded.

'No – at least – not the flesh-and-blood ones,' he chortled.

I arrived at this moment. 'Well, make sure you let us know if you see any,' said the older officer, sternly. Then, barely missing a beat, he turned on me and demanded brusquely, 'What's that car doing there?'

He was pointing to a bamboo grove where a rusting old wreck had weeds curling out through the windscreen.

'That's where we keep the sheep feed – so the rats can't get it,' I answered.

'That one, then. What about that one?' He indicated another forsaken old banger at the end of the alfalfa field.

'That one works,' chipped in Manolo, enjoying the exchange enormously. 'It's for getting stuff to and from the bridge.'

'There's another one up the hill there. Why?' The *civiles* were getting infuriated.

'That's for spares for the one that runs to the bridge and back,' I replied.

'Well, let me tell you, *señores*, that it's illegal to have old cars lying about in the countryside. Get rid of them, and quick. If they're still here next week, I'm denouncing you and there's a big fine.' And with that, the duo marched off to their car.

GRANADA WELCOMES

T HE PLIGHT OF THE YOUNG MOROCCAN men brought home to me just how vulnerable immigrants can become when forced to live and work outside the legal sector. I felt that I had to try and do something to help. But I wasn't at all sure what that something should be; I'm a bit of a non-starter as an activist, possessing none of the qualities I presumed essential: I can't hold the attention of a meeting, and my administrative skills are hopelessly poor. Yet what did aptitude matter? The point, surely, was to try. So, grasping the bull by the horns, I signed myself up as a volunteer in an organisation called *Granada Acoge*.

Granada Acoge – 'Granada Welcomes' – is the local branch of an immigrants' welfare organisation that exists throughout Andalucía to look after the interests of immigrants, legal or illegal, wherever they have come from. In Granada, you can find them – a largely voluntary, part-time team of lawyers, social workers, doctors, translators and teachers – in a cramped office, really just a small house, in a back alley called Aguas de Cartuja. Three telephone lines or more ring constantly, the waiting room is crammed to bursting with hopeful newcomers from all corners of the globe, and every ninety seconds the doorbell rings and someone comes in. Somebody leaves about every half-hour, so by the end of the morning the place is bursting at the seams.

I was to work as a general-purpose volunteer, and the first morning I turned up bright and eager and was placed under the tutelage of Mati, the rather sexy woman who ran the telephone and the door. Mati chain-smoked and spoke in a husky drawl, and I could tell by the way that she peered sideways at me through sultry-lidded eyes that she was wondering what a middle-aged Englishman was doing in a place like this. At length she decided that I was like some kind of foreign child and began to establish a way of dealing with me. She spoke slowly, enunciating her words with care and regarding me closely to see if I had understood.

Usually, I hadn't. The system they had, and there had to be a system, was so utterly impenetrable that, no matter how many times she repeated it, it still lay way beyond my grasp. I had been too long outside the orbit of offices, organisations, routines and fitting in with established patterns of work. Indeed, my last 'proper job' ('proper', I suspect, disallows farming or writing), was half a lifetime ago, in my twenties, working night shifts in a paper-clip factory in Utrecht.

'*Bueno,*' enunciated Mati slowly. 'Your first job is to answer the telephone…' I heaved a sigh of relief. Surely I could make the grade as a telephone receptionist. I didn't tell Mati that I once spent ten minutes trying to phone Spain from my sister's house in London before my five-year-old niece took the 'phone' out of my hands, pointed it at the telly and switched channels.

'First', Mati continued, 'you must establish if a client has been here before, then if they already have an appointment, then what their problem is, and, according to what they tell you, you must do one of the following: If they have not been here before you must put them through to Juanma. That's number six... unless of course it's his illegal day, when it's line four... or if he's not here – he might be in court, for example – then put the call through to Inma. Inma will be on Juanma's line – four that is – until coffee break, then you'll have to try her on her own line, which is five, but she's often not there and you'll have to ring Eduardo to find out where she is. Eduardo is line two and sometimes you have to press the button more than once. Are you alright so far?'

I nodded eagerly, not altogether grasping the finer points.

'Now, that's if they haven't got an appointment. If they have got an appointment, you must check it in the appointment book...'

'How do I do that?' I asked, thinking I ought to be asking an intelligent question or two.

Mati pulled hard on her cigarette and narrowed her eyes. 'You ask them for their name and then see if that name is written down in the book. If it is, they have got an appointment, and if it isn't, they haven't. You got that?'

I wasn't sure: this was moving outside my league.

'Because there are some who will try and fool you into thinking they have an appointment when in fact they haven't...'

'Is there no depth to which people won't sink?'

Mati didn't think that comment worth noticing and, stubbing out her cigarette, opened the door and lit another one. Having dealt calmly with an agitated Senegalese woman who had burst in armed with a sheaf of forms, she lit yet another cigarette and continued with my induction.

'Now, if they fulfil both the conditions of having been here before and having an appointment, you must find out what they want. If it's a legal problem, then Fatima will deal with it, but you must be careful because often what sounds like a legal problem is in fact a social problem. Our social worker is Erminia and she's only here on Mondays, Wednesdays and Fridays. She shares a room with Eduardo, so if his line's working that's where you'll reach her.'

Mati opened the door as she said this, in response to a spirited and prolonged ringing of the bell. A group of Peruvians poured into the tiny room, each wearing bright weaves on top of assorted denim and shouting loudly over each other in what I took to be Quechua.

Lighting another cigarette, Mati swung round the desk and joined them, sounding firm and conciliatory at the same time. The telephone rang. She looked back at me suggestively. I looked at the burbling telephone as if it were a box with a snake in it. There was no room for doubt, though: she wanted me to answer it. Hitherto I had been busying myself with opening the door, looking blankly at the groups of needy clients as I tried in vain to understand some shred of their excitable introductory speech, and then, with relief, handing them over to the omnicompetent Mati.

'Go on, answer it,' she said.

Timidly I lifted the receiver. '*Hola*,' I said... Nothing, silence.

'Nobody there, Mati,' I explained thankfully and made to put it down again.

'You have to press the green button to open the line.'

I pressed the green button and arrived halfway through an impassioned tirade in what I thought may have been Hausa, or perhaps Swahili, but anyway with the unmistakable tones of the African continent. I couldn't make head nor tail of it. Soon there was a breathy hiatus.

'Could you say that again, please… in Spanish?'

There was an unfamiliar oath and my interlocutor launched into another language. This was closer to home – it sounded like Egyptian Arabic with an element of Portuguese – but it was still hard to tell what was being said.

'*Vous parlez français?*' – problem-solving on the hoof.

Now there came a fluid but totally incomprehensible French, almost as bad as my own.

'Do you have an appointment?'

'*Oui… oui… oui!*'

Now I was getting somewhere. The line, though, was bad and I was surrounded by a constant and raucous babble.

'Tell me your name.' I frowned and strained, pressed the receiver to one ear and stuck my finger in the other. 'Sorry, can you repeat that, please?' We tried again. It seemed more like a poem than a proper noun.

'How about you spell that out?' I removed the finger from my ear and fumbled among the pages of the appointments book. A group of Moroccan students was crowding around a couple of middle-aged Romanian women and trying to pore over a city plan on the wall. The Moroccans were getting some tart words from the Romanians for pushing.

'*Quoi?*' came the voice from the other end of the line, incredulous.

'Spell it out – you know, letters.' It was only then that I realised what a ridiculous suggestion this was, as whatever tongue this name belonged to, it would be more than likely written in Arabic script, or some baffling ideographic system. But, as Mati had by now settled things with the Andean contingent, she took the telephone from me and, with an indulgent grin, calmly and swiftly sorted it all out.

It had been a poor showing, and I hung my head a little. Mati was kind to me but I could see that there was a slight element of condescension in her smile. 'Jeezus,' I thought, 'if I can't even do my bit answering the phones, then what good am I? Where do I go from here?'

I carried on for a while, opening the door, occasionally taking the phone, when there was nobody else within range. But things didn't improve much, and at lunchtime I went to seek out Charo, who runs the show, and who manages in her quiet, confident way to keep the lid on the whole heaving shebang. Now, Charo is one of those people who exudes charisma and charm, and along with Mati she is the compelling attraction of *Granada Acoge*, inspiring bright young lawyers, social workers and interpreters to sign away their free time to the cause. I suspect Che Guevara had a similar magnetism, though perhaps less of the feminine warmth.

I sat across the desk from Charo, she like a gentle and beautiful headmistress and me the hopeless pupil, but a good bit older than her. 'I'm afraid I've not been of much use,' I mumbled. 'I don't think I was cut out to be a telephonist.'

Charo was looking at me curiously, trying to fathom out what was going on in my mind. I have this recurrent waking nightmare that women are different from us men in a whole heap of sometimes terrifying ways, the worst being that they can actually read your mind – and no matter how close or intimate you get with a woman she will never *ever* betray the sorority and tell you the truth. I know this because I've often taxed Ana on the subject, but to absolutely no avail. But this terrible suspicion has never left me and probably never will. It's one of a number of reasons why I'd like to be a woman for a week…

'I'd really like to be useful to you,' I fumbled on. 'But if I can't fulfil the most basic function of your organisation… Well…'

'Well,' she echoed, leaning back into her chair, 'we do have a magazine, you know. You said you were a writer…'

'Well, yes…' I smiled modestly.

The telephone rang. Charo answered. 'It's for you, Cristóbal…'

'For me?'

'Yes…' she held out the receiver. I looked at it aghast. Oh Lord, I wasn't going to have to go through another fiasco like the last one in front of Charo.

'Go on, take it. It's only Mati…'

Relief flooded over me. '*Hola*, Mati?'

'Do you speak German, Cristóbal?'

'A bit. Why?'

'Get yourself down here, I've got a job for you.'

Thus I found myself creeping among the wards of the Virgin of the Snows hospital looking for a German girl called Lotta, who had had an accident and spoke not one word of Spanish. I felt pretty important: I was actually on a mission.

I found Lotta, without a problem, in a second-floor ward. She looked like an enormous porcelain doll, her head swollen and bandaged, and she lay staring in an agitated sort of way out of the window. She was fine, she said, in spite of a crack on the skull, but was desperately worried about her dog. It transpired that she was hitching around Spain with her dog and had taken the animal for a walk one night, when it upped and took off after a cat. It heaved her over the side of a bridge and she fell into the dry riverbed. The dog rocketed off after the cat, and when she regained consciousness it was nowhere to be found.

The accident had taken place a hundred kilometres to the northeast, but she had been brought to the Granada hospital for a spot of remodelling on her poor swollen head, which had taken a hell of a blow. She didn't seem to mind about that at all, even when I told her, translating for the charming young doctor, that if things didn't go right she might need extra surgery to make sure her eyes stayed in line.

'I've got to get out of here and find my dog,' she said.

In her ward, across the aisle, was a little girl, sad and quiet and sick and hooked up to a number of bottles and electronic devices. Beside her bed sat her mother, a tiny countrywoman. She had sat there for three days and nights, she said. That's what you do in Spanish hospitals: you have to provide your own nursing. This woman was the very essence of tenderness and care, and, as if it were not enough to comfort her poor little daughter, she was tormented with worry for Lotta's plight. My arrival and the opening of a conduit of communication released a torrent of concern. It had been unbearable for her, she said, to sit there and see poor Lotta so damaged and broken and so far from her mother, and to be unable to speak words of comfort to her.

Lotta said that the mother had in fact talked to her ceaselessly, but with her own lack of Spanish, communication had been limited to loving squeezes of Lotta's hand. Apparently, by barking, Lotta had managed to get the idea of the dog across, but what part the dog played in the drama had remained a mystery to Angustias, which the mother told me was her name. With Lotta's permission I filled Angustias in on the mysteries of Lotta's situation, and Lotta on the diagnosis of Angustias's daughter – a form of hepatitis, but one that seemed to be slowly improving.

Better news was to come for Lotta, too. A male nurse at the little health centre in Cuevas del Campo, where she had received initial treatment, had found her dog waiting outside and was looking after it in his own home. He reassured her that he would be happy to keep the pet until Lotta was well enough to make the journey back. This put Lotta's mind at rest sufficiently for her to promise that she wouldn't discharge herself there and then.

By the time I got back to Aguas de Cartuja, *Granada Acoge* had closed for lunch. I found the staff in the bar nearby, clustered in a group around Charo and Mati. Charo beckoned me over and, after hearing about the events of the morning, continued with her suggestion that I write something for their magazine.

I promised to think about it. Then I went home and thought about it. One of the things that had struck me about the Moroccan lads was the hardship of the journey they had undergone, through mountains and remote paths with scarce food or water, wearing just a worn pair of trainers. I decided to walk the route that they might have followed on their way through the mountains, and write an article about it for Charo's magazine. I got very excited about this idea and resolved, in order to give the undertaking at least the appearance of authenticity, to wear an old pair of cheap trainers, perhaps even flip-flops, and to carry my needments in a small sports bag – in short, the uniform of the poor Moroccan immigrant.

'That's a great idea, Chris. Maybe you could also sell it to one of the papers, and raise more funds,' Charo enthused. 'And think how nice it will be to do something different from all those light little comedies about sheep and parrots.'

●

It is a hell of a journey that the Moroccan and African immigrants undertake. Nothing perhaps, given that some travel up from Ghana or Sierra Leone. However, three hundred kilometres or more in mountainous country, as an illegal, looking out for the police, is not a Sunday stroll, as I found myself explaining, a few days later, to Michael Jacobs. 'Perhaps I'll compromise the purity of the concept a little and abandon the flip-flops,' I mused, dwelling on the detail. 'Flip-flops are hell in the mountains.'

'Well, I think we should... g-go for as much authenticity as possible. I wonder if it would help *Granada Acoge* if we each wrote a piece on the walk?'

'You mean, you want to come too?'

'W-well, if you d-didn't mind. Y-yes, I'd love to come.'

I thought about it briefly. It would be nice to have company on this lengthy and gruelling trip, and Michael was a serious person, in agreement with me as to the objectives of the expedition and its underlying philosophies. 'Of course. That would be great.'

And so our expedition was conceived. Two writers would set out in the footsteps of the Moroccans who had turned up at my farm, making their way through the hostile mountains of Andalucía to the promised land of El Ejido in the east. By this shift we would highlight the predicament of the illegal immigrant and air questions on the complacency of us denizens of Fortress Europe. It was a heady notion – at last, a form of activism I could act upon.

As is so often the case, Michael just happened to know exactly the person we should meet – a professor of Ecology called Manolo, who worked at the University of Seville and who was an expert on the Parque de los Alcornocales – Spain's largest national park – a swathe of forest that cuts north from the strip of coastline where the Moroccan launches tend to land. We arranged to meet up at his house near Seville, where he kindly supplied us with a compass and maps and drove us into the mountains to Alcalá de los Gazules, the start of our walk.

At Alcalá the rain came down in sheets, the streets were ankle-deep in rushing waters. I bought an umbrella. 'Vogue', it said – 'Vogue Windproof'. It seemed a somewhat inauspicious way to begin the journey.

AUTHENTICITY WILL OUT

A S THE RAIN LASHED DOWN ON ALCALÁ, we ducked
into a bar, but there were so many people in
there sheltering from the downpour that there
was no room to open our map. We went outside
onto a terrace protected by a canvas awning so that Manolo
could draw our route, but the air itself was so damp that
within minutes the map was sodden, and wherever he so
much as touched it with his pencil the point made a grubby
hole.

Manolo knew the Alcornocales well, having grown up
in the region and worked there as a park warden before
joining the University of Seville. He explained to us in
minute detail the route we should take. 'Now at the first
bifurcation of the path, by a big rock, don't take it, but keep
on until the main path turns left and starts to climb. The
important thing is at all times to keep the peak of Aljibe on

your left and the radar dome of Pico de las Yeguas on your right – that way you can't possibly go wrong.' And he made a couple of big wet holes with his pencil in the remains of our map. 'I must be getting home to my family now. Any problems, just give me a ring on my mobile.' And he sloshed off into the wet, black night.

I couldn't help but feel that we were already losing a certain amount of authenticity. Not many immigrants would have the benefit of a briefing from a former park warden. And none would have the luxury of spending a wet night, as we did, in the *hostal* above the bar. Not that it was exactly high life. In the room we were offered, water was dripping through the ceiling and down the wire to the dim bare bulb; the bathroom was soft and green with mould; the floor was awash; and there was an interesting design feature consisting of a window that opened directly onto a concrete wall. But the room next door looked even worse, from a glimpse through the open door, where a group of men in vests were sitting around coughing and watching TV. A good night's sleep seemed unlikely, so we set out for a last night on the town, before our journey.

Dominguito's was the place to eat in Alcalá, according to the barman downstairs, and when the rain slackened for a moment that was where we went. Dominguito was a lugubrious sort of a man with protuberant ears and thick glasses. He thrust a *tapa* towards us with our drinks. Michael, as ever, recovered his spirits. 'The seafood'll be g-good here,' he enthused. 'So we ought to try the prawns... Also you get fantastically good ham – the woods are full of p-pigs, so a *ración* of *jamón ibérico* would be nice. Cádiz produces interesting white wines, too, so we'll have a b-bottle or two of the Gadir Blanco...'

I was happy to leave the choice to Michael, who can talk of the regional gastronomy of Spain as others might discuss football. But again I was assailed by a shadow of concern that the purity of our expedition was being compromised by a very un-Moroccan feasting on ham and wine. Still, I like ham and wine a lot, and as all the Moroccans I know approve of a bit of feasting when the chance arises, I thought I'd indulge myself just this once.

That night, the electricity in our room kept on fizzing, even when the light was off. The water dripped irregularly through the hole in the ceiling. The men in vests next door had turned the television up so they could hear it above the sound of their coughing. Michael was fast asleep within thirty seconds of hitting the bed – and he snored like a bastard. I lay there, listening to all these noises and thinking in a disjointed sort of a way of what an interesting exercise it would be to write them all down in musical notation.

The morning found us back at Dominguito's, which had been recommended to us as the best bar in town for breakfast – again by the barman at the *hostal*, whose ears also stuck out a lot. I suspected him of being Dominguito's brother.

'What they have for b-breakfast in this region,' said Michael, 'is *manteca colorá*. It's wonderful – you should try it on t-toast.'

Manteca colorá is the orange pig-fat butter that in Andalucía you see the more Spanish type of Spaniard smearing thick on his *tostada* in the morning. He'll be washing it down with a *coñac* or two to get himself bounced into the day. I had always viewed *manteca colorá* with suspicion – it's pretty suspicious-looking stuff, coming as it does in white, off-grey or orange – and in all my time in Spain I had never once tried it. But Michael's features were suffused with pleasure as he stuffed the ghastly-looking mush into his face. 'G-go on,' he burbled with his mouth full. 'It'll set us up nicely for the day's walk.'

Gingerly I smeared a smidgen upon my toast and took a bite. In a rather gross, atavistic way, it was delicious. I helped myself to a little more, then a lot more, until my *tostada* groaned beneath the weight of livid orange fat. I felt a slight biliousness, and yet at the same time a hit of energy from the dead pig coursing through my veins. Michael was right: this was exactly what you needed to set you up for a day's trudge. Once again, though, I couldn't help noting that few genuine arrivals from North Africa would fancy pig-fat butter at the start of their day.

There were a dozen or so men at the bar. Michael regaled them all with the details of our projected undertaking, and asked for their advice. This was not such a good idea, I thought, as it would serve only to confuse the already convoluted directions we had got from Manolo. And, sure enough, the ensuing babble chased away my few shreds of certainty.

At least it had stopped raining though, and, pausing only to buy a few supermarket victuals (a cheese Michael liked the look of, some ham, a bag of olives, and another of dates) we hoisted our laden packs onto our shoulders and trudged off along the road. If truth be told, I was actually the one doing the hoisting, because, instead of the authentic sports bag, I had brought with me a proper backpack, whereas Michael had borrowed a bright red cotton duffel bag, with straps that were just bits of string. This was authentic gear, and, even with just a toothbrush and some food, the straps were already cutting into his shoulders.

As we walked, the sun burst through a gap in the rolling black clouds and in an instant the air was thick with huge flying ants. There were so many of them that you couldn't help breathe them in – although they were so large that they didn't quite fit up your nostril and thus were able to make good their escape. It was an eerie scene, and the more so as the sun dried the vegetation and the very earth started to steam.

Soon we reached a *venta* – a roadside inn. 'We could stop for a c-coffee here, perhaps, no?' suggested Michael. 'And we could ask the way…'

'Heavens, man, we've only been walking for fifteen minutes… But yes, why not?'

So we stopped and dropped our packs. There was nobody about except for a fat lout who was propelling a mop about the place with a pronounced lack of enthusiasm. The lout looked at us without interest and shambled behind the bar to get a head of steam up in the coffee machine. Michael got the map out, and the notepad upon which Manolo had sketched the route. In the cold light of day and at the head of the trail it looked more baffling than ever. There was a sketch of what looked like railway sidings, a pine tree (beside which Manolo had written '*pino*') and a rock (labelled '*tajo*'), then a long, wiggly dotted line that passed neatly through the spiral binding of my notebook to our destination on the next page.

'Hmm,' said Michael in an unconvincing sort of way.

'What we know for sure,' I assured him, 'in fact the only thing we know for sure, is that we have to keep the peak of Aljibe on our right at all times.'

'N-no, left,' said Michael.

'I'm sure he said right, Michael.'

'N-no. He said we had to keep ourselves on the right of it... thus it'll b-be on *our* left.'

'I'm not so sure. But how are we to know which one Aljibe is?'

'It's got a radar d-dome on the top.'

'No, that's the Sierra de las Yeguas, and we have to keep either right or left of that...'

Michael looked uncertainly at the map and scratched his head. 'What's that p-pine tree there for?'

'I can't remember what Manolo said about the pine tree. It's very nicely drawn. Maybe it's just a particularly good one.'

We finished our coffee and Michael tried asking the lout for directions, but to no avail. Still, with our hearts full of ill-founded optimism, we plunged into the park. Within an hour, we had lost all trace of a path and were blundering about up to our chests in the exuberant vegetation of the cork oak forest.

Now, a cork oak forest may be a pleasant thing to look upon, with its exotic tangle of flowering cistus, dog roses and gorse, but it's a rotten place to be blundering about in. It was no longer a matter of keeping peaks on our right or left; we couldn't see beyond the next tree trunk, let alone out of the woods. Our boots had become caked with heavy mud; we were scratched and bleeding, confused and a little irritated by the way things were going.

We came to the top of a rise, where we could see above the trees. 'B-bloody hell,' said Michael. 'It looks like the middle of the Tasmanian rainforest.'

It was an odd parallel to draw, as neither of us had ever been anywhere near Tasmania, and what we were looking at was cork oaks. But I knew what he meant. On all sides of us stretched an unbroken forest of trees, seemingly track-less, without clearings or breaks. A small flock of vultures circled aimlessly above a distant rise. A little disenchanted, we plunged back into the trees, heading, insofar as possible, to the northeast – where in sixty kilometres or so the forest would come to an end.

We clambered carefully through barbed-wire fences, scrambled in and out of overgrown ravines, and slogged up steep slopes, all deep beneath the canopy of trees. I stopped for a minute, obeying the call of nature; then, hurrying along to catch up, burst through a clump of oleander to find Michael rooted to the spot, staring intently ahead.

'What's the matter?'

Without speaking he indicated a sign nailed to a tree: '*Toros Bravos*', it said – Fighting Bulls.

'We can't p-possibly go on through here...' Michel hissed. 'I'm terrified of *toros bravos*.'

'Don't you worry about it,' I said putting my arm on Michael's shoulder. 'That sign is just there to frighten us.'

'I don't think so, Chris,' he replied, with studied calm. 'I think it's there so if we get gored to d-death we can't blame anyone.'

'Look,' I said, reassuringly. 'There's no bulls in sight, and besides, there are lots of trees... If anything should happen, all we have to do is find a tree and shin up it. That's what you do with bulls.'

The truth is that, if aroused, the *toro bravo* is one of the most aggressive animals on the planet – they are, of course, selected for the trait – and an awful lot more people get gored in the Spanish countryside than in the bullrings. So Michael's fears were pretty well founded. However, we had to get through this place, and besides, as I reassured him, there are often signs indicating the presence of *toros bravos* when in fact there aren't any bulls at all. Michael still seemed reluctant to move, but after I changed tack and suggested that the bulls were most likely to appear close to the sign where we were standing, he agreed to keep going. As we tramped on apprehensively, I mused over whether this would be a good moment to mention the unhelpful colour of his rucksack – which, you may recall, was a vivid red.

The bulls failed to materialise, and who could blame them? For although the Parque de los Alcornocales is held in high esteem for its beauty, wildness and the variety of its flora and fauna, the corner that we had chosen to explore was distinguished by little other than heavy mud, aggressive vegetation and the apparent absence of any paths.

After what seemed like hours of beating our way morosely through this ill-favoured landscape, we came to a farm, where a short man with a moustache and a cheese-cutter cap appeared from beneath a tree and eyed us in an unfriendly fashion. 'You want to be a bit careful if you're planning to walk further,' he growled. 'They're hunting today and there's a lot of guns out on the hills. You want to stay on the track there and cut up the hill just before you get to the reservoir. Don't go past the reservoir or you stand a good chance of getting shot.'

'W-wonderful,' said Michael. 'Thank you very much.'

'Go with God,' said our man and returned to whatever it was he had been doing.

Michael looked at me meaningfully. 'G-God, what an accursed b-bloody place! If you aren't lost forever in the trackless forest, you get gored to death by b-bulls – and if the b-bloody bulls don't get you, the goddam hunters'll shoot you down! I tell you, Chris, this place is a d-death! Give me the city any day.'

It was hard to disagree just then. But I reminded Michael that this was not intended as a nature ramble. And getting lost and uncomfortable made things, well, almost authentic.

We struck onwards along a dull track for an hour, and then came to a reservoir. 'We're not supposed to go p-past the reservoir... That's where we get shot,' Michael groaned.

'Yes, but there's been nowhere to turn off until now. We'll just go a little bit further and see if we can find a path uphill.'

We walked on until suddenly, rounding a tight corner, our way was blocked by a group of horned cows.

'Oh J-Jeezus Christ!' cried Michael.

'They're cows, Michael. They don't mean us any harm.'

'How do you know? Oh, God – they're looking at us!'

It was true. The cows were looking at us in a bovine sort of a way, and seemed reluctant to move out of our path.

'But that's what cows do, Michael. They look at you with those big limpid eyes...'

'They're looking at us LIKE THEY WANT TO KILL US!!'

'No they aren't. I mean, they don't. They're not bulls – they're cows, man.'

'Oh yes? And what about those bloody great horns?'

'Horns, Michael, contrary to popular belief, are not a defining male characteristic. These are cows – look, they've got udders.' (So I confidently assured him, though I have since been told by a man who breeds *ganado bravo* – fighting cattle – that the cows are the most dangerous. The ferocious aggression for which they are bred, coupled with their maternal instinct, can make an extremely disagreeable companion on a woodland walk).

We skirted round the edge of this group of underrated beasts and cut up through the scrub, a hideous slope covered in chest-high cistus, brambles and gorse. 'I reckon if we just keep on going up we can't be far wrong,' I said breezily, to comfort my agitated companion. It was already abundantly clear that his navigational skills were even poorer than my own, so I thought it best, for the good of the expedition, to assume command.

We climbed up and up and on and on. The breath burst from our lungs and our aching muscles begged us to stop, but still we climbed. After perhaps a couple of hours of battling through the beastly scrub, we found ourselves on the edge of a steep muddy track. Not caring a fig where it led, we followed it on up. Every now and then there were scatterings of fresh grain. I decided to keep quiet about this, as Michael, with his poor understanding of country ways, would be unlikely to recognise it as hunters' bait. But after we passed the fifth or sixth heap, curiosity got the better of him.

'What d'you suppose this stuff is, Chris?'

'It's just stuff.' I figured that my friend was a man so irrepressibly urban that he was unlikely to know what wheat and barley even looked like. And he was silent for a bit. I heard his heavy mud-clogged boots squelching on behind me. I could tell he was thinking.

'But then why is there stuff, and to my untutored eye it looks like fresh stuff... Why are there regular heaps of fresh stuff?'

'That's just the way it is in the country: there's fresh stuff all over the place – it's seeds.'

'You know what it makes me think of?'

'No, tell me...' I asked, bracing myself for trouble. His answer surprised me.

'It makes me think of the years of hunger under Franco,' he said. 'Life really was desperate across this province in the 1940s.' And Michael went on to tell me of a father and his fourteen-year-old son, who in desperation had left their mountain village to seek work on the coast. They had walked for a day and a half until they got to Málaga – the best part of a hundred-and-fifty kilometres. 'And not only that,' he continued, 'but they spent five hungry days in the city looking for work, and when they didn't find anything, they turned around and walked back – with no money and nothing to eat, just the figs and prickly pears they could pick as they passed. Just imagine... It's one thing walking with your belly full of food and hope. But to trudge on starving and discouraged like that... How terrible that must be.'

I hadn't seen this side of Michael before – he had always been the bold and witty raconteur, drawing out nuggets of erudition and displaying them with all the panache of a street performer. But there was a pared-down quality to his speech now and to the stories that followed, as if he were reaching for something elemental. Walking does that for you: it beats out a different pace for your thoughts to follow.

We talked on – of the miners of Órgiva who would gather and plait esparto grass, to fashion shoes to walk with the next day, as they tramped up the hill to work each morning. The paths were so long and rough that their shoes only lasted a day's journeying. And I remembered a story that an elderly couple in Torvizcón had told me, of how in the year of their marriage they had rented a farm high in the mountains above Trevélez, and staked all the money they had on some sacks of potatoes to produce a crop of 'Papas de la Sierra', which are highly prized as seed potatoes – or were, as nobody sows them any more. They worked all through that long summer nurturing the crop, their hope for a start in married life. But when it came to selling the fruits of their labour, the price they were offered by the wretched local merchants did not even cover the cost of the transport down from the hill. Pepe told me that even fifty years later he could still remember the misery he had felt as he climbed back to tell his wife the news of their destitution.

Michael listened. 'I think it's time for some lunch,' he said.

We threw ourselves down on the track and unpacked the food. Soon the olives were caked in mud and there was mud on the bread. Tiny ants swarmed over the ham and sausage. We didn't care, though. We just slumped on the ground and ate the ants and the mud along with the rest.

We had climbed above the woods now and could see all the way down to the sea at Barbate. The sun glittered through the mist and the Mediterranean shone as a sheet of white at the foot of the deep forest. 'That's where we

really ought to have started, down on the beach at Boloña,'
I suggested.

'What!? Walk through even more of this beastly forest?
Not b-bloody likely!'

●

It's amazing how quickly one recovers with a bit of rest
and food. With just a few false starts, we stumbled upon a
path leading down into one of the typical 'cloud valleys' of
the park, lush and dripping with mists. The sun broke out
through the thick canopy of trees, hung with lichen and
mosses. A clear stream meandered in its deep cleft.

We scrambled on down the valley, which had now
thinned into a chestnut forest, until finally, at dusk, we
entered the village of Sauceda. Michael knew all about
it. In 1936, the first year of the Civil War, this village in
the forest had become a hide-away for Republicans and
for a while had flourished as a model community run
along communist lines. Then, at first light one morning,
Franco's air force had bombed and strafed it to rubble,
slaughtering hundreds of men, women and children. The
only building to survive was the *ermita*, the little stone
church.

The village now was used mainly as a summer camp but
with the holidays still a few weeks away it was empty and
had a ghostly feel. Worse still, the cabins all stank of bleach
and there was not a single bar. We were reduced instead
to cajoling the warden into selling us a box of ready-made
sangría. Michael's face as he carried this box of foul liquid
back to our cabin could have been used as a study for Christ
Carrying the Cross.

Night came on and we sat in the dark on a stone wall, outside our chlorinated hut, and addressed ourselves to our muddy olives, *chorizo* and bread. We grimaced at one another as we washed it all down with the *sangría*. 'Lord,' I exclaimed, 'if this was Morocco, we'd be sipping a delicious glass of mint tea right now; not poisoning our livers with this chemical muck.'

'Ngraaughh,' Michael agreed. He was gnawing hard on a hacking of *chorizo*.

I looked at the horrible, mud-caked sausage with distaste. 'And why is it that we always end up eating some part of a pig?' I demanded. 'Surely we ought to make some efforts to be a little more authentic. No?'

'W-well...' answered Michael, taken slightly aback by my assertion. 'It depends what you mean by authentic. Five hundred years ago converted Muslims and Jews were obliged to display a *jamón* swinging from their rafters as proof that they had genuinely adopted Christianity. Otherwise, they'd have been slung out of the country by the Inquisition. Why do you think the meat has achieved such iconic importance in this country? Anyway,' he paused, 'it makes sense that, as hispanicised Brits, we follow the same habits.'

He had a point. I took the slice of *chorizo* he'd balanced for me on the point of his knife, and settled back for a long, contemplative chew.

A sad fact about a long walk is that it tends to be repetitious and somewhat dull to relate. The scenery varies, as does the weather, and occasionally you run into a fellow traveller. But mostly it's just a matter of walking: marvellous for meditation, less so for dramatic narrative. And so it was for Michael and me. We trudged on. Michael became as foolishly nonchalant as I was about cow encounters and we talked a lot about our sore and weary bodies and – as you do when you're hungry and have no prospect of a decent dinner – about the deliciousness of food.

Next to history and art, gastronomy is the subject that Michael most excels in. And he talked with great passion about El Rey de Copas, the restaurant of his friend and neighbour, Juan Matias, a chef who Michael insists is touched by culinary genius: a man who can slice, heat, mix or beat the edible bits that co-exist with him in his particular corner of the planet like no other cook. In the way that a really fine wine can touch the nerve endings of the soul and lift you briefly above the quotidian woes, so can his food. Or it can on a good day. For Juan Matias isn't always in the mood for haute cuisine and the foodies who seek him out from as far afield as Madrid can, on occasion, find themselves presented with a dish of steak and chips. 'But what steak! What chips!' Michael enthused, kissing the ends of his fingers.

Not that we spent all our time on this walk discussing our favourite restaurants. No, indeed. There were moments when food, wine or even a decent bed for the night were mere passing thoughts. One was when we stumbled upon the Roman road that zigzags steeply up through dazzling mountain scenery to Benaocán, with its white stones, gutters, culverts and drainage systems almost entirely intact; and another on the high pass of Puerto Boyar just above the town of Grazalema, when we were treated to an extraordinary fiesta of birds.

We had stopped to guzzle oranges in the grass beneath a huge crag, pockmarked with little caves and nesting holes, when suddenly the air came alive with the beating of wings: there were choughs cawing, bee-eaters flashing the colours of the rainbow as the sun caught their feathers, crag martins racing hell for leather among the rocks, kestrels mewing, hawks hovering. Then, from somewhere in the upper air, came a whooshing sound, a great shadow passed over us, and with a sudden downdraft a huge eagle landed on the ledge not twenty feet above our heads. I looked up and gasped in wonder and, as I looked, down came another. They were so close that I could see the fierceness in their eyes, see the claws on those terrible talons, talons that could effortlessly crush the bone in your wrist. To see these magnificent creatures land on their nest so close to us was perhaps the most dazzling sight I had ever seen.

'Jeezus, Michael! Did you see that? I'm telling you, you could live a hundred years and you'll never see anything like that again. Bloody hell!... I mean, God... I mean... I can't believe I've seen what I've just seen...' I babbled on.

But even Michael, one of the least ornithologically aware people I knew, had stood up, open mouthed, letting the orange knife clatter down the hillside.

●

At last, on our fourth day of trekking, we crossed the plateau that leads to the valley below Ronda – which we had revised as our target, a waymark perhaps one quarter of the immigrants' way to El Ejido. The hill town was a most welcome sight, although from a distance, through my sweat- and dust-caked spectacles, it looked like a smear of white guano on the top of a rock, such as you'd expect from a colony of gannets.

We slogged across the valley, and little by little the euphoria induced by the sight of our goal started to vanish and gave way to a morose silence. As we approached Ronda, I became ever more conscious of how dirty, evil-smelling and sore I was. My companion looked, if possible, even less edifying than I did. He was limping and blistered, and the string that held his pack had lacerated his shoulders. I kept a good distance ahead of him, so I wouldn't be affected by his groans of pain.

As we reached a curious no-man's land down by the town dump, the way parted and there was a signpost – the first we had seen since Alcalá. One way said '*Ronda – 20 minutos*', and the other '*Ronda – 30 minutos*'. Tired and sore though we were, we chose the longer, which Michael thought looked more promising from the landscape point of view.

An hour's limping later and we had crossed the great gorge and were hobbling into the nearest bar. One drink led to another, and the rich smell of the tapas and the jollity of the bar soon entrapped us, weakened as we were. We forgot our pains and our filthy state, and steeped ourselves in food and drink. It was unthinkable to imagine what it must be like to arrive tired and hungry in such a town and to stay hidden until a safe way out presented itself.

For Michael and me, the route on was simple: we caught an early-morning train to Granada. As the train threaded its way through those hidden parts of Andalucía where it seems that only trains can go, I opened a heavy-lidded eye and looked at my walking companion, who was deep in a book he was supposed to be reviewing.

'Y'know what?' I said, in a ruminative frame of mind. 'I can't help feeling that we lost track of the original purpose of our journey.'

Michael looked up and studied me thoughtfully.

'Hmm,' he said. 'Maybe you're right, but the truth is that you can't really get to grips with the difficulties Moroccans have in Spain unless you know a bit about the life they leave behind, don't you think?' And with a grunt and a readjustment of his eyebrows, he returned to his book.

GRAHAM GREENE AND
THE COBRAS

I N AN EFFORT TO MAKE ENDS MEET when we first came to
Spain, seventeen years ago, Ana and I used to collect
seeds for our friend, Carl, who ran a mail-order seed
company from his home in Sussex. As Ana knew
something about botany, I tended to be the unfortunate erk
who had the brains boiled out of him on hot Spanish hillsides, bent with my sacks and secateurs, while she toiled
amongst the reference books and told me where to go and
what to look for. If the location was somewhere nice and
the picking not too disagreeable, then she would come
along too.

Once in a burst of optimism, ill-founded as it turned
out, we took an order for ten kilos of lavender seed. The
seeds of the lavender in question, *Lavandula stoechas*, are

like dust, and we spent weeks cutting plants in the hills, stuffing them into sacks, and emptying them onto our flat roof to dry in the sun. The whole roof was covered in a scented cloud of lavender. We dried it and trod it and sifted and fanned it, and little by little, grain by grain, the black pile of infinitesimal seeds started to appear. It was like panning for gold, because for each kilo we were to be paid £200. If we could achieve the full amount, then the boost to our fragile economy would be enormous. But we never did quite manage the order – like Zeno's paradoxes, the pile of seeds accumulated at a slower and slower rate, and was periodically depleted by gusts of wind.

We might have despaired if Carl hadn't come up with an even better route to financial security. We could collect an order of Moroccan broom instead. Now, Moroccan broom, or Cytisus battandieri, is a lovely plant – a big silver-leafed bush with sweet-scented yellow racemes draping down like wisteria blooms – and Carl had seen the most beautiful specimens carpeting the forest floor in a clearing just outside a small Middle Atlas town called Azrou. It would be easy to find, he assured me. He had jotted down some directions and drawn a map of sorts, and there would be no problem picking or shipping them out, as no restrictions existed between Morocco and Spain. He'd pay me the princely sum of £3,500 for ten kilos – and the same again the following year if all went according to plan.

Well, we were in no position to turn down an offer like that. So, at the end of August, which is just about when the broom starts to release its seeds, I crossed over to Tangier and took the night train to Fez, where I could pick up a bus to Azrou.

It was late morning and the heat at the Fez bus station seemed to come straight from the desert. At length I found the Azrou bus, clambered in and slid into a spare seat. It seemed about to leave, but there we sat, slowly baking in the midday sun, while passengers squeezed into the aisle until further movement was impossible. The sweat poured off me in rivers and my head was pounding by the time the driver climbed in and started the engine. He looked around at the multitude of passengers, eager for motion and air, then got out again and disappeared for another twenty minutes, leaving us half asphyxiated by fumes. Nobody seemed to mind, though, and eventually he returned and we set off slowly across the shimmering stony hills towards Azrou. The wind that came in through the window was so hot it seemed to shrivel the very hairs in my nostrils.

Azrou means 'rock' in Berber. It takes its name from a huge rock in the middle of the town, upon which is written AZROU in huge letters. Below the rock there is a line of cheap cafés and basic hotels. I checked into one of them, on the promise of a cold tap in my room, and, after a splash, set off in the soft evening light in the direction suggested by Carl's map. I had two photos of the plant I was seeking and a photocopied map of the area. For an hour and a half I climbed uphill and into the forest. The holly oaks and hawthorns that grew along the lower slopes soon gave way to the great blue Atlantic cedars. It really was like a fairytale forest, the traveller dwarfed by the immensity of the huge trees. The air was still and hot, but the distant blue fronds at the top of the trees lifted and fell in the gentlest of breezes.

I wandered here and there, startled occasionally by scufflings and slitherings, and awed by the beauty of the forest. But there was no sign of *Cytisus battandieri*, and as the gloom settled deeper and the first star appeared in the jagged shreds of sky above the treetops, I decided to give up and return to the town. I was disappointed and a little uneasy: I had invested what for us was a substantial sum of money in this trip and, if I didn't come home with these seeds, we would have a seriously hard winter.

Still, I had only just arrived and maybe the next morning, after food and rest, things would turn out right. I settled into one of the cafés below the hotel; open to the street, they were bathed in the scent of smoke, roasting meat, coriander and diesel fumes. I picked a table in a tiled room at the back, where I could sit alone, and ordered a tumbler of sweet green tea – stuffed with mint like seaweed in the Sargasso Sea – and a mutton kebab from the grill outside. A ceiling fan hummed lazily, doing its best to keep the flies on the move, and, slurping my tea in anticipation of the meal ahead, I took my book out from my bag and read all the extraneous bits on the cover and inside, delaying the pleasure of beginning.

It was *The Captain and the Enemy* – Graham Greene's last novel. I savoured its opening sentence: 'I am now in my twenty-second year and yet the only birthday which I can clearly distinguish among all the rest is my twelfth, for it was on that damp and misty day in September I met the Captain for the first time.' Well, what an opening! I had read once that the *New Statesman* ran an annual competition to submit the first line of a novel in the style of Graham Greene, and that Greene submitted these very words under a pseudonym. Amused when it failed to win, he had the delicious satisfaction of using the words at the start of his next novel.

My dinner was before me now and I sighed a sigh of contentment as I slipped beneath the glorious spell of being alone and far from home, well fed, and embarking upon a new book.

'Hallo, my friend. Where are you from?'

I froze, then buried my head deeper into the book. I wanted to read and eat. I was too tired to deal with some stranger's curiosity. Maybe he was not addressing me and would soon go away.

'Is the book you are a-reading a good one? Tell me, my friend. Where are you from?'

My interrogator had drawn so close I could feel his breath on my face. Without looking up, and with a very bad grace, I grunted, 'I'm English,' and read determinedly on. But it was no good: I'd already lost the thread.

'Aha, English,' echoed my irrepressible interlocutor. 'English from England. Many books I have read from your country.'

'Good,' I growled.

'Yes, many books. I enjoy particularly the novels written after the war.'

The words were overenunciated with a crazy relish, crisp and clipped, and addressed directly into my ear as the man, who was sitting at the next table, had pulled his chair out and was leaning across the narrow space between us.

'And what is that book you are a-reading?'

Rudely, without raising my head, I said, 'Graham Greene!'

The man's eyes lit up. 'Ah, Graham Greene, I like this author very much... *The Captain and the Enemy*. This was a later book and not so interesting as *The Power and the Glory*, but it is very...', he paused, searching for the words, '... provoking of thoughts.' And then the man embarked on the most astonishing resumé of the Greene oeuvre: *Brighton Rock*, *The Lawless Roads*, *The Comedians*, *Travels with my Aunt*. He'd read the lot. 'Perhaps,' he concluded, 'I may buy this book from you after you have read it? I would like to use it with my students.'

It was time to throw in the towel and, besides, it was becoming a privilege to be called a good friend by this fellow Greene fan.

'May my friends and I join you at your table?' he asked.

'Please do.' I dissolved and smiled as my new friend and his two friends and a friend of theirs and the latter's cousin all pulled up chairs and sat down with me.

'My name is Mourad; this is Ali; and this, Aziz and Abdullah and Hamid.'

'I'm Chris – Christophe.'

We all shook hands and, in the face of such evident good-will, my churlishness vanished.

'You are here for holly-days?' asked Mourad with an earnest smile as he inclined his head to listen intently to my answer.

I had never seen anyone revel so much in a simple exchange of words, and found it disarming. Mourad must have been in his mid-twenties, though his neat moustache, meticulously laundered clothes and polished lace-ups made him seem older.

I put away my book and we sat and sipped mint tea together, searching in a mixture of French and English for common ground. Mourad told me that he had recently finished an MA in English Literature at Meknes University, hence his erudition, although his peculiarly clipped enunciation came from hours hunched over the radio listening to the BBC World Service. He had hoped to teach at the local college, but as there were no vacancies he tried to get by giving private lessons.

'And what sort of living is that?' Ali cut in. 'No one here has any money to pay him, though they want to pass their exams sure enough! And he keeps lending them his books! So he has to work like me in the peach harvest to make ends meet.' He emphasised his words, and Mourad's folly, by suddenly grabbing hold of his friend's shoulder and squeezing it fiercely.

But Mourad was not the only one of the group struggling to make a living. Most of them, it seemed, did a variety of irregular jobs, labouring or harvesting, as well as trying to pursue their 'professional' work. Understandably they were intrigued by my seed-collecting mission and, after I had paid the bill, we all strolled down the road to the Pâtisserie Central. Here we installed ourselves at a little melamine table beneath the stars and watched the evening promenade swell to fill the street, as we ate those sweet Moroccan pastries called gazelle horns, and sipped juice made from almonds.

●

The evening promenade was dazzling to watch. It was August, so the town's population, normally around 25,000, had doubled, as *émigrés* returned from France and Germany for the summer holiday. This made for an extraordinary mix of cultures and dress. Whole families would promenade up and down the road, maybe a couple of dozen strong –

the older women veiled from head to toe, the teenagers provocatively dressed in skimpy singlets and the tightest of jeans. In between ran the whole gamut of European and Moroccan fashion, from exquisite silk caftans through Parisian haute couture to the coarse and shapeless sacks of the hardliners. Darkness fell suddenly and the heavy throng was illuminated by the lights from the cafés and the odd car cruising carefully through the crowd. The streets were thick with families milling and dust and warm darkness, and the sound of laughter and pleasantries. And there wasn't a beer in sight.

At our table, the conversation was spirited, if disjointed, as every few minutes an acquaintance of one or other of the group stopped at our table and embraced or kissed everyone with a show of profound affection. I shook hands with each arrival and held the shaken hand sincerely to my heart. Every time, after the embraces, there commenced a lengthy formula of greeting – *labass, veher, hamdullillah* – with earnest hopes as to the well-being of all the family and friends of the recipient, and commendations to the care of Allah.

The intensity of the pleasure that Mourad showed to one friend in particular, the fervour of the embrace and the warmth of the commendations, made me wonder if perhaps they had not seen one another for many years. 'But no,' said Mourad, surprised. 'We were together this afternoon. He will come to see us here tomorrow; I have made an arrangement for him to join us in your agricultural work.'

Mourad had earlier established that he, Ali and Aziz would become my team of seed-pickers in the morning, and as well as that he would not hear of my staying at the hotel. 'I know that Hassan who runs the hotel,' he warned me. 'He is the king's spy. You must stay at my family house.'

So, laboriously, we made our way up the street to the hotel where we gathered my bag and left the spy Hassan fuming. And thus I found myself, after ducking and twisting down dark alleys in one of the more crowded neighbourhoods of the town, in the bosom of a Berber family.

Mourad's family house was a combination of partially built and dilapidated, a structure of reinforced, chipped concrete and shoddy brickwork, with steel rods sticking out all over the place. The floor was concrete, too, and the windows were mostly just unornamented wire grilles. Yet, within the shabby exterior, you could discern the elements of a small Andalusian palace. There was a central courtyard open to the sun, with a tap that ran into a drain in the centre, and around the drain was gathered a little crowd of old oil tins with basil, coriander, thyme and mint and a couple of spindly marguerites. The rooms were arranged on two storeys around the courtyard, and were furnished with rugs and, all around the walls, low beds covered in cushions.

This secret palace was peopled by a family of extraordinary complexity, to whom I was slowly introduced over the next few days. Mohammed, who was Mourad's brother, was easy enough to fathom. At nineteen, and the youngest son of the family, it fell to him to pour the tea and serve and clear the table. He was a beautiful, shy young man who, with help and encouragement from Mourad, had just gained a place to study at the university in Meknes. Then there was an older brother, Hassan, who had a car repair workshop – almost completely devoid of tools – around the corner. Hassan employed Little

Mohammed, who was ten and also lived in the house. Little Mohammed had no family of his own and had just turned up one day, alone and utterly destitute. They had taken him in – although they were not too far off destitution themselves – and he was now part of the family. So too was cross-eyed Abtisa, who haunted the house like a tiny wraith. She had arrived through Latifa, the younger of Mourad's three sisters, who worked as a nurse in Azrou hospital. Six years before, a young couple, on their way to give birth at the hospital, had suffered a car accident. The husband died immediately, but the wife survived in hospital just long enough to give birth to Abtisa, before joining her husband. Nobody at the hospital knew what to do with the little girl, so Latifa took her home. Abtisa was the prettiest little six-year-old, but cross-eyed to the extent that it was a job to know which way she was looking or at whom she was smiling.

Presiding over this enormous family was Aïsha, a huge woman with skin like polished ebony. She drifted imperiously about the rooms in brightly coloured robes, making sure everything was immaculate and well done and to her liking. She welcomed me warmly to her home.

The money to run the household came from wherever and whoever, as fortune dictated. Mourad had brought in a little from some back-breaking work on the peach harvest, as well as some presents – spices, cloth and coffee – from his students; Hassan's tool-less workshop provided occasional sums; Latifa worked for pennies at the hospital; Mohammed, when studying was over, did whatever turned up. Mourad's father was a logger working in the cedar forest and spent most of the time living away on the timber camps.

Mourad told me something about his father's work: how the pay was negligible but the tasks demanded of the men almost superhuman. Local worthies – 'friends of the king' as Mourad put it – would buy the logging concessions on tracts of cedar forest, and then put in poorly paid and ill-equipped teams to do the work. And there was no mechanisation at all in the forest: no cranes, chainsaws or caterpillars – just levers and chains, axes and cross-cut saws and sheer human strength. Mourad pointed out this forestry work to me over the following days and it was staggering. There were logs of cedar eight feet in diameter and twenty feet long, which made a massive load for one of the trucks to haul from the forest. And these logs, weighing as much as five tons, were loaded by hand, all the men getting together at the end of a day's cutting and rolling the monsters up ramps into the back of waiting trucks. 'There are many, many fatal accidents in the forest,' Mourad told me. 'The foresters are very lucky just to survive.'

Having heard all these things I expected Mourad's father to be a great bull of a man, but I was wrong. He showed up later in the week, a small, slightly built character, very quietly spoken and utterly dominated by his galleon-like wife. In fact, I hardly heard a sound from him other than a few welcoming grunts, but then exhaustion often does this to a man.

In the morning, I showed Mourad, Ali and Aziz the photos I had of *Cytisus battandieri*. 'Yes,' said Mourad. 'We will find this plant; it is not a problem. Today we will go to the forest of cedars to i-dent-ify it. Then we return with sacks for the seeds.'

By the time we escaped the clutches of the town, the sun was hitting its zenith and it was a relief to plunge once more into the shade of the cedars. My companions, however, seemed rather nervous and, as we drew deeper into the forest, looked timidly around them, jumping every time they heard a scuffle or a rustle. And there was a lot of scuffling and rustling.

'Cobras,' explained Mourad. 'Black cobras, and they do not just wait for you to stand on them, but they attack you.' And by way of illustration he showed us a wicked scar that ran right across the meat of his thumb. He had been about ten years old, he said, and out in the woods with his father, when – as is the way with boys – he stuck his hand into an interesting hole in some rocks. Unfortunately, there was a snake in there and it bit him. The snake was a black cobra. Mourad's father, seeing the snake, whipped out his knife and slashed his young son's hand deep to the bone. Apparently the venom of these particular cobras will kill you in a couple of minutes, and it was only this instant reaction that saved young Mourad from death.

Of course we all felt very much better after this story, as we walked hither and thither through clearings and thick forest, through stands of young trees and amongst the more thinly spaced old giants. And there was still no sign of the *Cytisus battandieri*, or *hällehäll* as it seemed to be called in Berber.

Mourad appeared from behind a tree, sucking a piece of grass. 'Show me once again the photograph, Chris,' and he looked at Carl's broom photograph for perhaps the fifteenth time that morning. 'I do not know this plant, Chris. Why your friend does want it?'

'Well, it has beautiful flowers and it smells nice, and it's very much in demand as an ornamental plant in Europe.'

'Aah, in Europe,' Mourad echoed in a knowing manner, then studied the photograph a little more. 'I myself do not find it very beautiful. For example, it has no flowers at all.'

'That's because the photograph was taken when the plant was in seed; the flowers have all fallen.'

'Ah, now I see. But I know plants that are much more beautiful, and, what is more, I know where they are.'

'No, it has to be *hällehäll* – that's what my order is for.'

Mourad looked disappointed. 'We must continue seeking,' he said, and we shambled on until we reached a clearing, in the middle of which stood a thin man in a worn dark suit and a thick woollen hat. He carried an umbrella and he was thoughtfully picking his teeth with a knife.

'Who would this be, Mourad?' I asked.

'This man is the *gardien du forêt*. He will know where we can find *hällehäll*. But to ask him could be dangerous, for this is the king's forest and he might decide to report us to the authorities, or he might want some money and we will have to pay him. But now we have no seeds – so let us ask him.'

The *gardien du forêt* didn't seem in the least surprised to see us. Mourad greeted him with the standard formula and then they continued a long animated conversation, the final moments of which showed signs of a breakthrough. Finally the *gardien* stepped across, shook my hand and beckoned me to follow him along a path at the edge of the clearing. 'He knows where to find *hällehäll*,' said Mourad happily. 'And he does not mind us picking it; in fact, he will help us.'

We called for Ali and Aziz and together we climbed a hill and crossed a track into another part of the forest. I walked at the back with Aziz, who was a tall, refined-looking young man with slender fingers. Aziz spoke no English but beautiful French. '*Ah, mon ami Christophe,*' he said mournfully. 'There is nothing in Azrou for a man with my talents. I am only waiting for the letter of authorisation and some money from my girlfriend, who lives in Lyon. And then I will return to France.' As he spoke, he wrung his hands, as if in supplication.

But just then, we burst into the light of another clearing and there was the *Cytisus battandieri*, hundreds of bushes stretching away in all directions. I grabbed a branch and picked some seedpods. Some were greenish still, but others split, cracked and twisted in my hand, spilling little black seeds. Our timing was perfect. A load lifted instantly from my mind: I would have something to show for the trip, after all.

It was right in the middle of the day just then – too hot to do any picking, and besides, we had no sacks to put the seeds in. But all around we could hear pods bursting in the hot sun, a sharp little crack and the patter of tiny seeds scattering among the dry grasses and the hard earth.

'It is lunchtime,' said Mourad brightly, and clapped me on the back. 'It has been a most successful morning's work, no? We have established the whereabouts of the *hällehäll*. Yes – and tomorrow we shall gather the seeds. In the meantime we shall address ourselves to the purchase of some sacks.'

One of the things that struck me about Aïsha's household was that nothing was kept that was surplus to daily requirements. There was no cupboard or larder for food, nothing that might go off, or that you could nibble at – not even the staples like salt, garlic or cinnamon. Whatever was needed for a meal was brought in fresh every day, and every scrap of it finished off.

I was often treated to chicken at Aïsha's, as there was a poultry farm attached to the house next door. This urban farm, of which there were dozens in Azrou, was a source of fascination to me. It was a garage building, with the doors open to the street during the hours of trading. On the floor lived hundreds of white chickens on a bed of sweet-smelling cedarwood sawdust. There was no fence or wall to stop them nipping out onto the street, just the watchful eye of the manager as he slumbered at the entrance. When a buyer came along, the boy would be sent among the milling, meeping chickens to find a good fat one. He would grab one and bring it to the buyer, who would expertly feel it all over as it squawked and flapped. If she gave it the thumbs-up, it was dispatched in an instant, plunged for fifteen seconds into a vat of boiling water, whipped out, excess moisture shaken off, and into the plucking machine.

This machine was a masterpiece of intermediate technology. It consisted of a tin box with a chicken-sized hole at one end, and, inside, a set of fast-moving rubber rollers that gribbled the feathers – loosened by the boiling water – off the bird. A deafeningly loud fan blew all the feathers into a sack. The plucked chicken was then plonked on a scale. Skilled fingers went in at the vent, and with one swift pull divested the bird of its guts, which were plopped into an evil-smelling bin. And that was that – not as much as five minutes had elapsed between selection of the chicken and its sale, gutted and plucked. It was a very slick operation.

On our return from the forest that first day, we dived thankfully into the cool shade of Mourad's house, performed our ablutions at the tap in the courtyard and collapsed onto divans. We had just enough energy to sip a glass of mint tea and pull apart a large pizza made of dough and flakes of shredded mutton fat that Aïsha had brought in on a tray along with some small bowls of tomato and beetroot salad. All was quiet in the hot afternoon – the streets had shut down. A quiet squabbling came from the chicken farm next door, the distant grumble of a lorry. I closed my eyes, wriggled a bit to get comfortable, and fell asleep.

Perhaps I dreamed of the splitting of seedpods in the sun, the scattering of my precious harvest, or maybe of the disagreeable black cobra that comes racing at you through the grass just for the pleasure of killing you. But anyway, when I awoke the light was fading and the streets were in full, noisy babble. Cocks were crowing (people don't seem to realise that cocks don't just crow the dawn but keep going all their wakeful hours); tin-makers were banging their pots; circular saws were screaming as they ripped through cedar logs in the carpentry shops; neighbours were exchanging views from window to window across the street. Altogether, it was almost like music, as it blended and squeezed through the high window of our room.

'*Bonjour, Monsieur Christophe,*' said Aziz as he raised himself from beneath his blanket. Mourad stirred and sat up. 'First we shall drink tea,' he announced, 'then we shall go to the town in search of sacks.' He disappeared from the room and shouted down the stairs for the tea tray.

'Listen, Mourad,' I said, over the second glass of tea. 'I've not gone into details about this, but I would like to employ you all properly for a couple of days and pay you a fair wage.'

'But my dear friend, it will be our great pleasure to help you.'

'That's very kind, but we need to fix on a sum in advance.'

Mourad studied me earnestly for a moment and put his hand on my arm. 'Let us not speak of such things, for we are brothers, no? And now let us go to the town.'

●

I've always thought that the most important piece of equipment to take on your travels is your nose, and its attendant olfactory receptors. The sense of smell is one of the most immediate and tactile we have – and surely to perceive the smell of a thing we must actually ingest microscopic particles of it, whether it's the heady scent of camellias or that of a long-dead dog in a ditch. A smell revives the memory and transports you to a time and place more powerfully even than music. If I ever need to return to Azrou, all I would have to do is mix together some mint, cedar, diesel and a hint of drains, and take a good long sniff.

Mint tea is the fuel that Morocco runs on. A glass of sweet mint tea is surprisingly satisfying on a day of heat and dust, and no meeting or transaction, no coming in or going out, is complete without it. A pot accompanies each meal, too. It makes a wonderful and effective substitute for alcohol because the ritual that surrounds it is so satisfying. It is brewed with gunpowder tea from China, a huge handful of pungent mint (or in winter a sort of southernwood) and an enormous block of sugar. The sugar comes in tall glittering cones of a kilo and you knock what you want from the cone with a special hammer; generally, you stuff it in to take up the remaining space after the tea and the mint. Then, you pour boiling water into the pot and leave it to infuse. Mind you, that sounds too simple, for it really is a ceremony, and the keener practitioners will make a preliminary brew to warm the pot, throwing it out before the final tea is prepared.

To service this obsession Azrou, like most Moroccan towns, has vast mint gardens on its outskirts, and every morning mountains of fresh mint are barrowed and donkeyed and trucked through the streets to the markets and shops. This provides the town's base perfume. Next is the cedar. Each street has a dozen little carpentry workshops that process cedar logs from the forest that cloaks the mountains above the town. Here they make benches and divans and tables and chairs and wooden boxes and pots and, whenever a drill or a saw or a plane bites into the wood, it releases a sweet scent that literally fills the air. To have one's own furniture made from perfumed wood, that would be a pleasure indeed.

As for the darker notes of the perfume of Azrou, well, there are old trucks everywhere – *Bennes-Marel*, they're called – and they belch fumes into the hot air and dribble diesel and sump oil into the dust. It's not as bad as it sounds: it seems somehow appropriate and gives a feeling of animation and industry to the town. Likewise the drains, which are not as foolproof and effective as they might be, but again as a counterpoint to the mint, the cedar and the smell of cooking smoke and spicy chicken and lamb – even the whiff of a drain can be a subtle pleasure.

Mourad, Aziz and I threaded our way through the hot evening streets luxuriating in these smells and keeping a look out for sacks. Every five minutes there were people to be effusively greeted: *labass, veher, hamdullillah*, each side would intone. And then, suddenly, Mourad recalled that he had a student to attend to, and suggested that he leave me in the capable hands of Aziz to conduct our purchase. I agreed, happily enough, though it transpired that Aziz was not the best person to delegate the task to. Having steered me first into a sweetshop, then a carpet store, a shop selling what passes for lingerie in Azrou, a haberdashery, and the shop of his friend who sold baby clothes, he seemed drained of ideas. I suspected him of putting his social life ahead of our mission, but then he did actually ask for sacks in each place, so who knows?

'Why don't we try a hardware or animal feed store,' I suggested at last. He was astonished at the idea.

'But those places do not have sacks for sale. I know this,' he insisted. 'And tomorrow is Thursday, the day of the *souk*. At the *souk* we will buy sacks.'

So we wended our way to the Café Central where we had arranged to rejoin Mourad. It was crowded and Mourad waved to us from a corner table, where he had been sitting marking an essay. As soon as I drew up a chair, he summoned the waiter and introduced him to me: 'Hamid, meet my new friend and brother, Chris. Christophe, Hamid is my oldest friend; we were at school together.'

We shook hands earnestly and, with the shaken hand on our hearts, bowed to one another. Hamid was slightly built with rather mournful eyes. He wore a white shirt and a red waistcoat and was quite the fastest-moving waiter I've ever seen. We gave him our order and he weaved off amongst the tables taking two or three more as he went. Mourad leaned closer towards me and explained in a whisper: 'Hamid looks sad because he is sleepy. He commences at six o'clock every morning and does not finish until sometimes later than ten at night.'

'You're joking. That's a sixteen-hour shift!' I exclaimed.

'Listen, I am telling you: he does this six days a week and he earns… How much do you think he earns?'

'I wouldn't like to guess…'

'He earns fifty dirhams a week.'

It was hard to believe. Fifty dirhams was the equivalent of about four pounds. 'But it is true,' Mourad assured me. 'If you do not believe me, ask Hamid himself.'

'This place is making plenty of money; surely they can pay him a reasonable wage.'

'It is making a fortune – you are right. You see that man by the till, the fat bastard who does not move all day from the money, and whose eyes are moving everywhere. He is the owner. He is the richest man in the town. He is rich because he pays little money to Hamid and to those who work in his bakery.'

'So why doesn't Hamid leave and find a better job? He's an amazing waiter.'

'There are no better jobs in Azrou – and if Hamid asked for more money, well, there would be ten men asking for his job. He cannot leave Azrou, as he looks after his widowed mother. The two of them live on his fifty dirhams a week. He would like to have a girlfriend, perhaps to have a family, but he cannot. He has neither time nor money to get himself a girlfriend. He is a very sad man, very kind and good, but sad.'

As Mourad spoke, Hamid appeared, placed our orders on the table with a smile and, signalling to some customers who were vying for his attention, whisked off again. Two young boys with shoeshine boxes quickly took his place. They had been looking in dismay at all the trainers and canvas sneakers before honing in on my scuffed leather lace-ups, caked in dust. As one of the boys cleaned my shoes, he kept up a spirited and what sounded like a rather adult conversation with Mourad, who seemed to know just about everybody in the town.

I love having my shoes cleaned and have always found highly polished leather rather beautiful, although the shine would last only ten paces or so out on the street before the dust dulled them again.

I asked who the boy was. Mourad made a helpless gesture. 'He has no family, no mother or father,' he said. 'He lives on the street. Many of these children do. In the winter it is very cold in Azrou, snow lies on the streets, and it is hard to survive. There are many old people who live on the streets, too, and of course it is even harder for them. Many die.'

As I digested this information, I realised that Aziz was studying me closely while clicking his finger joints. 'We become very skilled at this, the clicking of the fingers,' he commented wryly. 'It is because we have nothing else to do. In Azrou it is very hard to be positive about the future.'

'Now, enough,' said Mourad, suddenly impatient at this gloomy turn in the conversation. 'If we cannot be positive about the future, then let us be positive about the present. Here we have Chris, the night is young. Let us find a car and go to Amrhos.'

'Amrhos?' echoed Aziz, with a note of surprise.

Mourad blushed. There was something iffy afoot. 'I'll get Ali and Hamid and we'll rent a car. It won't be too expensive and things will be just warming up in an hour or so.'

What things, I wondered. Then a thought struck me. 'Mourad,' I demanded. 'You are not taking me to a place of ill-repute, are you?'

Both Mourad and Aziz looked shocked. 'How can you ask this, Chris?' Mourad lamented. 'Amrhos is a party of Berber drumming and dancing. It will be an unforgettable experience. You yourself told me you love the drumming. We must all go.'

There was a slight edge to his voice that bothered me still, but two hours later eight of us stuffed ourselves as best we could into an ancient Mercedes taxi and set off for the outskirts of town. It didn't feel quite like a normal taxi ride, and there was a reluctance to discuss openly the evening ahead. I pondered this as we sped – for some reason without lights – along roads crowded with people and donkeys. After about fifteen minutes of this, we arrived at an unfinished roadside hotel, seemingly in the middle of nowhere. I paid the taxi driver. It seemed to be understood that I was the one bankrolling the operation, and indeed I was probably the only one among us with any cash.

To my relief, there was both drumming and quite a crowd. The drummers had already begun their set and as we entered a brightly lit bar, with a stage along one wall, the room seemed to vibrate to the sound. There were maybe thirty or forty other people there, most of them men, but with a family or two as well. As the waiter came for our order, I asked Mourad what there was to drink. 'Fanta or Sprite, or tea if you like.' Then he added quietly, 'There is also beer, I believe.'

Everybody ordered beer. And that, of course, was what all the cloak-and-dagger stuff was about. It was a drinking expedition. Azrou was officially dry and the Amrhos was the one place in town – or, rather, out of town – where you could drink alcohol. And it was a lot of fun. As our beers arrived, I watched the three young men on stage: one a singer, the other two playing Berber hand-drums. These are big deep tambourines without jingles, which you hold with your thumb through a hole in the rim and attack with your fingers; as you approach the centre, the boom is deep like a marching band's bass drum, while closer to the edge there is an endless variety of tones.

These drummers knew their stuff, creating a gutsy excitement with their complex rhythms and, as they drummed, three young women in floor-length dresses, belted at the waist with scarves and glittering with jewellery, walked onto the stage. The crowd applauded and the singer, a stocky man with fists the size of small barrels, burst into song. The song seemed to have no melody but employed the guttural sounds of Berber to harmonise with the drummers. It was exciting but also slick and disciplined, with a tight pace. Some of the songs that followed were question and answer, with the dancers wailing and ululating in response, setting their necklaces, bangles and ankle jewellery jingling. Even without amplification, the singer and drummers filled the large room and held the audience entranced.

The dancers swayed at first to the music, but little by little they started to echo the complexities of the rhythms

with their feet and arms, and hips. It was the hip move-
ments that got the crowd going – and it was hard not to sit
with your eyes glued to those lubricious hips that swivelled
and writhed with such speed and grace. The dancer nearest
our table seemed to be putting on a special show just for
me, fixing me with her deep, dark eyes and gyrating her
hips with absolute confidence in her allure. Mourad and my
table companions kept nudging me and giving me looks, as
if I were supposed to play some part. Which, of course, I
was. For every now and then one of the men in the audience
would leave his table, walk over to the stage and insert a
note into the cleavage of his favourite dancer.

Mourad leaned across to me with a grin: 'You, too,
must give – she is dancing for you and it is how they earn
money.'

I'd never done this sort of thing before. I fumbled about
in my pocket and pulled out a fifty dirham note. Those eyes
continued boring into me as I stumbled across the floor and
inexpertly slid the note into the dancer's dress. It wasn't
so tricky a manoeuvre, but failure would have been deeply
humiliating – imagine the note sticking to my sweaty palm
or fluttering off into the crowd. The note, anyway, found its
home, and it must have been one of the better tips, as for
the rest of the performance the dancer remained near our
table and kept her eyes fixed on me, triggering pokes and
sniggers from Mourad and his cronies. As for me, it seemed
somehow rude to look away, but exhausting to keep up the
rapt appreciation of a fan.

Eventually, the last number came to an end and my
dancer cast a meaningful look at me over her shoulder as
she left the stage.

'I think she likes you, that dancer,' said Mourad gaily.

'Oh don't be so foolish, Mourad. That's her job – she dances for money.'

He looked hurt at the thought. 'Fifty dirhams is a not a large amount of money to give to a dancer. It is generous but no more. At these dances some men go crazy and give them really big money. No, she is interested in you because you are different.'

I hung back a little, but Mourad had me by the hand and was not going to let me get out of this. He moved to the next room, where a disco was starting up, and keeping hold of my hand, steered me towards the dancer.

'But I can't speak any Berber...' I hissed 'Only 1, 2, 3, 4, 5 and...' – I racked my brains for another word that I knew how to say – '...Ah, yes. Donkey.'

'Leave it to me,' Mourad hissed back, 'I'll translate.'

We reached the dancer, who clamped her eyes back onto my face as if she'd been raking the crowd looking for it. 'Um.. you danced really beautifully, thank you,' I said in English, looking between her and Mourad. Mourad then translated this, at great length, into an impassioned outpouring of Berber. The scene reminded me rather of Cyrano de Bergerac, when the big-nosed hero supplies sweet words of courtship to the friendly moron that the heroine has taken a shine to. Perhaps Mourad was reciting stanzas from the *Rubaiyat of Omar Khayyam*, or maybe even a choice passage of Graham Greene. When he finally drew to a close, the dancer smiled at me, slightly condescendingly, as one would to a flirtatious adolescent, said a few words to Mourad and moved away.

'I'm afraid she has to leave now, Chris,' he translated. 'Her husband, you see. He is waiting for her.' And he indi-cated a large man standing beside the door. I turned and he nodded at me, holding up a huge fist in a gesture of farewell. It was the singer. I returned the gesture, grateful we were communing at a distance, and retreated to a seat in a poorly lit corner where I could wait while Mourad and his friends had their fill of the disco and the novelties of the bar.

●

As Aziz had promised, the next day was Azrou's market. A slope of waste ground near the centre of town had been transformed overnight into a medieval encampment, a labyrinth of stalls and huts and booths, or sales pitches marked simply with a sheet spread on the ground. It was already mid-morning by the time we arrived and great vats of dye were bubbling and steaming away, overseen by Berber women in full regalia. Mourad, proud of his local *souk*, assured me that they were natural dyes, rather than the common chemicals. You could buy the wool nearby – hot, smelly, tangled mounds of it, raw from the shearing. Beyond it, the smoke from cooking fires rose and hung in a thin blue cloud, at times giving a scanty brown shade from the full intensity of the sun.

We had arrived amongst the aisles searching for sacks but I was sidetracked by a thousand things. And then, among the storytellers and the often unidentifiable stalls, we heard a wild reedy music, soaring above the general noise and the Berber hand-drums again. 'Come,' said Mourad, his hand on my arm. 'This is something we should see.'

A current had been created amongst the crowd by the insistent wail of the music. Mourad and I joined it and were propelled into a clearing, where a trio of snake charmers were at work, belting away on their trumpets. They were playing in the shade of an awning, rigged up to their battered white van, and one of their colleagues was placing boxes and baskets around them on the floor. A furious thundering of Berber hand-drums told us that the show was about to begin. Then, with an energy at odds with the blistering torpor of a late morning, the principal player launched into a chant and began striding about and drawing lines and circles with a stick in the dust.

'What's he on about, Mourad?' I asked.

As I spoke, the head man spotted Mourad and me, and insisted that we move to join those squatting in the dust in the front row. I wasn't keen, preferring to blend in with the crowd; however, blending in wasn't really an option that morning as I was the only foreigner there, with sunburnt ears and nose. Fearing the worst, I allowed Mourad to lead me through the parting crowd to the place normally reserved at a public spectacle, for children. I squatted on my hunkers like everybody else – not so easy to get away if things cut up rough.

Then suddenly from somewhere there was a snake. God knows what it was but it was as thick as my upper arm, as long as my leg, and covered in the sort of markings that nature uses to proclaim 'Danger!' – and it was slithering through the dust towards us. I breathed deep and watched it philosophically as it approached. Just before it got to us, one of the assistants – who had been pretending he hadn't noticed it – snuck up behind and, catching the snake gently round the neck and supporting its huge body with his arms, slipped it neatly inside his shirt. My heart was thumping fast, the crowd was spellbound. Another snake, thick as a slender wrist, long and grey, slipped out of a basket and moved across the dust towards the semicircle of wary onlookers. It was caught neatly with a stick, and into that same shirt it went. It was a voluminous shirt. The man strolled around for a minute and then nonchalantly slipped each snake back into its box or basket. More snakes appeared and lay quietly in the sun – more frenetic music. The excitement grew and grew.

The head man was explaining something to the crowd, and a number of men were coming forward and standing rather apprehensively in a smaller semicircle. 'Come,' said Mourad. 'We will join them.'

'What? I asked. 'Are you crazy?'

But Mourad had already volunteered us both. 'We must do this, Chris. It is for our protection in the forest. Come.'

There were about twelve of us. The head man, with a rather episcopal look, bade us all kneel. Oh Lord... I knew what was coming next... and, sure enough, the assistants started to move among us with boxes and baskets of snakes and things. I watched as they approached me, distributing various denominations of snake and draping them around the necks of the men kneeling in the dust. There was no way out of this.

My knowledge of herpetology is not extensive – you don't need it much in the temperate climes of Sussex. I can identify with a fair degree of certainty the difference between vipers and grass snakes; I have a hazy idea as to the morphology of anacondas and boa constrictors, but that's about as far as it goes. I had no idea at all of the name of the snake that was being coiled twice around my neck by the grubbily robed snake charmer. It was a sinister-looking customer, slender and greyish and about as long as a useful scarf. Behind its head was a suspiciously loose flap of skin, which I feared might be the stuff of which a hood is made; but I didn't want to think of the word 'hood' because the next word that comes into your head is 'cobra'.

The stony ground was hurting my knees and I could feel the sun roasting the top of my head. My snake, which seemed tranquil enough, despite the frenetic rhythms and the atonal wailing of the trumpet, actually had the effect of keeping the sun from burning the back of my neck. I thanked it quietly, and almost took a little comfort in its being there, warm and smooth and not actually unpleasant. I looked round the semicircle of kneeling figures, dark-featured and earnest, some in denim jackets and baseball caps, most cloaked in *djellabas*.

Mourad, anxious for my well-being, looked over to me and smiled – but his smile froze as he was told to hold out the palm of his hand, and upon it was placed a large, black scorpion. I've heard it said that the sting of the black ones is lethal, and I felt pleased that I had not been the one selected for the honour. And then I felt bad: it was wrong to wish such a thing on anyone, let alone someone as charmingly ingenuous as Mourad. Even if it was entirely his fault and served him right...

Unlike my snake, Mourad's scorpion was an adventurous type and within moments began moving up his arm towards the inviting opening of his short-sleeved shirt. It moved slowly for a scorpion, dulled by the intensity of the sun, but nonetheless soon reached the comfort of the sleeve and set about moving into its shade. I winced a little on Mourad's behalf, as did the couple of hundred people now watching.

Mourad was desperately trying to catch the attention of the lead charmer, but he was too busy working the crowd with yet another energetic monologue, emphasising the rhythm of his speech with beats of the hand-drum. Suddenly he caught sight of the beseeching Mourad and his plight and, stepping swiftly across the space made by the kneeling men, took the scorpion delicately between thumb and forefinger and returned it to Mourad's outstretched hand, where it sat still.

My snake, meanwhile, had gone to sleep, bored no doubt by the next part of the proceedings, where the snake charmer placed a piece of paper in our outstretched hands. Apart from Mourad and his scorpion, all the rest of us kneelers had snakes of one description or another draped around our necks, leaving our hands free. Mourad was kneeling on stony ground with both his hands outstretched: one for the scorpion, the other for the paper. This was a gruelling posture to maintain for any length of time. I hoped it was going to be worthwhile.

Drawn on the paper, which was lined and torn from an exercise book, were what I took to be runes. I'd never seen runes before and had no idea what they looked like but I was sure that that's what these symbols were. They were drawn in blue biro and I found myself wondering about their efficacy; I'd have preferred them carved in stone or perhaps drawn in blood. Everyone seemed to be taking the ceremony absolutely seriously, though, and my fellow initiates had their faces bowed in earnest concentration, trying not to show their fear.

I was working hard on this, too. I recalled that wild animals are goaded by the smell of one's fear, and that, while you can fool a fellow human being into thinking you're not afraid, you can't hide the smell of it from an animal. Still, I was trying my best to fool this sleepy snake into thinking that I wasn't afraid of it. I was thinking as hard as possible of things other than snakes. And perhaps it worked – for, apart from a brief interest in the openings between my shirt buttons, it didn't stir... until, amid a climax of drumming, chanting and music, the ceremony came to an abrupt end, and the snakes and scorpion were collected up and put back in their various receptacles.

We initiates dispersed back into the crowd, and I was left with that sense of deflation you get as a child, when a show is over or you have completed some absurd dare. But it was short-lived, for Aziz came bursting through the crowd holding a dozen perfect sacks. 'You'll never believe where I found these,' he announced, still evidently doubting the fact himself. 'In the hardware shop!'

'Come,' said Mourad, putting his arm round my shoulder. 'Now we are ready to make our fortune in the forest. Let us walk up to the Café Central and celebrate.'

SACKFULS OF TREASURE

THE FOLLOWING MORNING, after only the most perfunctory round of greetings and salutations in town, Ali and Aziz and Mourad and I set out up the track to the cedar forest, through the ilex woods and up into the domain of the magnificent blue Atlantic cedar. We found the *hällehäll* and I showed my pickers the highly technical contrivance I had developed for the work. You take a walnut-sized stone, cover it with a part of the sack, tie a string round the resulting knob, and take a turn round the waist – this leaves both hands free to pick the seedpods.

The first few minutes of picking are pretty exciting. You grasp a handful of pods, which on *Cytisus battandieri* grow like Indian feathered headdresses, and you break them off and stuff them in the sack. As you grasp them you can feel the ripe ones burst inside, and you see the little hard black seeds spatter into the sack. There's a certain satisfaction in feeling the weight of your sack grow infinitesimally with each handful, maybe a gram. And then a pleasure each time you find a heavily laden plant – you can see the ripe seeds through the almost translucent pods when the sun is low. Your mind clears and you hear all the sounds of nature: the cobras slithering contentedly to and fro in the dry grass, and troupes of monkeys – the Middle Atlas is heaving with monkeys – jabbering in the trees.

After about an hour you start to feel the tedium of the work. Your hands are a little sore, you're a tiny bit frazzled by the heat, your eyes are stinging, and your nose and forehead are a little burnt from constantly looking up at the sun as you reach for the high-growing pods. After two hours you never want to see another seedpod as long as you live and you're stuffing sacks like an automaton. After four hours Mourad and I sort of drifted together. 'I think we should stop for lunch now. It is hot and we are tired,' he suggested.

We slumped in the shade of a cedar and drank water and ate olives and bread and little triangles of Laughing Cow cheese spread. Then we lay down in the soft cedar needles and slept away the hottest hours of the day. I hardly need to tell of my contentment as I woke and watched my pickers fast asleep around the tree, and considered the swelling harvest of ripe seedpods. The expedition looked like being a success: I would come home with the goods, the hunter home from the hill. But not only that, it was turning out to be such a pleasure, too – new friends, a new world to get to know. Granted, the picking was grim, but you can't expect everything to be effortless and, besides, who would want to be anywhere else but here in the Middle Atlas, lying in a bed of soft needles in the Forêt des Cèdres, a gentle breeze cooling the air and lifting the great blue branches, and tonight to sleep in the friendly bosom of a real Berber family? I reckoned it a fair deal.

As I observed the sleeping pickers, lying lost to the world in various poses, I noted how thin they all were. There was not a hint of obesity – these young men were lucky when they could find enough to eat. They were poorly but neatly dressed; they could afford only the cheapest clothes but they wore them well and, although we were out in the woods for a day's seed-picking, they were clean and neatly pressed. All of which stood in stark contrast to my own rather disgraceful appearance and incipient corpulence. Especially neat and fastidious was the tall, elegant Aziz. He had picked about a third as much as anybody else, but no matter: he was an engaging character and I loved his formal French. 'Monsieur Christophe, you cannot know how I suffer,' he would tell me in confidence. 'Aziz?' Mourad would say. 'Aziz is not only utterly lazy, but also crazy.'

Looking at the sleepers, I wondered about wages. Mourad had been disinclined to discuss pay with me but this was a crucial issue for us all. I stood to gross £3,500 from this trip, which was a vast amount of money for me, and we needed a reasonable chunk of it to make ends meet at home. If I returned with nothing we would have to endure a certain amount of hardship – we would not go hungry or unshod – but it would be what is meant by hardship in our European society.

Hamid the waiter was earning about £4 a week – maybe £7, with tips, in a good week – thus the money I would gross would pay poor Hamid and his widowed mother for seven hundred weeks, the best part of fifteen years. Mourad had been lamenting to me the wretched lot of Hamid, but he was even worse off himself: he didn't have a job at all. As he told me, he got the odd bit of translation work, and otherwise waited for whatever would turn up, while giving lessons for a pittance or for free. I figured that, at Mourad's present perilous state of affairs, the money could support him for twenty-five years.

Aziz had no work and no prospects until his shadowy French girlfriend showed up with the imaginary visa. I didn't know much about his financial position, if it could be called that, but he wasn't a rich man. Then there was the *gardien du forêt*, with his lean frame, shabby suit and air of destitution; well, I dreaded to think what he was paid by the king to guard this little bit of the forest. ('Against what?' I asked Mourad. 'Seed collectors, perhaps,' he replied.)

I needed my lads to do the job – I'd need them even more later on, as it turned out, for the drying and processing. I could not do the job without them and I wanted it to continue – to come back every year or every other year to pick an order, and increase the variety of plants. Perhaps one day I could turn it into a business that Mourad's group could run from here. But, for now, I decided I had the following options:

[1] Give them the whole lot.

[2] Split the money four ways (and pay the *gardien* daily).

[3] Pay outrageously good wages – say, £100 a day each. I was reckoning on twenty man days' picking, which, leaving

myself out, made £1600 between them, and thus £1900 for me before expenses (and the bill at the Café Central was building up);

[4] Pay the current day-labourer´s rate at home in Andalucía, which was then about £15 per day. A doctor in Azrou would be lucky, very lucky, to earn £15 a day, and it was eighteen times what Hamid earned at the Café Central.

I mulled over all this as I lay there beside my new friends, who for all their poverty seemed to bear me no ill will for the monstrous divide that lay between us. Well, what would you decide? In the end I opted for the Spanish labourer's rate – £15 a day, irrespective of whether it was a whole day or just a part of one – and when the pickers awoke, I told them the deal.

To my relief, everybody thought it was a magnificent emolument, and the *gardien* was thrilled. I gave all the money to Mourad, who said he would act as paymaster, and I added a fee on top for his administrative and organisation work. I don't know if he was taking a cut from the others, too, for fixing them up with the job; it wouldn't have been unfair as, after all, he was the one who had read *The Captain and the Enemy*.

●

'*Eh bien mes amis, on recommence?* Let's get started,' I called, and we tramped out into the forest again. We picked for a couple more hours until the light began to fade, and then, stuffing the day's harvest into four sacks, we shouldered them and trudged down the edge of the scarp to Azrou. It was dark when we entered the town. We took the sacks of seeds straight up to the flat roof of Mourad's house, tipped them out and spread them out in the moonlight.

For three more days we left the town early in the morning, after the obligatory session in the Café Central, and spent the whole day in the forest, returning at sunset. The great heap of pods on the roof grew and grew. At night we shovelled it into a pile in the corner, to keep it from the damper night air, and in the daytime we spread it all out for the rays of the fierce sun to bake the pods dry. As the sun warmed them, there was a constant cracking and splitting, and everywhere, as the pods dried, cracked and twisted, they leapt into the air, scattering their seeds over the dusty concrete roof.

On the morning after the picking was completed, we spread the seeds and then spent the rest of the morning lounging in the Café Central. I learned a little Berber and, by constant repetition and example, gathered the correct and proper formulae for greeting people one had not bumped into for, say, an hour.

Towards midday we slouched home for lunch. Mourad's house was not as strictly Muslim as some and, now that the family knew me, I was able on occasion to go to the women's part of the house. As we arrived they were preparing lunch in what passed for a kitchen, although we from the Western world would hardly recognise it as such.

There was no sink, drainer nor tap, for example; neither was there a cooker nor a hob; and the only work surface was a low wooden table, around which the women were squatting in the gloom. The immense battery of tools and utensils, pots and pans and plates so necessary for our European cookery was quite absent. There was a sieve for sieving flour, a big plate, a knife, a big *tagine* dish, a battered old pressure cooker, a clay pot and a camping gas stove. The tap was in the yard. There were, unsurprisingly, no recipe books.

I thought of all the various meals we had eaten in Mourad's house – delicious *tagines* and salads and home-baked flat breads. The cooking was a communal activity, shared by all the women of the house and conducted with grace and skill. It all served, somehow, to emphasise the prima-donna-ishness, the frippery and petulance of our more economically advanced societies. Here was a family without a car, a fridge, a telephone, a camera – the only ornament in the house was the obligatory photograph of Hassan II, the (then) king – and yet they took in orphans off the street, and looked after their old people with a natu-ralness and clear-sighted sense of duty unthinkable among their North European counterparts.

'Chris, my friend,' said Mourad after we'd polished off some flat bread and baked aubergine and were reclining away the afternoon hours, 'I am thinking that tomorrow we shall make an ex-ped-di-tion.' He emphasised this last word heavily; clearly he liked the sound of it. 'And what did you have in mind, my friend?' I answered lazily.

'I have in mind that I shall find a car and that we shall all have a *pique-nique* at Aït Oum er-Rbia.' He obviously liked that word, too – as you would, for it is one of the most delicious names I have ever come across in any language. Say it for yourself – *ayit-oom-err–rr-bía* – and don't forget to roll those 'r's.

●

I had decided, perhaps hastily, that as well as stumping up for the expedition to Aït Oum er-Rbia, I was going to cook the lunch. A picnic in Morocco involves something more than squatting in the grass with an egg sandwich and a bottle of beer. There must be a bit of cooking, otherwise it's not a proper picnic. So in the morning, Aïsha, Abtisa and I went shopping. Aïsha chose the unfortunate chicken, giving it a thorough going-over with practised fingers before agreeing a price, and I watched the process philosophically as our *pique-nique* was boiled, plucked and gutted before our eyes.

Then we continued along the street and, accompanied by a great deal of haggling and tutting and spirited disagreement about prices and qualities, we bought the remaining ingredients for the way I figured a chicken *tagine* ought to be. We bought some ready-shelled almonds – despite Abtisa insisting this was a waste of money, as she could easily shell ours for us – a screwed-up newspaper full of raisins, some dried apricots and figs, an onion or two and a head of garlic, some potatoes, a heap of fresh coriander and a chilli pepper. Finally we added some olives, bread, a jar of honey and also a preserved lemon, and a bottle of olive oil.

I was surprised to find, given the rock-bottom wages that are paid in Azrou and the fierce haggling of Aïsha, that none of the items came cheap. But then our ideas about food prices are so distorted by supermarket competition, agri-business and global subsidies that we forget what it must be like for small producers and farmers trying to sell their own crops.

About midday, with the sun as high in the sky as it was going to get, we all bundled ourselves into the car that Mourad had arranged. We started by discussing the price. The driver, noting my presence among the merrymakers, quoted a price that would have actually bought his car in Europe. 'I think this is good price, Chris,' said Mourad.

'No, it's not good price, Mourad. It is an outrageous price. I'm not trying to buy his car!'

'Outrageous price,' repeated Mourad, and haggled weakly with the driver. 'Chris, he has said that he will reduce this outrageous price a little because I have said to him you are my friend. He will take us for nine-tenths of what he originally asked.'

'C'mon, Mourad! You must be joking.'

By now everyone was itching to get on with the expedition, and the children – Abtisa, Little Mourad and another very small girl I couldn't put a name to – were literally hopping up and down with excitement. There were ten of us. The taxi was the usual enormous Mercedes, but even so it was asking a lot to get ten passengers in. The venal beast of a driver saw me reckoning this out and said something to Mourad. 'He says we are also very many people and he will have to pay the police – if not, he will be imprisoned.'

'Tell him I'll give him half,' I told Mourad, anxious now to get things moving.

The driver scowled, said something that was probably best left untranslated, and climbed into the driver's seat. 'He accepts your offer. Now let us go.' At half the original price I was still paying the man over £100, so I didn't feel that I was cheating him out of his living.

Somehow we managed to get all those people in the car – a truly extraordinary feat, because, although the children were small and elastic and the boys were thin, some of the women were pretty voluminous. At last the expedition got under way, the taxi racing through the town, hand on horn. I hoped the door mechanisms were in good order or we might all burst from the car at speed.

The bodies were so tightly packed, it was difficult to see anything out of the windows. After about half an hour, things also got a lot bumpier, as we left the asphalt and joined a sinuous *piste* that wound upwards through the cedar forest. The car bounced and lurched and skidded round the bends, and the cabin filled with hot dust. It was hell, but from the squeals and yells of pleasure it seemed everyone was having a good time.

We drove on through the forest for the best part of an hour and then stopped by a lake. As soon as we stopped, everyone exploded from the car to stretch their limbs and discover which ones were still working. Mourad and Mohammed, his younger brother, stripped to their underpants and dived into the lake. I followed and then in went Little Mohammed too.

Aziz stood on the bank clicking his fingers. '*Non, mon cher ami*,' he announced. 'I shall not bathe; I fear that the water is not clean and also dangerous.'

It was glorious. Swimming in a clear lake among the cedars on a hot Moroccan summer day. The boys howled about and splashed and yelled and swam way out into the middle, while the poor perspiring women shouted encouragement from the shade on the bank. Little Abtisa rolled her skirt up and paddled up to her knees, but that was as immodest as any of the females got. Oh, the cooling of that wonderful water! We were dry within minutes of climbing out and, stuffing ourselves back into the car, we set off on the final leg, over the hill to Aït Oum er-Rbia.

After a while we started dropping down a steep hill through open farming country and crossed a bridge over a raging river. Then a couple of kilometres upriver we stopped and burst once more from the car. Spirits were high at the thought of the coming feast, and we strode gaily up the hill for our first glimpse of this supposedly magical *pique-nique* spot.

Aït Oum er-Rbia was a truly extraordinary sight. There was a tall cliff of golden rock, a spectacular geological fault, and bursting forth from the foot of this cliff was not just a spring but a full-blown river. The clear, icy water leapt from a dozen caves and coursed swiftly down a steep slope, where it formed a fast river dotted with islands. Stairways had been cut into the cliffs, and little bridges of wood and stone constructed between the islands.

On each island and in shady clefts cut into the banks, teahouses had been built, using the materials that lay to hand: eucalyptus branches, string and wire, sacks and twigs for the roof. The floors were of beaten earth spread with rugs. Everywhere were families sitting in the shady teahouses, some idly trailing an arm in the racing water, others making tea on charcoal burners or preparing the *pique-nique*. The air inside was blessedly cool. Sweet smells rose from the cooking fires along with thin plumes of blue smoke. And, in spite of the tumult of the waters, there was the most glorious sense of peace.

Perhaps this derived from the beauty of the spot, or from the natural unsophisticated ease with which these families were enjoying themselves – just the simple pleasure of being together in a place of dazzling and strange beauty. In part it came from the absence of anything packaged. Even the normally ubiquitous Coca-Cola sign was nowhere in evidence; there were no plastic chairs, tables or umbrellas emblazoned with global logos. This was a piece of our lovely planet just as it ought to be seen and enjoyed: no turnstiles, no advertising, no muzak, no health and safety railings to stop you falling in.

We negotiated a fee with the ragged old man who owned our particular tent-pavilion. A little too much, but I was past caring: I was ecstatic about this idyllic place where I was to cook a *tagine* for these gentle, generous people. The fee gave us the use of an island pavilion with a charcoal stove for the rest of the day. Like figures in a Chinese painting, we tripped across the bridges to reach our island. Aïsha and Latifa, concerned at first at the thought of me doing the cooking, began to relax when they saw how much I enjoyed preparing the *tagine*. I oiled the dish, added all the ingredients – as many of them as possible stuffed into the cavity of the accommodating fowl – put the conical lid on, and placed it on the cooker on the floor. Then I lay back to wait the hour and a half or so before it was ready. Aïsha had brought the camping gas stove and all the wherewithal for making tea, so soon we were contentedly sipping the sweet minty brew.

We dozed and murmured contentedly, trailed fingers in the river, swatted flies and daydreamed – all those things you do on a hot summer afternoon in those bright haunted hours suspended somewhere between waking and sleep. And little by little the smell of chicken cooking with coriander and onions and garlic, gently gurgling in the oil over the charcoal embers, became more intense, until finally we could resist no longer and we fell upon it, all of us burning our fingers as we tore at the hot sweet flesh. Then we dozed some more, had another brew of tea and went to explore the cliffs and waterfalls.

It was not until evening fell, and the air filled with bats and their peeping, that we packed up our stuff and piled again into that long-suffering car for the two-hour ride back to Azrou.

Early the next morning we went up to the roof to have a look at how the seeds were coming on. If you listened carefully, you could hear a sporadic popping of pods, which gradually increased with the heat of the day until it reached a frenzy at midday. The frenzy continued all afternoon, a frantic leaping and twisting of pods as they hurled the little black and brown seeds high in the air, often over the parapet or down the stairwell. The house was full of seeds and there was a fair smattering on the street outside.

But there were countless seeds still in the pods, and it was time to move on to the next stage, of treading. Mourad and I spread the pile out all over the roof and set to work marching about, dancing and stamping, to crack open the recalcitrant pods. The most effective move was the Twist – the Chubby Checker dance – which involved raising yourself up on the balls of your booted feet and, from the hips, giving a twisting motion, while graunching the pods on the concrete. It was exhausting but satisfying, in that you could see, amongst the fine fluff and dust, even more seeds.

For hours in the hot morning sun we danced upon these seeds to our own cover versions of Twist classics, then we swept the whole lot into a pile and set to sieving. With a coarse sieve we separated the dust and the seeds from the whole and broken pods. But there was so much dust that there was no sign of the seeds, so we took the fine-flour sieve from the house and tried again. Imagine the pleasure as the dusty heap slowly turned to a mass of hard little black seeds. I looked at Mourad with his shiny black hair and moustache – all entirely grey – as the dust stuck to the sweat on our arms, hair and faces. We were both wearing handkerchiefs tied over our noses and mouths to stop us breathing the stuff in.

We repeated the process all through that long hot day, reducing the pods to ever-tinier particles, increasing the dust, and seeing the pile of seeds grow and grow. Later in the afternoon Aïsha and the women came up with wide, flat-tish baskets of woven rushes. These they filled with seeds and the dust and particles we had been unable to sieve out and, by shaking them in a certain way that only they knew how – I tried it but achieved nothing – they produced a pile of perfectly clean seeds. This was the method they used to clean grain. I was feeling elated, excited by what was look-ing like a great success.

There was no such thing as a pair of scales in the house, so we took the bag of seeds round the corner to a grocery stall. Eleven and a half kilos! We'd done it! Mourad and I treated ourselves to an evening at the local *hammam*, where we lay enveloped in steam, soaking and scrubbing away the strains of the day and several layers of encrusted grime.

Emerging into the warm night air, I felt an altogether new and different person. The dusty, careworn me, laden down with worries about cobras and forests and fair pay, had been sloughed off and a freer version had taken its place. Relishing the feel of the breeze on my new, pink face, I walked with Mourad to the Café Central where Ali, Aziz and the usual entourage were waiting for us. Normally after such a long absence from each other we would clasp hands and wrap an arm around each other's shoulders, but that was not enough for the depth of feeling welling up that evening. I was clamped to each in turn in a firm and affectionate embrace.

We were celebrating a job well done and the start of a business partnership, but of course this was also a parting. Very soon I would be heading for Tangier with our consignment of seeds. There I could do what the scruffiest, most inept tourist could do with ease: I could walk onto a boat bound for Spain and enter Europe. My new friends, however, could do no such thing, though they often talked of it. The enormity of this injustice struck me afresh. Surely there must be some way I could help?

'We could try the Spanish consulate at Tangier, perhaps,' said Mourad. 'Chris seems a lucky person. If he accompanies us then maybe we shall succeed in getting our visas. It will be good for all of us to earn some money over there.' Ali shook his head. He'd tried for a visa several times, as indeed had various other men grouped around the table. The odds were stacked heavily against us. Still, it was worth giving it a try.

The trick it seemed was to get to the consulate early. So we took the bus to Tangier, stayed the night in a cheap hotel in the Medina, and got up as the first glimmer of dawn was spreading across the skyline. I checked my watch as we rounded the corner to the consulate building. It was 5.30 am – and thirty people were already settled into a line ahead of us.

A notice on the wall announced that the visa section would open at 9.30 am and close at noon. By the time nine o'clock came the queue stretched round the corner and down the road – maybe three hundred people or more. All of them were clutching various documents that they hoped might give them an edge; letters of recommendation, long-expired visas belonging to other members of their families, photocopied bank statements, and the exorbitantly priced passports that the Moroccan government allows people to buy but which gain them entry only to two countries, Mauritania and Algeria. What you need to travel on a wider scale is a visa – a simple piece of paper that is denied to almost all who apply.

The window from which this precious document was to be issued was mounted low in the wall so that applicants were forced to adopt a humiliating half-crouching position to talk to the official on the other side. As 9.00 am moved towards 9.30, most of those waiting slipped off in relays for coffee, so the queue was constantly waxing and waning. Then 9.30 came and went and a murmur of impatience rippled through the crowd. At 9.45, the hatch opened and the business of the day commenced. It took a long time to deal with each applicant, often accompanied by shouting and impassioned gesticulation; and, to cut a long story short, by the time twelve o'clock came, and we had been queuing for six hours, there were still thirty people ahead of us. We hadn't moved forward one single place. Mourad and Aziz kept disappearing to count the numbers, but it was clear that there wasn't any possibility of being seen.

There were a number of policemen keeping order of a sort, and finally Mourad had a word with one of them. 'Of course you're still in the same place,' he said, looking at Mourad as if he were some sort of half-wit. 'You have to pay if you want to be attended to.'

So the three of us left the line and shouldered our way into the tumultous gaggle that now surrounded the nearest hatch. It was soon obvious who the policeman taking the money was. Mourad spoke to him directly and I slipped him the suggested amount: two hundred dirhams – £16. Immediately we were ushered through the crowd; not to the service window, but to a small door beside it where I alone was told to enter and take a seat.

The man at the desk cut short his half-hearted attendance to the poor man crouching on the other side of the hatch and turned towards me. 'Yes?' he demanded gruffly in Spanish. 'What do you want?' I could tell that two hundred dirhams wasn't going to buy us much time so I hurriedly explained that I was standing as a sponsor for my two friends who wished to visit me at my home in Spain. Of course the thing was as transparent as can be; nobody could doubt that as soon as Mourad and Aziz entered Spain then they'd be off and into the vastness of Europe, where they would most likely stay.

'I see,' he said. 'Your friends must return to their home town and there procure the following documents.' And he proceeded to enumerate a whole heap of improbable papers. A Certificate of Absence of Criminality from the police, a Leave of Absence signed by their employer, a Social Security bond – the list went on and on, covering documents that possibly did not exist and, if they did, were entirely beyond my friends' grasp. For a start, neither Mourad nor Aziz had an employer to sign them off. 'There will be no problem,' the official assured me. 'Once your friends have assembled all these documents, they just bring them to me and I will authorise their visas. Okay?'

That 'Okay' had a finality to it: we had wasted our two hundred dirhams. Mourad and Aziz immediately recognised the brush-off and were crestfallen, but there seemed no use hanging around and insisting. We walked slowly along the edge of the port, talking of possible stratagems. I remembered once, while queuing on the quayside for a boat to Algeciras, noticing a dishevelled looking youth covered in axle grease and engine oil dodging between the cars on the quayside. As I watched, and beneath the very noses of the Port Police, he crawled underneath a truck and started exploring for handholds and footholds. The police ignored him until the truck was due to move onto the ship; then they ordered him out. He came out and they gave him a half-hearted cuffing. He lurched about, slack-jawed, like a drunk, intoxicated by his desperation and by the constant dashing of his hopes – and then crept beneath the next truck. I hoped that Mourad and Aziz would never be driven to such extremes, though it was easy to see how obsessive the need to travel can become when it is so flatly and unjustly denied.

As we were talking, a couple of youths approached us. They were deep black and so shabbily dressed that they stood out. There was a haunted look in their eyes and they addressed me hesitantly in very shaky English. They had travelled, they told me, all the way from Liberia, where a civil war was raging. Their families had been slaughtered and they could not return for fear of their lives. They were utterly destitute. They believed that, if they could just get to Europe, they could find work and start to rebuild their lives, with enough to eat and freedom from terror. I was the only European in the crowd, so they had sought me out. Surely I could help them?

I could do nothing. They walked off slowly, not knowing where to go or what to do. I can still recall the faces of those poor boys – neither of them would have been as much as twenty years old – wandering aimlessly among the lorries; the fear in those youthful eyes, the momentary light of hope, and the disappointment. I hate to think what became of them.

Mourad and Aziz stopped with me at the pier. We bade each other a fond farewell, swore vows of undying friendship and swapped all manner of addresses. Then I shouldered my baggage and walked apprehensively towards customs.

The bags of seed, gathered with such care and with present and future hopes riding upon them, suddenly made me profoundly nervous. Although I knew I was doing nothing illegal – as Carl had explained, there were no seed-exporting regulations in place between Morocco and Europe – there was guilt written all over me. I oozed paranoia and was already preparing for my arrest and trial. I was sure I wouldn't get a fair hearing. The system in Morocco was such that officials in public employ – policemen, customs officials, administrative officers – were not paid well enough even to feed and clothe their families. Corruption was thus a necessary way of life. There seemed a strong likelihood that, carrying all the broom seeds, I might find myself thrown in jail, and would be obliged to buy my way out. I could probably afford the bribe, but even so it would be very disagreeable and inconvenient to find myself in the slammer, or indeed to risk the fruit of our recent labours.

At the customs control, I trembled and blushed, stammered when spoken to, looked nervously to left and right and cast the odd distracted glance behind me in case I was being followed. The three uniformed customs officers stared at me knowingly as I approached the inspection... but did nothing; not even a poke in my bag. A short walk up the gangway and I was on my way back home to Spain.

●

Carl was thrilled by our haul, and listened with interest to my plans of starting a seed-collecting partnership with Mourad. This was precisely the sort of operation he wanted to support and, although Ana had some reservations about covering the entire expanse of northwest Europe in *Cytisus battandieri*, she too thought it right to shift the project to a local enterprise.

With the omens all in place, I entered into an erratic correspondence with Mourad. As neither of us had easy access to a phone, we wrote letters, which introduced a rather formal note to our relationship, Mourad using an elaborate literary English. It also showed us both up as appallingly inept entrepreneurs. One thing we agreed on, however, was that we would meet the following summer in Azrou and collect some seeds.

In the event we didn't, because the winter before that Mourad took it into his head to smuggle himself into Europe. As proof that the worst-laid plans just occasionally work, he had hunkered down under the seat of his cousin Naïma's van, covered himself in rugs and the sprawling legs of her children, and sailed serenely through customs. He'd done it. He'd reached Europe, the promised land. And his first thought, touchingly, was to visit me at El Valero, and take up my offers of hospitality. But, by some mischievous twist of fate, he chose the one month that year that I was away, shearing in Sweden.

Ana was at home and recounted the brief visit as soon as I got back. Apparently Mourad had persuaded his cousin, who was on her way back to her home in France, to make a detour to our farm. Finding it almost impossible to work out the right road to our valley, they accosted the first foreigner they met in the street for directions. Luckily this was Sam Graves, a kind and gracious British expat who knew us very well, being the father of the agent who had originally sold us the farm. He was also the son of Robert Graves, which, had Mourad known, might have led to much literary discussion.

But the talk, it seems, was all about how to reach our farm: not an easy thing to explain. Poor Sam tried every means to get across the complicated directions, but to no avail, and in his typically generous manner ended up taxiing Mourad, his cousin and her husband, and their four children, along our rutted mountain track, even fording the river to the farm. At last they rounded our final bend and parked just below the stables. Mourad and his group emerged from the car and looked slowly round at the few traditional buildings and ramshackle outhouses that comprise our home. Nobody said a word, but each wore a slightly puzzled frown. The farm, as Mourad explained to me later, reminded them all of one thing: Morocco.

Still, the party made their way up towards the house and were greeted by Ana on the way. She had never met Mourad before and he stepped quickly towards her through the dust, anxious to effect the introduction, and to discover where I was. The news was a blow. It hadn't occurred to him that I might be away. Ana invited him to stay until I returned, but he wouldn't hear of it. Not only would it have been a gross breach of etiquette to stay with Ana on her own, but I think he was also worried about incriminating her with the police.

By the time I came back, Mourad had disappeared from his cousin's home in Lyon and embarked on what sounded very much like a grand tour of Europe. It was typical of Mourad that he refused to limit himself to working behind the scenes in a restaurant kitchen or sweatshop, making discreet forays around the city under cover of night. Instead, as soon as he earned a bit of cash he embarked on the sort of travels that only the most avid literary tourist might contemplate: hopping trains and buses and popping into bookshops en route to read up on each new city's attractions in a guidebook. Following up contacts he'd been given by friends in Azrou, and trusting that his outrageous luck would continue, he sallied over the border from France to Italy and on to Switzerland, where he had a hankering to see the Alps. Eventually it was in Switzerland, in the shadow of the mountains, that his luck faltered. He was caught dawdling near the border in broad daylight, thrown into jail for a fortnight and deported. 'Ah, but Chris,' he told me, his eyes dancing at the memory, 'I would do it all again.'

Later on, I had my own reason for delay. Chloë was born the following year, so I tried to pare down foreign trips to a minimum and find work closer to home. Carl came up trumps with a large order for the extravagantly blossomed *Retama monospermum* which thrives on the Costa de la Luz, and some euphorbias, which grow even closer to home, on the hillside high at the head of the Trevélez River. But, even with local shearing jobs thrown in, it was tough trying to make ends meet, and when autumn came I was left with no choice but to head for Sweden again for a month's shearing. I remembered once asking a friend of Mourad – one of the lucky ones with a visa in his passport – how he could bring himself to leave his young family for a year at a time to work on construction sites in Germany. He shrugged: 'But I'm Moroccan. For us there is not a choice.' And yet my own short stints seemed hard enough to bear.

It turned out that we never did repeat our seed-collecting enterprise. Back in Azrou, Mourad, with another timely piece of fortune, managed to land himself a job as a teacher. The money wasn't much but it was enough to enable him to marry. His wife was a Berber whom he'd known since childhood, named Aïsha like his mother, and the couple moved to a rented house in the district of Sidi Assou. He was delighted – this was much closer to the life he'd hoped to lead – and when Aïsha became pregnant with their son Ilyas he wrote in glowing terms of the 'new generation we are both producing that will forge in harmony a new culture'.

I considered asking Ali to join me instead in the seed-collecting work, but I wasn't sure we could establish the same rapport. And then I, too, found other work. A publisher in London accepted my first book and with a few strokes of ink at the bottom of a contract turned me into a bona fide author. Mourad was tremendously pleased and impressed. He knew, he assured me, that I was destined for the literary life.

We still write to each other and, on rare occasions when Mourad takes me up on offers of help, I cross to Tangier with a few necessary medicines or books for his growing family of two boys and a girl, the latter of whom suffers from asthma. While we sit together at a harbourfront café talking, as men of our age do, about our health and the sort of future we hope to steer our children towards, I sense how much the travel constraints still weigh on him. Of course he would like the extra consumer power that goes with working and living in Europe. But he insists that even more than this he would like to be free to dream: to plan trips, and adventures and opportunities for his children, without having them so categorically denied. It would be nice, for instance, to think of taking his children to Brighton and tasting that famous rock.

CASA & CAMPO

S OME YEARS LATER I FOUND MYSELF reflecting on Mourad's reaction to our home, after a phonecall from one Eduardo Mencos. El Valero had looked depressingly like a Berber farm to Mourad yet here was the director of *Casa & Campo* – one of Spain's glossiest home and garden magazines – asking to come and view our garden. It seemed a ludicrous notion, but Señor Mencos was not a man to be gainsaid. 'Didn't you tell him that we don't actually *have* a garden?' Ana asked incredulously. 'And this is just your average mountain farm with a vegetable patch on one terrace?' I assured her that I had, but that this had been dismissed by my interlocutor as typical British modesty.

'And you mentioned the old wrecks of cars scattered about the place, and the bedsteads used as gates?' she continued.

'Well, yes, I think I might have. Anyway, all farms have old cars and bedsteads on them,' I countered, neither of the two having featured prominently in the conversation.

'And that the swimming pool's a pond full of frogs?'

'Yes, I said all those things, but he's read some article about us and is convinced he should come and see the place for himself. He's not bringing a photographer, though – this would just be to, well… to meet us and have a look around.'

Ana groaned. *Casa & Campo* specialises in features and photos of salubrious dwellings with impeccable borders, topiary, gravel drives, zen follies and the like. 'It'll be a waste of everyone's time,' she insisted. 'El Valero just isn't a *Casa & Campo* sort of place. And I'm not sure I'd particularly want it to be.'

She was right, of course, but it seemed ungracious to cancel the visit now. Perhaps we could make some improvements. Standing on the terrace, outside the kitchen, I cast a cool appraising eye around our farm. 'We could get rid of Custard,' I suggested.

Ana came and stood beside me, and together we gazed down at the ancient yellow carcass of our old Renault 4 rusting away just beyond the steps to our house. Wasps were buzzing in and out of the jagged hole that had once been her sunroof; for some reason hot yellow tin is irresistible to wasps. 'Well, at least it will keep the Guardia happy,' she reluctantly agreed.

●

It's wrong to get sentimental about cars, especially their battered old husks, but the truth is that you can't help remembering them fondly. They head my personal hierarchy of inanimate objects, along with guitars, walking sticks, the odd cooking pot and a beloved cherrywood corkscrew... Thinking about it, I seem to be consumed with sentiment for a whole array of objects, though cars are very much ahead of the pack.

Custard was the very first car that we bought when we settled in Spain: a canary-yellow Renault 4L, or a *Cuatro Latas* ('Four Tins') as the locals call them. We were seduced utterly by her spotless bodywork and the sparkle of her windows, which we were assured was the work of one devoted lady owner, a pharmacist from Armilla. And in an automotive way Custard trod lightly upon the earth: she didn't use a lot of fuel and she didn't weigh much, and like the *Deux-Chevaux* she was a car designed to transport a basket of eggs the wrong way across a ploughed field with a peasant at the controls. That suited us fine, and also the price was right – the equivalent of £600 – which was as far as we could stretch at the time.

We took Domingo along with us to buy it, because he knows everything about cars. He slithered about beneath the car on the showroom floor for half an hour, then pronounced himself satisfied that she was in good order. And so the three of us clambered aboard and clattered proudly back to the Alpujarras. 'I'm glad we've got a car like this,' said Ana as the engine strained up the steep mountain track, bouncing in and out of the ruts. 'We don't want our neighbours to think we're grand.' At that time not many of our neighbours owned cars at all, but the look on their faces as they stopped their mules to wave us past held not a glimmer of envy. We called the car 'Custard' because it was that sort of yellow – well, the yellow you find in packets, at any rate; personally, I make custard with brown sugar and cinnamon, so it comes out a sort of dull ochre.

Coming to live with us was a big lifestyle change for the car, with daily runs to the pharmacy replaced by the merciless battering of our track, the fording of the river and heavy loads of animal feed and building materials. Little by little the pristine yellow coat faded, bits began to drop off, and Custard was transformed into a most singular vehicle. The exhaust pipe fell off altogether and the slightest incline made the engine roar like a battle tank; the wheel bearings, as a result of constant soakings in the river, went rusty, so that as the wheels went round they did so with a sound like the twittering of many small birds; and the doors had been damaged by repeated blows and opened with the sound of braying donkeys. Ana found it a little embarrassing when people stared as we roared and twittered through the town. But despite the fact that the car sounded like a mobile zoo, we developed a great affection for her. She would go anywhere, in the foulest of conditions and with huge loads.

Domingo gave me a couple of lessons in how easy it is to maintain a Renault 4. You just buy the bits from town or from the dump, and bolt them on. To me it never seemed quite as easy as it looked when he did it, and the job was marred by my sloppy workmanship and complete mechanical incompetence. So, with the battering and bodging, Custard started to go downhill – metaphorically speaking.

It was a state brought home to us, with some melodrama, the following New Year's Day, when my sister treated us to a wildly generous Christmas present of a night in one of Spain's fanciest five-star hotels. We arrived late and not a little frazzled, having rattled all the way from El Valero to Salinas near Loja, a journey of about three hours as it was then. Finally we pulled in through the hotel gates and clanked on along a drive that curled through groves of holm oaks heavily populated by rabbits. Turning a final corner, we came upon the gleaming white towers of the hotel, set amid sweeping lawns and pools with fountains that glittered in the evening sunlight. I pulled in amongst the rows of huge Mercedes and BMWs with blackened windows and gleaming paintwork. As if from nowhere, a flunky appeared, a superior-looking cove dressed in an archaic uniform and top hat. Grasping the passenger door, he opened it for Ana. It says a lot for the sort of place this was that, as the door slid off its hinges and clunked onto the ground, he batted not an eyelid. 'Welcome to La Bobadilla, Madam, Sir,' he said.

The next day we fixed the door back on with a judiciously placed nail, and limped back to El Valero. It was, however, to be Custard's last major journey and within weeks she had spluttered to a halt by the old threshing circle above the house, where she rusted away beneath her shroud of wasps' nests and plants.

Even Ana had to acknowledge that this current state was of no use to anyone, and we agreed to have the car cleared away. So a few days later, Pepe Pilili's awesome JCB reduced Custard to a loveless lump of barely yellow metal, hoisted her up and dragged her across the river to the dump.

The ground still bore the indents of Pepe's machine when Eduardo Mencos roared into the valley in a low-slung BMW estate. I met him at the bridge, a great bear of a man, very blond for a Spaniard, and with a frank and genial manner. I could tell by the way he looked around him that he was a man with an eye for landscape. It was early summer and the heat of the sun was still melting the last of the snows in the high mountains, so the river was tumbling full and clear out of the narrow gorge. He had been gazing at the river-banks lined with tamarisks in feathery flower, the yellow profusion of the *gayomba* and *retama*, and the poisonous pink blooms of the oleanders.

'You've found yourself a Garden of Eden,' he announced, striding forwards in a cloud of dust and enveloping one of my hands in his. 'Even Spain, which is clearly the most beautiful country in the world, has little to offer as good as this. You live in Paradise. I am certainly looking forward to seeing your garden.'

'Er, well, in a sense this *is* our garden,' I said lamely.

Eduardo laughed heartily and slapped me on the back. 'No, this is your farm,' he said. 'Let's go and look at your garden.'

We crossed the lower *acequia* and walked between the thick bramble hedges that border the field of alfalfa, towards the eucalyptus grove. 'Nice-looking crop,' he commented, but was still casting about for telltale signs of our more decorative patch of earth. 'Ah!' he exclaimed, climbing the stone steps that led up to the pool. 'This is better – definitely better.' The pool stood before us, dark green with the excrement of frogs, its still surface dusted with fallen yellow petals of broom. The great iron water-wheel grumbled quietly on its axle as it revolved slowly, heaving great quantities of water, fish shit and algae up into the stone filter bottle.

Eduardo stopped: 'Now, this is the way a pool should be. This is magnificent.'

I looked at the dark water, at the host of frogs burbling upon the rim, at the dragonflies flitting amongst the lilies and the flags. 'It's a bit on the grubby side at the moment,' I apologised.

But Eduardo was having none of it. 'What does it matter?' he exclaimed. 'If the water were clear, you wouldn't get that wonderful effect of the blossom against the greenness, nor that reflection of the rocks and hills. And it doesn't smell of stagnant water or chlorine. This pool is a work of art.'

I was beginning to warm to the man. I tore him away from the pool and led him up to the house. Eduardo took in the muddle of vernacular architecture with one sweeping glance. 'There are a lot of buildings here,' he commented. 'Did you build some of them yourself?' The question seemed ambiguous somehow, and not altogether admiring. He paused to peer through a gaping black hole, with a door swinging off its hinges. This was what I liked to call my workshop.

Somebody once said to me that a man's workshop is a good indication of the state of his mind. This was a rather unkind cut, for mine is perhaps better described as a wildlife reserve rather than a seat of industry and creativity. There are ants, cockroaches, earwigs and, though I've never encountered them, I know there's the odd scorpion and centipede. It all lends a certain frisson of excitement to scrabbling around in the dark – there are no windows – among the chaotic heaps of tools and rubbish that litter the floor.

When more rational and wholesome folks come to visit, they are appalled at the state of things. 'Why don't you clean it out?' they suggest helpfully. 'Get a shadow-board, put up hooks, make shelves, put a light in...' and so on. What these well-intentioned people don't seem to realise is that to do any of these things one needs tools – and I can't find the tools. Also, this represents my natural state of being, and I feel that once you start to tamper with how you operate naturally you are sailing into dangerous waters; that way lies despair, nervousness, and the unleashing of the dark beasts of the spirit. Better it is to suffer a few imperfections than risk lousing up all your better qualities by trying to rise above yourself.

I steered Eduardo determinedly away from this unappealing revelation of my innermost being, and led him down to the house to meet Ana, who was engaged in chopping up an elaborate but unappetising salad for the chickens. He considered this activity with some surprise.

'It's the way the chickens like it,' said Ana with a grin. 'They don't have fingers like we do, so I chop it up for them in beakfuls. After all, it's not much fun being a chicken.'

'But if you had to be a chicken,' observed Eduardo, 'then I think that perhaps this wouldn't be a bad place to be one.'

Ana took this as a compliment and suggested we sit down in the shade and enjoy a drink; it was still far too hot to go traipsing round the garden.

'So you've come to see our famous garden?' she said, looking at him quizzically as she placed a bowl of olives on the table to accompany the cool beer.

Eduardo took a big slug of beer and narrowed his eyes with pleasure. 'I have always admired the English and their gardens,' he replied, after a long pause. 'So, when I read this article about you and your garden, naturally I was intrigued. And so here I am, drinking your beer... Mmm, these olives are good.'

'We haven't quite got a garden,' said Ana, firmly. 'It's my dream to make one and I work on it daily, but I want it to grow organically, in its own time, rather than shipping in a whole load of ready-made trees and shrubs.'

'A very laudable philosophy,' agreed our guest, helping himself to another olive. 'And so...'

'And so', continued Ana, 'that's why we haven't got the sort of garden that you might want to put in *Casa & Campo.*'

Eduardo smiled indulgently. 'Ana, I think I realised that as soon as I met you both. But please believe me when I say yours is just the sort of garden I enjoy. May we go and have a look?'

Eduardo's charm had the effect of dispelling Ana's reticence and embarrassment, and before long they were chatting easily together and setting off down the path. (It's something to do with speaking the same language – horticultural Latin – and sharing a genuine appreciation for such matters as mulching and compost.) I decided to string along too, because I can't think of a nicer way to pass a summer evening than wandering around in a garden.

●

Ana's kitchen garden is her comfort and joy, her retreat from the cares of home and family and, if it's not too fanciful a notion, the nearest thing our farm has to a soul. There are others in the Alpujarras whose gardens may produce a greater abundance, but for me the deliciously anarchic tangle of flowers and trees and crops, and the idiosyncratic notions behind their planting, reflect the essence of Ana – in a similar way, I suppose, that the disreputable chaos of my workshop may reflect me. A rather chastening thought.

Eduardo carefully shifted the bedstead gate beneath the huge fig tree that stands at the garden entrance and then gazed admiringly around him. Ana's eccentric creation really did seem to take his breath away. A blaze of marigolds – bright orange and the most vivid of yellows – had spread itself across the front of the garden, giving way beneath the canopy of orange trees to a haze of green from the filigree fronds of fennel, while at the back there hung a mist of blues and pinks from delicate *Nigella* or love-in-a-mist. The fence was covered with scented roses, little pink ones and big white tea roses, and a great amorphous rambler of a honeysuckle that clambered all over the ancient olive tree at the end.

Among this apparently random tumble of flowers and plants were tiny vegetable beds, arranged so that they could be cultivated without stepping on and compacting the soil. For years Ana has worked those beds, digging them and assiduously removing every stone, working in copious quantities of moist black dung and compost, then mulching with the scraggy wool produced by our sheep. Eduardo ambled amongst them, casting an appreciative eye on the fine tilth as he went, and nodding in response to Ana's explanations of what lay hidden beneath the surface, the patterns of planting and the arcane systems she employed.

Chief amongst these was her particular system of crop rotation. Cabbages, for example, being capricious, don't like to grow where cabbages have grown the year before, and nor do tomatoes and quite a few others. In order not to offend these vegetable sensibilities, Ana makes complex charts and, during the winter, anguishes over the locations and successions of the various crops. She is often to be found poring over these charts as she tries to cajole the various recalcitrant vegetables into their allotted places. It's a sort of vegetable solitaire. (Of course, there are times when she loses and has to move one or other crop to a brand new patch she's created by the alfalfa field.)

As well as this, Ana follows the Rudolf Steiner method of 'biodynamic agriculture', where each operation in the garden has an auspicious day depending on the alignment of the planets. This began with a 'biodynamic' chart that a friend sent her from London, which she initially scoffed at and then decided to try in a limited way, on the basis that people round here have always attended to the phases of the moon when planting, so why not the rest of the solar system, too. Suffice it to say that Jupiter and Mars came through for the broad beans and carrots so convincingly that she continued the experiment. Ana doesn't, however, stick assiduously to the biodynamic teachings, but simply follows those tenets that suit her and discards those she finds inconvenient or downright ludicrous.

The main thing is that the work satisfies her spirit, and the pleasure we get from its anarchic beauty goes deep in all of us. When Chloë was a baby, we used to dangle her in a sort of baby-bouncer thing with elastic ropes from an orange tree while we were working in the garden. Later she gravitated to a sandpit I built her, my first venture into the world of home architecture. Now she takes her friends down there to root among the marigolds for early strawberries.

It's hard to say just how many of these philosophical elements Eduardo picked up on, but being a man of horticultural perspicacity, he seemed to discern what it was all about, and made appropriate admiring comments as he ambled along in Ana's wake. At length we moved on up the steps to the rockery.

Now the rockery was a creation I was particularly proud of, having expended a great deal of energy the previous year, hauling interestingly shaped but extremely heavy rocks up to the terrace from the Cádiar riverbed. To make it more interesting I also gathered a load of aesthetically pleasing driftwood, which we incorporated into the design, along with some exquisite blue glass bottles that had entered our lives in the form of a crate of organic wine. It took a while to get the relative orientation of each element of the structure just right and fitting snugly before packing the interstices with earth. Just as I was putting the finishing touches to the work, directed by my wife, Manolo appeared as if from nowhere. He stared at the rockery, then turned with a baffled expression from me to Ana. 'Ah, yes! A garden made with old rocks and bottles,' he chuckled, and continued on his way, shaking his head in disbelief.

A year later and the rockery is an unqualified success. Ana has planted it with carefully selected indigenous plants, and one or two outrageous cacti, like lifeforms from some improbable planet, and it dazzles all who see it – except, of course, Manolo, who sees the succulents and cacti as weeds. 'They have a garden full of rocks and bottles and planted with weeds,' he tells the amazed villagers of Tíjola. 'Ay, these *guiris* – foreigners,' they reply.

But Eduardo was made of different stuff and was entranced by it all. 'Ana,' he enthused, 'I love this rockery; this is just how a rockery should be in these dry mountains. These indigenous plants will survive the very worst conditions, and because they are cared for and nurtured here they will give of their best. Look at this beautiful little sedum, it's exquisite.'

Later that night, after a skinful of wine and a warm, animated exchange of stories and ideas, Eduardo showed us some photos of his own garden in Castile – which turned out to be more of an avant-garde sculpture park – along with a brochure for an exhibition he was organising in Madrid. The exhibition was called 'Gardens for the Soul' – and it was about the most baffling bit of post-futurist modernist deconstructivism that I had ever clapped eyes on. 'But do you write about this in *Casa & Campo*?' I asked, bemused.

'No, *por dios*,' laughed Eduardo. 'It would be like, er, like...' He cast about for a good simile. 'It would be like trying to get across the attractions of El Valero. I couldn't possibly put that sort of stuff in the magazine; our readers just aren't ready for it.'

ALL ABOUT OLIVES

NOT LONG AGO I WAS IDLING AWAY an hour or two, in the way that one does, leafing through a book on Moorish Spain, when I came upon an account of a fifteenth-century Arabic treatise on agriculture. It brought me up short, for it offered a solution to a conundrum that I had been wrestling with: what to do when a favourite tree stops producing olives. It's a knotty problem. You have an ancient tree, a thing of ineffable loveliness, providing shade from the summer sun – but no olives. Well, according to Abu al-Jayr, the Moors worked it out like this…

The owner of the tree enlists the assistance of two friends. With the first, he enters the grove, and the two of them, holding hands, amble in a contemplative way amongst the olives. As they pass beneath the recalcitrant tree, the friend stops and admires it, whereupon the owner says loudly, 'Oh, that one; I'm going to chop it down, it produces nothing.' 'A shame, it's a fine-looking tree,' says the friend. 'Yes, but there's no place for idlers here. Its time has come.' And so saying, the pair pass on through the grove. Now the second friend enters. Taking the same route, he pauses beneath the tree and, looking meaning-fully up into its branches, says, 'He means it, you know.' All being well, the tree will mull over this threat and return to the fold.

The story set me thinking about the Arabs' skill with agriculture, and their attitude towards nature. For, although modern wisdom has taught us that it is a fine thing to drench the earth with fungicide, pesticide, growth retarder and broad-spectrum systemic herbicide, there does seem to be a revival of interest in the simpler and less noxious ways of the past, a return to a more even-handed exchange with the land that nourishes us. Abu al-Jayr would certainly have approved. He might also have noted, with some satisfac-tion, how much has endured of Moorish cultivation of the olive in the Alpujarras. The landscape is still very much as it was terraced and planted by the Moors at the end of the fifteenth century.

There is no time when you are more aware of this legacy than at harvest, which begins in October, when all the olive terraces are trimmed and rolled flat as pool tables, and their water channels and banks and walls cleared of all vegeta-tion, lest a stray olive should seek to escape its destiny. The terraces that surround the villages, and the bigger olive groves that fold over the hills and valleys, take on the look of a well-tended garden.

The countryside gathers a new life and momentum, too, as people come out from town to work their patches of land – for everyone has at least an olive tree or two – and gather the harvest for the coming year's oil. All through winter the Alpujarras ring to the sound of the beating of trees, the unmistakable hollow clack as the long poles, cut from canebrakes in the river, strike the hard wood of the olive branches. It's a family affair, full of the chatter of children, and also a bit of a festivity. Everywhere there is the blue smoke of fires and the irresistible smell of roasting meat – for it would be unthinkable to go to the country for the day without having a picnic, and to a Spaniard there would be little point in having a picnic without roasting some meat.

But inevitably things are changing, in ways that might bemuse Abu al-Jayr. Those *olivareros* more receptive to the march of progress have exchanged their flimsy canes, or *barras*, for more durable and harder-hitting rods of glass fibre. These are coloured a dazzling dayglo green, so you don't lose them, and they change the music of the winter countryside by making a thunk rather than the traditional clack. And the seriously modern-minded growers have taken things a step further, adopting the Honda tree vibrator, a device that shakes the living daylights out of a tree to dislodge even the most fiercely persistent fruit. So, for much of the winter, the country-side rings to the whining of shoulder-mounted Japanese petrol engines.

We have about fifty ancient olive trees, and about a hundred young ones that we put in three years ago. Most of our trees are *picuales*, the variety best suited to the Alpujarras, as it will hang on tight to its fruit right through the violent winds that can lash the region in winter, yet the olives obligingly fall when you want to harvest them. The others are mainly *manzanillas*, which produce the most delicious of all the eating olives. They are the ones you get in tins and bags, industrially processed and stuffed with a pepper, anchovy or almond.

We're not what you'd call scientific about the blending of our olive crops, and I suspect any chef worth his salt would throw up his hands in horror at the contents of our extra virgin. We just chuck the whole lot in – *picuales*, *manzanillas*, a few *de agua*, as the local eating olive is known, and a scattering of *acebuches*. This *acebuche* – pronounced *athi-boochi* – is the wild olive from which all olives are sprung. Its fruit is tiny and charged with an infinitesimal drop of tangy green oil, in which the palate with an inclination to sentimentality and bombast may detect four thousand years of Mediterranean winds, heat and dust and the pungent aroma of numberless aromatic plants. It's hardly worthwhile to harvest the *acebuches*, but there's a thrill to including a little of that ancient line in your oil, leading you to muse at breakfast time on the antiquity of the earth as you drench your hot toast in thick green oil.

Acebuche is used, too, as a root stock for grafting the more delicate, modern olives onto. It grows ponderously but solidly, and will give you a tree that will survive the worst excesses of heat and drought and cold, cold winters, squeezing up from the very bowels of the earth all the sweetness and pain of the world. (You have to have good bread to appreciate this.) Wild *acebuche* also makes the most beautiful walking sticks. Its young growth is perfectly straight, with a uniform alternate branching, and, when prepared, picked, peeled and polished, has the feel of fine silk. The sticks are much prized by country people, and everywhere, even in the remotest and wildest places, you see *acebuche* with its branches bent and tied into rings, to be cut a year or two later with the graceful curve of the stick's handle neatly grown.

I can clearly remember when I first visited Spain, thirty years ago, and found myself wandering in an olive grove somewhere near Córdoba. Olives hung enticingly everywhere and, not having a clue what the little green fruit was, I picked one and popped it in my mouth. Of course, it tasted foul.

Worse than foul, in fact, for the bitterness of a raw olive is truly bestial, and it seems a miracle that anyone ever worked out what to do with this strange fruit; when to pick and how to pickle the 'eating' ones, and how to leave them for longer, if you intend to crush them into oil.

As an olive producer – albeit one who doesn't register on any conceivable European Union statistic – it is the olives that we pick and pickle that give me greatest satisfaction. These begin the season in October, and you gather them, shading from green to purple to black, by hand. What you do is 'milk' the tree, combing its tresses with a rake or your fingers; the business of thrashing the daylights out of the tree with a stick won't do here. Then you steep your olives in spring water (no chlorine), changing it every day and ruxing up the fruit to clear the slime. After twenty days or so, you taste an olive for bitterness.

It'll still be wickedly bitter – it takes about a month to dwindle to an acceptable level – and the trick is to retain just a hint for flavour and bite.

Next, when you deem it right, you make up a seven percent brine solution – you know, seventy grams of salt to a litre of water (thank heavens for the metric system); or, if you are Alpujarran, you could add salt until a fresh egg floats upon the surface. You then place the olives in the solution and they will keep for pretty much as long as you want. That just leaves the *aliño* to add – the mix of oil and herbs that give the preserved olive its particular flavour.

You want to do this every few months, after you've reckoned the number of olives you're going to get through in the near future. You rinse the salt away in a dozen or so changes of water, and then pour in your *aliño*, flavoured as your imagination dictates. The Alpujarrans, being conservative folk, tend to stick with salt and garlic, but in more adventurous parts of the country there is no end to the variety. To start with the least agreeable, they might include a sprig of bitter rue – one of the foulest-smelling plants, though some people swear it imparts the subtlest of nuances to the mix. Less conventional but more attractive concoctions might feature lavender, rosemary, thyme, oregano, fennel seeds, coriander, caraway, harissa, chilli, lemons (fresh or preserved *à la marocaine*), orange and lemon peel.

It's a matter of taste, of course, but after a decade or so of experimenting, I can report that the orange and the olive go together like a dream, and that the combination of Moroccan preserved lemons and harissa is, as the Spanish would have it, *para chuparse los dedos* – 'to suck oneself the fingers'.

So, the *aliño* decision made, you create your mix, add it to the olives you've already stuffed in jars, top up with olive oil, leave for a week... and start eating. Cookery books state rather primly that you can keep this stuff in the fridge for up to two months, but I reckon it's okay out of the fridge for two years and more, albeit that they do gradually lose something of their bite.

●

Picking the eating olives is, for most farmers, just a prelude to the real business of producing oil. This takes place a month or so later, in the weeks leading up to Christmas, and it is when the sticks and Honda vibrators come out in earnest. There is no more of the delicate milking, but instead what seems like an all-out assault on the trees, whacking them until every last olive has fallen. Afterwards they look a sorry sight, like beaten boxers, with torn and broken branches hanging limp.

This sight – so at odds with the beauty of the silvery leaves, the sheep nibbling grass around the ancient trunks – always haunts me a little when we begin the harvest, and each year I find myself starting off by milking the trees for the by now purpley-black fruits. I climb the first tree and run my open fingers down each laden branch to send a shower of olives pattering down onto the nets spread below. There's a glorious sensuousness to the feel of the perfect little fruit, glistening with oil as they slip through your outspread fingers. The smell, too, of being high in the crown of an olive tree is incomparable. Bernardo across the river says it's like green tomatoes, and the very essence of olive oil. Then there's the peace of it, the sound of the pattering olives, the breeze in the leaves, the rushing of the rivers, and you up there dappled with warm winter sunshine.

But Manolo, to whom this sort of thing is typical of the bizarre notions brought by *guiris*, considers my performance with blank incomprehension, and sets to in time-honoured fashion with his *barra*. And before long I am at it, too, whooshing and clacking my cane at the branches. If you milked a tree for oil olives, it would take you the best part of a day to pick just one tree. And, although you might think that a very agreeable way to carry on – being under the impression, as you probably are, that there are no deadlines, timetables or stress in the countryside – it's simply not viable. Once an olive falls, it ceases to be nourished by the tree and the acidity starts to develop, and for the best olive oil you want your acidity to be as low as possible. The ideal is to press your olives within twenty-four hours of picking them, though this is seldom practicable unless you have your own mill. If I were to milk all my trees by hand, the first olives picked would be over a month old, and completely rotten, by the time I'd sacked them up and taken them to the mill.

Time, then, is of the essence for all olive farmers, and with this in mind I try to tempt my friends from the city to come and help with the harvest. For the price of a few bottles of olive oil and a week of good food and wine, I've established that you can have a cheap and contented workforce and, if the weather is right, then everybody has a wonderful time.

It's hard to make a living – or indeed anything at all – out of small-scale agriculture, and olives are no different. When I bought El Valero, however, I was certain that our olive harvest, along with the flock of sheep, would provide the backbone of our fragile economy. It didn't matter that we had sold our entire first orange crop for a paltry £50; olives would be different.

Unfortunately, the odds were stacked against us. For a start, our olives hardly seemed to be growing. I sought advice, as usual, from Domingo, who assured us that this was no fault of our own – it was simply a *vecería*, that curious phenomenon where, every other year, groups of olive trees decide amongst themselves to gather strength for the following year by yielding little or no fruit. That year most of the trees on our farm seemed to have opted out, and of the pitifully few that hadn't, the bulk of their olives dropped in the winter winds and were wolfed by the sheep. When it came to the reckoning, we had collected barely a couple of hundred kilos to press.

We cast about for someone to mill such a tiny quantity, and were directed to Manolo El Sereno, in a village north of Granada. His *apodo* – Sereno means 'nightwork' – refers to the fact that, somewhere back in the last century, he was the lamplighter for his village. He had long retired, though, and was now, as he told us proudly, the owner of the smallest olive mill in the world.

Driving up with our sacks, I humped them into his mill, which was set up in a little room next to his bathroom. With a saucepan he ladled the olives, glistening and oily black, into the funnel on top of the mill, and started up the grinder. I jumped back and opened my mouth (which is what you should do to prevent your eardrums splitting in the event of high-volume sound), for the noise was unbelievable. The grinder is a powerful hammer-mill that graunches up the olives and shatters the stones, preparing the pulp for the pressing.

I stared in open-mouthed stupefaction at the awesome machine with its horrendous roaring, its sound amplified still louder by the tiny tiled room. Manolo, who seemed impervious to the din, busied himself down in a corner of the room, messing about with the arcane paraphernalia of home olive-milling. Then suddenly a tiny gobbet of flying olive mash whizzed past me and spattered on the white tiles. Then another and then some more. Perhaps this was the way the thing worked, but soon my glasses were caked with a thick layer of olive pulp and there were purple splodges all over the gleaming white walls. I backed into a corner, shielding my eyes from the flying sludge. Surely this was not the way it was supposed to be.

'Ay, Manolo!' I shouted into the ear-splitting roar. But he didn't hear me. The grinder raced on. If it carried on at this rate, then the whole of my olive harvest was going to end up on the walls of Manolo's mill. I ventured from my cover to tap Manolo on the shoulder, but just then a thick lump of flying olive flesh caught him square in the ear.

He looked up in consternation. '*Hostia!* – The Host!' he cried. 'I've left the door open!' He leapt to the switch and shut the monster down, leaning on the door as it whined slowly to a stop, thick clods of purple sludge oozing round the edges. Then he cleared the muck from round the door, shut it tightly and started the whole process over again.

From the grinder, the *masa* – a thick sludge of olive flesh, skins and shattered stones – was ladled into a great tub to rest before going into the press. Vile brown muck, it looked about as unappetising as a thing can look. There it reposed for a few hours. I got fed up with watching this part of the process, and repaired to a bar in search of faster-moving entertainment. When I returned, the sludge was in the press, a tall steel cylinder with a mesh at the bottom and a spout. From the spout dribbled a thin stream of viscous liquid.

'This is the first pressing,' said Manolo. 'The oil's coming out under its own weight. This is the extra-double-virgin stuff. I'll put it in separate bottles for you.'

We watched the oil dribbling out for a bit.

'How long will it take for it all to come through?' I asked.

'I'll leave it tonight and all day tomorrow, then I'll let it stand to let the *jamila* settle out. The *jamila* is the water that the olive contains along with the oil. The oil is lighter than the water, so it floats on the top.'

A few days later Manolo rang to say our oil was ready. He had put it in neatly labelled plastic Coca-Cola bottles. I don't know quite what I expected, but its arrival, and our first tasting, was not as exciting as I'd hoped. I'd never been that sophisticated a connoisseur of oils; indeed, to speak plainly, I'd hardly have known nor cared about the difference between olive and sunflower. These days, I can talk olive oil as passionately as the next man, and can appreciate that at the gastronomic end of the market its production and maintenance is as delicate and complex a matter as that of wine. But back then, one oil seemed much like another to me, and the stuff in the two-litre plastic

Coke bottles, fruit of our first harvest, did little to convince me of any magical properties.

●

Still, the year after Manolo's milling, things looked better, as we had been assured they would. In fact, it looked like there was going to be a bumper harvest – far too big for Manolo's tiny mill to deal with – so we cast around and made enquiries about other local mills. The one thing everyone told us was that all commercial millers are thieves, and will stop at nothing to screw you. It seemed that there was no way to avoid this, as all millers are the same, always have been and always will be.

When I pressed Domingo for an explanation, he suggested that millers always had an advantage over their public, as they were cunningly well versed in the ways of counting and weighing, while their customers were often illiterate and unskilled in the finer points of mathematics. When times were hard – which they usually were in rural Spain – it was difficult for the millers, finding themselves in this position of power, not to be corrupted. Something of this proclivity had found its way into the millers' gene pool, and thus to this day honest millers are scarcer than hen's teeth. Domingo illustrated his contention with examples of dastardly behaviour. And, as well as cheating their customers, it seemed there wasn't a miller in the area who hadn't been fined for adulterating his olive oil with cheap bulk oils.

The thing looked bleak, and we made careful enquiries as to which crook to entrust with our business. Domingo advised – for a 'cleaner, more honest sort of deceit', as he put it – the appealingly named Cuatro Culos, who performed the deceit so neatly and seemingly ingenuously that it was almost a pleasure. 'The good thing about Cuatro Culos', he told us, 'is that he admits that he screws everybody. He can't help it, he says; he was made that way. And he's a very nice man, generous and charming. If you're going to get ripped off – and you certainly *are* going to get ripped off – then you might as well be ripped off by somebody nice.'

It was a well-marshalled argument, and there was a sense of fun about Cuatro Culos's very name – which, of course, is really his *apodo* or nickname. It means 'Four-Bums' and Domingo explained that it was a nickname passed down, along with the proclivity for deceit, from generation to generation. It has, as have many of the best *apodos*, an appealing ambiguity about it. This particular *apodo* usually indicates the occurrence of gluttony somewhere in the family history, but it could also be taken to mean someone who is capable of crapping on you in a big way. Either interpretation could be suitable for a miller, of course.

We chewed over all this, and I was on the point of driving off to be fleeced by Señor Culos when, for some reason I can no longer recall, I plumped instead for Miguel Muñoz of Las Barreras, a miller with a reputation for utter and shameless venality.

The crop that year was as good as any I have harvested: over two thousand kilos, beaten and plucked from the trees by a band of pickers that included a Swedish professor of Cultural Anthropology, a marine biologist and a teacher of comparative religions. We stuffed the crop into old sheep-feed sacks and stacked them under cover from the rain that by good fortune started to fall just as we finished the harvest. I rang the mill to ask when I could bring them in. 'I can't possibly do them this week,' said the miller. 'I'm stuffed up solid with a backlog. Bring them in next Tuesday.'

The rain stopped and the temperature rose a little and the week ran its course. On the Tuesday morning I rose before dawn in order to be the first man at the mill and avoid the rush. I heaved the sacks into the trailer and headed across the valley for town; I had a niggling sense, throughout the journey, that I might have trodden in some dog shit.

The sun was just touching the tops of the Sierra Nevada as I pulled into the mill yard. There were trucks and tractors, cars and trailers and mules already there. Mountains of sacks and crates of olives were stacked up in every available space, and scores of big-built, bovine-looking men with caps on were standing around in what looked to me like chaos. So much for my early start. I thought about turning round and trying Cuatro Culos, but this course of action was made impossible by the fact that I couldn't actually turn round; it was too tight a manoeuvre, and I couldn't unhitch the trailer without unloading it – and, once I'd unloaded two thousand kilos of olives, I certainly wasn't going to load them back on again.

I launched myself instead upon that sea of milling men and tried to discover what I was supposed to do next. 'No mate, not a clue...' 'Sorry, can't help you...' Some muttered and mumbled, while others just shook their heads unknowingly. Others still seemed baffled and disconcerted by my

Spanish. Finally a man in a blue boilersuit suggested that I 'try down below'.

I walked down the hill to the lower part of the mill, where in a cavernous shed the furious machinery of oil extraction was roaring and clattering and thumping. I stepped gingerly in amongst the howling shades – the floors in these mills are slippery as ice from all the spilled oil. 'Is the chief here?' I asked a small brown man in a T-shirt with the slogan 'Marbella Yagtht Club'.

By gestures he indicated that the chief was to be found high upon a catwalk suspended in the shadows, ministering to the raging machinery. I slithered up the steel stairs and stopped. Here was the chief and another man. Neither acknowledged my presence. The other man watched while the chief helped out a huge and terrifying machine. The noise was deafening. THUMP THUMP THUMP went the bit that punched up the olive-caked *capachos* or pressing mats. As each mat burst to the top of the pile, a puncher-slider rammed it across to the next part of the machine with a hellish hiss of oily air. Here great steel teeth gripped the mat and shook it like a dog shaking a rat. Some of the *alpechín* (the spent mush of pips and skins) fell off. The mat flapped up and was jerked across to the third part of the process. Here the chief picked off any bits of mush that had survived the shaker, risking his wrists and forearms as the terrible rams, pistons and thumpers worked their pitiless way with the *capachos*. Finally a layer of thick brown olive mush was slurped onto the mat by a giant nozzle. On and on it went: THUMP hiss crash clonk, THUMP hiss crash clonk blurp.

I watched the process for a bit, spellbound. The mill chief was too involved in his process to notice me, or to follow the usual conventions of nicety. He was, in effect, part of the machinery, and, as he was standing on an oily steel catwalk without any kind of protection, I reckoned the probability of his actually becoming part of that machinery was pretty high. Eventually, though, I tired of the spectacle, and remembering that my car and trailer were slewed across the narrow yard in such a way that nobody could get in or out, I shouted across the middleman at the chief, 'ARE YOU THE CHIEF?'

I know it sounds silly, but what other opening gambit *could* I have used? In any case, there was not a flicker of response. 'ARE YOU (formal form) THE CHIEF?!' I tried again.

'Yup,' he said, pulling off a torn mat.

Silence, while I weighed my next words. You have to get this right when you're shouting at the top of your voice in a foreign language at a man who seems determined to ignore you. But there's no alternative. You have to just take a deep breath and brace yourself for humiliation.

'I'VE BROUGHT A LOAD OF OLIVES AND I WANT TO KNOW WHAT TO DO WITH THEM,' I yelled.

Flap went the machine, thump hiss crash clonk blurp gloop. I couldn't be sure the chief had heard me. He was still concentrating on the machine.

'I'VE GOT A LOAD OF OLIVES. I RANG YESTERDAY. YOU SAID YOU COULD MILL THEM TODAY!!'

The chief muttered something across the middleman.

'WHAT?' I shouted.

The middleman turned to me and said: 'How much you got?'

'A couple of tons.'

'Can't possibly do them today,' said the chief at last. 'I'm short-handed and we've got a big backlog. Stack 'em in the yard with a piece of paper with your name on and the number of sacks.'

'WHEN, THEN?'

'Maybe tomorrow...'

I had no option but to do as bidden. So I scrawled my name on the sacks, left them in the yard and went home, resolving to come back next day and watch them being milled.

●

Next morning I managed to arrive before the mass of *olivareros*. '*Hola, buenos días,*' said the chief, friendly as you like now we had got to know one another a little. 'We can start on your olives right away. You want to tip them in the hopper over there?'

I put the first sack on the sack-barrow and rolled it across to the hopper. I flipped it over onto the edge and untied the string. I paused. There was an unmistakeable smell. I checked my boots for dog shit... Nothing there, oddly enough. I opened the sack... Inside was a putrid mass of evil-smelling brown sludge. That was where the smell of dog shit was coming from – the whole damn lot had gone mouldy.

'*Hombre!*' said the chief in my ear. 'You don't want to store olives in plastic sacks. That's what happens; they go mouldy. I can't pay you much for these.'

'Pay me?! You mean, you'll accept this muck to go in with the oil?' I was incredulous, looking at the steaming brown slime in the sack and then at the chief.

'I can give you a *duro* a kilo for that stuff,' he said, wrinkling his nose in distaste. 'Otherwise you might as well throw it out; nobody else is going to give you anything for it.'

'Okay,' I said, crestfallen – a *duro* was five pesetas, about 2p. 'I guess that's a bit better than nothing... What shall I do with it?'

'Just tip it in the hopper,' he said.

'What! In there, with all the good stuff?'

'*Claro*. Just tip it in.'

Slowly, reluctantly, I took the sack by the bottom and rolled the disgusting contents into the hopper. I watched as it slithered slowly down to the bottom, and then went to get another sack. Sixty sacks there were – it took me half an hour to cart them across the yard, untie them and tip the muck into the hopper. A queue began to build behind me, half a dozen men with their hands in their overalls, idly scratching their crotches and looking with mild curiosity, but not much surprise, at the mephitic sludge I was pouring into their olive oil.

'You don't want to store olives in those feed sacks,' said one. 'They go rotten.' This particular conversational form – the statement of the obvious – is one at which the Spaniard excels. 'Yes, but he's a foreigner,' explained another. 'He does not know the olive.'

With each new sack I hoped there just might be a few nice, shiny, black olives, so I might salvage the tiniest bit of self-respect. But no: each sack seemed worse than the last. The men seemed more indifferent than hostile, or even critical, and when the horrible business was over I felt pretty bad about taking the paltry 10,000 pesetas (about £40).

I returned home with my tail between my legs and the foul-smelling sacks in the trailer, to tell Ana of my foolishness. I suppose she should have known as well as me, but somehow the matter of sacking and storage of bulk products seems to be the man's department. I slept badly that night, wracked with remorse. What made my transgression feel worse was that the oil you got from Muñoz's mill was not your own oil. As with most of the bigger mills, all the oil goes together into the great storage tanks and, if you want oil rather than – or as well as – cash, you go to pick it up when it's settled and bottled.

Later in the spring, my shame had settled sufficiently for me to go and collect a few bottles of oil for the house. A little to my surprise, the oil seemed fine – nice and clear and a light gold in colour. I couldn't imagine what they had done to achieve this, what filters and fierce refinements they had employed – but there it was, and it tasted alright. Not what I now know as a gourmet oil, but serviceable.

•

The year after, we had another fair harvest, and this time we picked it fast, stored it carefully and got it to the mill as quickly as possible. There wasn't too much of a queue, and I parked the car, anticipating with some pleasure the tipping of my sacks of clean, glistening olives into the hopper and watching them hop and hobble up the conveyor belt into the cleaner that would blow out the twigs and leaves.

'Where might a man go who wanted to take a leak?' I enquired.

'Round the back there,' indicated the harassed chief with a jerk of his thumb.

I wandered round the back of the mill. There was a curious smell. I checked the sole of my boot once again, then pulled up short. Here was a mountain of olives forty-foot high. An evil-smelling steamy vapour was lazily rising from the pile, which was covered with a thick, oozing mat of pallid mould. The smell was the smell of my olives of the year before, only worse, and the olives in the pile, which had clearly been building up for weeks, had become an indescribable, mouldy mush.

'Always happens when we get a backlog of olives,' the chief reassured me, when I returned to the mill. '*No importa* – the refining cleans it all up.'

I decided not to go back to that mill again, and cast about for somewhere to take our olives that was more in line with our hale and wholesome principles. I stumbled eventually upon what's known as the 'Muslim Mill', a new outfit, rather nicely located in a dense olive grove to the west of the town. There's a sizeable Muslim community in Órgiva, composed mostly of Spanish *conversos* and a miscellany of Sufis from all over the world. They have a rather enviable co-operative philosophy and, perhaps as a result of this, had pipped to the post all the other ecological and agricultural groups in setting up their own mill.

Although a modest little place, the Muslim Mill is equipped with the latest in Italian oil-pressing technology. That makes its practices not quite as traditional as they might be, in that the oil is centrifuged rather than crushed out by the towers of *capachos*, and your hardliner would have it that this damages the oil's finer properties. But to me it tastes pretty good, and the important thing is that you can be sure of getting your own oil from your own olives, so the skill you employ in harvesting and caring for your trees comes home to reward you. That's become increasingly important to me as our farming has slid imperceptibly into gardening.

As for the Muslim millers – well, they are far from cheap, and in all probability are on the make just like everybody else. However, Abd'l Khalil, the chief, is a first-generation miller (and a first-generation Muslim, come to that – he was once a José), so he has been spared the gene pool. And those draconian injunctions in the Q'uran against usury and suchlike give you a certain confidence – a hope that if you're being ripped off, it's done cleanly.

Salad Days

GASTRONOMIC ACCOLADE was the header of Michael Jacobs' email. Yes, in the past year, even El Valero has joined the digital age – at least, whenever the radio-telephone is in the mood. As the message appeared, I gathered that I had been invited to join El Dornillo, the gastronomic society of Valdepeñas de Jaén. This was a privilege indeed, for members are entitled to attend quarterly feasts created by Michael's neighbour Juan Matias, one of the great chefs of Andalucía. I had been elected, the email noted, for my 'efforts in promoting the food and wine of the Sierra Sur'. This was curious, for while I had certainly ingested and imbibed a fair bit of the food and wine of the Sierra Sur, I had no recall of having actually helped its dissemination. I suspected that Michael had rigged the election, though it may also have helped that as a schoolboy I played drums for Genesis, which, believe it or not, cuts a lot of ice in Valdepeñas de Jaén. There's even a Bar Genesis, somewhere in town.

My inauguration as a *pinche de honor* – an 'honorary kitchen help' – was to coincide with El Dornillo's April feast, which is traditionally held in an arcadian valley setting, furnished with a clear stream, a copse of tall poplars and a great bowl of mountains, just to the north of Valdepeñas. I arrived, as requested, at midday, with the sun shining from a chilly but pellucid blue sky. The Sierra Sur is high, and spring comes a little later than it does in the Alpujarras, so the trees had as yet only the palest of green tinges, the colour of the new buds.

A goat, or *choto*, was doing the honours for the society that day, the previous gathering having been graced by a couple of Iberian pigs. It made its appearance in two huge frying pans over a log fire. One contained the celebrated *choto al ajillo*, consisting of chopped goat with an armful of garlic, all boiled in oil. In the other was *choto a la caldereta*, similar to *choto al ajillo* but with the addition of red peppers and onions. Juan Matias, who seemed entirely at ease with cooking over an open fire for a hundred guests and more, explained to me the niceties of the different methods of preparation.

The smell of the goat and its attendant garlic sizzling away over the blazing fire was driving the company to distraction. The sun shone and the throng eddied and flowed around tables charged with wines from nearby Alcalá la Real and tapas of *embutidos* – small sausages and suchlike left over from the pig feast. And then the president called us all to attention for the inauguration of new members. A handful of us stepped forward to be presented with an assembly of gifts: a straw hat to keep off the bright

April sunshine, an apron that signified our status as *pinches*, and a *pergamino* – a most official-looking parchment in a frame with a little wooden *dornillo* (mixing bowl) affixed to the top left hand corner. The inscription on my parchment referred to me as Don Christopher Stewart, which had a nice ring to it. Michael, however, told me that his own, which he keeps mounted on the wall above his chimney breast, was even more impressive, inscribed as it is to a Don Michael Jackson.

The newly inducted kitchen helps stumbled through speeches of acceptance and thanks, as the collective appetites approached critical mass. But at last the business was complete, and with sighs of ravenous delight the company fell upon the perfectly cooked goat. More wine flowed, and as we had our fill of *choto*, fruits and pastries did the rounds. It was a glorious occasion in itself, but it was *amenizado* – which I used to think meant 'menaced', but in fact means 'enlivened' – by the band of the Valdepeñas Old Folks' Home. These characters made the Buena Vista Social Club look like striplings, with a combined age for the eight of them approaching seven hundred years (I sometimes wonder about the usefulness of 'combined ages' as a statistic). They gave it all they'd got and, as the afternoon turned to evening, and the company moved from wine to *Cuba Libres*, the music took on a life of its own. There were four guitars, two *bandurrias* (lutes), a saxophone and an accordion, and they were cracking for all they were worth through the dance numbers.

I found myself musing over how many guitarists you'd find for your band in your average British old folks' home; the Spanish seem to have it over us in this department. There was singing too, with songsheets, a number or two from each nearby village, including one that contained the memorable refrain:

Si tu me quieres

Meteré un pepino en tu buzón

which, roughly translated, means, 'If you love me, I'll slip a cucumber in your letterbox.'

The Spanish are fond of a salacious conceit.

For days afterwards I was fired up with enthusiasm for the simple country feast, the *déjeuner sur l'herbe* perfumed with the scent of roasting meat. I felt sure that I could emulate the Dornillo's cooking in our own valley: not with goat (for I 'do not know the goat', as the locals would have it) but with a couple of lambs as the main attraction. An occasion soon presented itself. It was shortly to be my fifty-first birthday – three seventeens for those with a fondness for prime numbers – and I felt that this was a pretty significant age to celebrate, the all-important half-century having slipped by with barely a cake and a candle.

I put the word about that I would be throwing a feast down in the valley by the confluence of the rivers. According to the local feng shui experts (who are legion in the Alpujarras), this would be a most auspicious place to have a bash – or anything else, for that matter – on account of the meeting of waters. Thus encouraged, I invited pretty much everyone I knew and, when a good number intimated that they might come, I chose and dispatched two lambs and hung them, in accordance with local wisdom, from an orange tree so that they should absorb the humours of the night air and the *azahar*, the sweet scent of the tree.

Having farmed sheep for the last thirty years of my life, I've become quite adept at cooking them. There are any number of things you can do with a lamb, but if the meat's good – and, though I say it myself, our lamb is tasty – then the simplest recipe is best. I just rub the whole thing over with olive oil and salt, then lay it on a spit over the hot embers. For the glaze, I make up a mix, warmed in a pan, of marmalade, honey, orange juice, soy sauce, garlic, cayenne pepper and whisky. I make lots of it and slap it on constantly right through the cooking process. If all goes well, when the cooking is done, I serve up a lamb like a big toffee apple, the skin looking like one of those bashed-flat ducks you see hanging in the Chinese eateries in Soho, while inside the crisp sweet glaze the meat is deliciously tender and succulent.

There was a minor problem, however, in that a good many of our friends do not eat meat. All of the local Spaniards do, but the expat community of Órgiva is engulfed in a raft of alternative diets, from straightforward vegetarianism through to vegan, ovo-lacto-vegan, macrobiotic and ayurvedic. There is also a small but significant minority of crudo-vegans, who eat only raw food – a fad which seems to be sweeping the alternative Alpujarras. It's a tough regime to keep up in the winter, they tell me, and not really a ball of fun in the summer, either; but apparently it makes you feel a whole lot better than you did in the dark old days when you fired your food, and there is ample evidence, for those who can see, that mankind was never intended to cook his food.

Not surprisingly the issue of what to serve a crudo-vegan guest is a vexed one. I settled on *tabouleh*, which, although it involves some serious graft at the chopping board, tends to be acceptable to everyone, and is a terrific accompaniment to the meat. I make mine, if anyone's interested, with an armful of mint, another of parsley, a bucket of tomatoes (ripe to the verge of putrefaction), a chopped head of garlic, a couple of jugs of lemon juice and a great heap of nutty bulghur wheat. To this vegan largesse I added a bowl of *salsa*, hot enough to lift the top of your head, along with some crisps to dunk into it, and some buckets of *baba ghanoush*, *humus* and other dainties. I was rather proud of the spread I had created until Ana pointed out that the crudo-vegans would have nothing to do with the bulghur wheat (which was boiled), or the crisps (fried), aubergines (baked) or chickpeas (boiled to a pulp). I rather defensively suggested that even crudo-ovo-lacto-vegans might feel an atavistic pleasure in sitting close to the smoke and imbibing the smell of roasting meat; it's something that goes deep in all of us.

The old folks' band of Valdepeñas lived too far away to invite, and I imagine their touring days are over, but a couple of friends had agreed to play guitar and flute and we engaged the services of a dazzling puppeteer, whose performance could keep the adults, as well as children, spellbound.

The morning of the festivities arrived bright and clear and I lit a great fire of olive and driftwood from the river, and kept it fed to produce a smouldering heap of charcoal. At the last minute, however, as the guests started to arrive, I realised that I had no spit to mount the lambs on, or at least the one that I had would hold the lamb over the fire but was useless for rotating it. What I needed was a couple of crosspieces welded onto the steel pole to fix the meat while I turned and basted it.

I had never done any welding before but I had always liked the look of it. Someone had left an electric welder on the farm after a building job and I figured it couldn't be that difficult to handle, so I started the generator, cut the crosspieces to length and set to the welding. Very swiftly I realised that there was a lot more to the job than meets the eye. First of all there is no way you can see what you're doing; the glass in a welder's mask is completely black, as well it should be, so you cannot see at all until you get the blinding spark of light when electrode connects with metal. Then, when you *can* see, you are invariably in the wrong place: you try and move the rod but it sticks to the metal and defies all your efforts at wiggling it about to free it. But that's only the very basics. The hard part comes when you do succeed in getting a proper spark in the right place, and the two pieces of metal actually stick together – whereupon you're supposed, for some unfathomable reason, to bash it with a hammer.

I smacked the spit rods hard with the hammer, as I had seen welders do, and with a clank the joined pieces fell apart. I cursed and rearranged them. I could hear the first merry- makers hooting and braying in the valley below; they would have to wait, I hadn't even started cooking the lamb yet; it would serve them right for arriving early. I peered into the blackness of the mask again. *FFZZSAPP* went the electrode and a great clod of molten metal formed nicely between the two poles. Rather pleased with myself, I put the mask aside, took up the hammer and gave it a gentle tap. With a tinkle the rods parted yet again.

An early guest suddenly appeared. 'Hallo there, Chris. What are you doing?' he enquired in a friendly sort of a way.

'What the hell do you think I'm doing?' I growled.

'My, you're in a party mood,' he said, and ambled off.

My incompetence with the welder was getting to me. Once more I rearranged the rods, slipped a new electrode into the holder. This time it worked. I blobbed more and more molten metal around the join and finally whopped it with the hammer. Joy of joys, it stayed together. I leaned the finished spit against the wall and set about arranging the second one.

Just then Ana came into view at the side of my mask. 'What on earth are you up to?' she asked incredulously. 'Everyone's here and you haven't even started cooking the lambs.'

'Stay cool,' I admonished. 'It'll be alright. I'll just weld this spit up and then I'll be ready to start the cooking.'

'Shall I take this one down to the fire?' She reached for the completed spit.

'No! Don't touch that, it's hot...!'

But too late: Ana had picked it up, yelped and dropped it. As it hit the ground it returned with a clatter to its earlier state as two separate pieces of iron.

'Jeezus-Christ!! *Now* look what you've done,' I shouted.

She gave me a withering look and flounced off to join the swelling multitude.

●

After another half-hour of cussing and swearing I decided to wire the wretched rods together. By the time I got down to the valley, the guests were all there, passing round the very last of the salads. They had cooked flatbread on the stones of the fire and with this they had polished off the bucketfuls of Middle Eastern delicacies that we had prepared for them.

The only person who was hungry now was me. I felt justifiably a little piqued; it was, after all, my birthday and, while I was buggering about with the welder, I had missed the music and the puppetry and every last leaf and grain of the side dishes. To make matters worse, everyone was singing the praises of a fabulous dish of 'sushi' – a delicately spiced roll of mushed avocado and pickled vegetables rolled up in seaweed and sliced – that the crudo-vegans had brought. In their generosity they had saved me a few delicious mouthfuls, fending off hungry hordes to do so. I swallowed them in the worst possible grace.

It took a long time to cook the lambs, but, as the fragrance of the roasting meat mingled with the night air and I sipped from a bottle of sparkling Barranco Oscuro cava, I began to relax and luxuriate in the atmosphere of growing bonhomie. Most of the guests had gone, leaving my family, some guitar-playing friends and a few Spanish carnivores to group around the warmth of the fire. The moon rose over the Serreta and a pale mist from the river swirled amongst the tamarisks and the rocks as we sat murmuring and masticating into the night.

STEPS AND WATERFALLS

THESE DAYS CHLOË NO LONGER spends Saturday
nights at home involved in edifying conversation
with her parents. She goes to town, and often
ends up staying the night there, with one of her
coterie of schoolfriends. Town is where the action happens,
and we have to drive her to and fro ever more frequently.
Being unsure as to the exact nature of the 'action', and seeking to be the responsible parent, I asked her one evening, as
we headed towards Órgiva, 'Just what exactly is it that you
and your friends do in town on a Saturday night?'

'Oh nothing really...' said Chloë. A silence while I
mulled over this surprising information. She had told me
that the previous weekend they had not gone to bed until
three in the morning.

'But you must do *something*, surely?' I prompted. 'I mean,
you can't spin nothing out till three a.m., can you?'

'No, I suppose not.' Chloë was playing with the buttons on her accursed mobile phone.

'Then what?' I continued my probe.

'*What* what?'

'What do you do?'

'Well, we... hang out...'

'Where do you hang out?'

A brief hiatus as she performed some tricky digital manoeuvre. 'Just now our place is on the *peldaño* – the steps – of the bank.'

'Which one?'

'Banco del Espiritu Santo – up the Plaza. But we're hoping to move somewhere closer to the centre.'

It all started to become clear. It was a phenomenon I had observed many times in Órgiva. As day turns to evening, the steps of the various shops and banks become occupied by gangs of teenage girls, who chew *pipas* – sunflower seeds – and gaze with regal detachment upon the world. The incumbents of each step receive visitors, mainly testosterone-sodden youths with space-monster haircuts and 49cc mopeds with the silencers removed. At times other gangs, or *pandillas* as they are called, temporarily forsake their own pitch to come and pay court to a rival, and then the pavement becomes impassable, blocked by the multitude of scantily clad girls, the shoal of *49ers* nudging the kerb, and the growing mounds of ejaculated *pipa* shells.

Although I had registered this scene, I had never imagined it as being a part of Chloë's life. It had all seemed a rather desperate business: the poor kids huddled in shop doorways in all weather, watching life – or what passes for life in a one-horse town like Órgiva – go by.

'So where are you thinking of moving to?' I continued my line of enquiry.

'We're hoping to get the shoe shop by the dentist, although I know that Claudia and her friends are after it, too. Mari and Lourdes are moving on. They've got one of the best *peldaños* of all – the driving school on the other side of the traffic lights. From there it's only one step to the top place in town, the *peldaño de la chuchería*, the sweetshop steps.'

'So how is it you all go moving round like this? Surely if one group has the best *peldaño*, then they're not going to want to give it up to anybody else.'

Chloë gave me a withering look. 'Oh, Dad, you don't understand anything…'

'Perhaps not, but I'd very much like to. I'm intrigued.'

'Sandra and her friends – you know, the ones who hang out now on the *peldaño de la chuchería* – well they're nearly old enough to be allowed into the *discoteca*.'

'So what do you do all night when you're hanging out on a *peldaño*?' I wasn't going to give up…

'*Charlamos* – we chat about stuff…'

'What stuff?'

'Oh, just stuff. You know… Hey, let's play *adivinanzas*…'

So we played *adivinanzas* – a guessing game in rhyme – for the rest of the journey. I had been given all the information I was going to get.

Thinking about that conversation on the way back to the farm, I began to see the business of the steps a little more from Chloë's perspective. What had appeared to me a dismal waste of time, sitting about with nothing to do and nowhere to go, was looking at things with blinkered English eyes, entirely forgetting that Spain has an outdoor and gregarious culture. The nights are usually warm, everyone's up late and, in adult life, you're expected to drift around the local bars together, endlessly joining and rejoining your friends. Hanging out in doorways and on steps with a few bags of sunflower seeds is just the way that a young Spanish teenager starts off.

Of course, I reflected, there are worries that the bags of *pipas* might one day get substituted for stronger substances, which are pretty rife even in the mountain villages of the Alpujarras. But there was no sign that any of Chloë's crew were going off those particular rails. And, being a small town, there's always someone looking out for you; it would be a reckless teenager who tried to give Chloë trouble, knowing that Manolo and his friends were in town. All in all, it seemed a definite improvement on the more intense and debauched teenage party scene in England. And it was certainly an improvement on my own upbringing. Packed off to boarding school on the first day I could tie my own shoelaces, I was confined to a lonely existence in the holidays, with no friends within a thirty-mile radius of my home. It was only by the merest stroke of luck that I managed to get a leg up into the business of mating.

Of course, there would be more worries ahead as Chloë grew older and hanging out on the *peldaños* gave way to *discotecas* – and a whole set of new baggage. But, right now, the *peldaños* seemed comfortingly benign and, in their way, they seemed a peculiarly graphic illustration of the stages of independent life. First the steps, then the discos, then the bars.

And then?

It dawned upon me that there was another *peldaño*, oddly close in spirit to the young teenage phenomenon. At the entrance and exit of every small town and village in Spain, you will see sitting on a bench a gaggle of old men with their sticks and hats. There they sit all morning, discussing the local issues of the day and watching the world as it passes. At lunchtime they rise slowly to their three feet and totter home. They sleep away the hot hours of the afternoon and, as the evening starts to cool, they return and remain there through the freshening hours of the night.

For the seventeen years I have lived in Spain, I have viewed these old folks with a certain detachment: a thing inconceivably far away in time and of no concern to me. But it seemed to me, as I reflected on the sweetshop steps and *discotecas* and benches, that the business of ageing is not a continuous process, like a river flowing steadily down to the sea. It's more a succession of waterfalls, some cataclysmic, some almost inconsequential, with peaceful stretches of flat water in between.

Not long ago I felt the pull of one of those falls, easing me ever downwards towards the latter *peldaños* of life. The plan for the day – and it was a hot summer day – had been for Ana, myself, Chloë and her cousin Lauren, who was over from London, to drive off to Granada and there improve our understanding of the universe by visiting the Parque de las Ciencias, a sort of high-class theme park devoted to the wonders of science. This could have been pretty exciting – at my stage in life, this is one of the few sorts of theme park you can get enthusiastic about – had the excursion not inexorably degenerated into a day-long shopping trip. I played along as best I could, but it soon became impossible to hide my dejection at being dragged along upon this most fatuous and detestable of human activities.

At some stage my increasing moroseness became intolerable to my shopping companions, and I was given a dispensation to slip off and sit in a bar. I found the right sort of bar in a shady corner near the Paseo del Salón, and sat down outside with a coffee. I had just managed to get my newspaper properly folded for a read when a doddery old boy shuffled in and asked if he might sit in the only remaining chair, which was next to mine. He was one of those urban Andalusians who wear a grey three-piece suit and matching *cordobés* hat even on the most blistering-hot summer day, and he brandished an elegant wild olivewood cane. 'You're most welcome,' I said, with the patronising smile one dishes out to the extremely aged, and then returned to my paper.

After a certain amount of huffing and puffing, he leaned over to me and announced, in the way that such people will, 'I'm ninety-five years old, you know.'

I looked at him critically for a moment, then said, in order to make him feel better about things, 'Well I never would have believed it; you're looking good, though.'

He didn't look too good, as a matter of fact. He was pudgy about the face and there wasn't a lot of hair on the top of his head; there was a wart on the side of his nose, and he wheezed a bit. But then, I suppose, at ninety-five – and here was a person who, if memory serves, would have been around not long after the second Carlist war – you're lucky to be here at all. 'Oh, I do what I can to keep myself going,' he informed me.

By now I realised that I wasn't going to get any more reading done, so I stuffed the newspaper back into my bag and eased my chair round so I was half-facing him. He peered at me with a quizzical look.

'You're not one of us, are you? I can tell from your accent. Where are you from?'

'I'm English,' I replied.

'Oh,' he said, nodding his head and peering at me. 'Retired out here, have you?'

That hit me a bit in one of the places where it hurts, but I decided to humour the old fool.

'Well, yes, in a sense I have, I suppose. Although I seem to do more work now than…'

'Your wife still alive?' the crap-noddled old boggart interrupted.

'Well, she certainly was when I last saw her,' I replied, getting a bit cross now.

'Got a family, have you, then?'

'Yes, as a matter of fact I have,' I said testily. 'I have a fourteen- year-old daughter.'

At this he drew back in astonishment and stared hard at me. I could see him mentally subtracting fourteen from ninety-five and coming up with the figure of eighty-one, and wondering how the hell I could have managed at such an advanced age to get it up.

I paid for my coffee and got up to leave.

'It's been very nice talking to you,' I hissed, and hurried off to rejoin the *pandilla* of shopping womenfolk, with my ego just the tiniest bit bruised.

THE ALMOND BLOSSOM
APPRECIATION SOCIETY

EN SACKS OF SHEEP MIX, one of barley and one of wheat for the chickens, some horse mix, and a bag each of biscuits for the dogs and cats. I looked at the great weight groaning in the back of the car and, satisfied with my agricultural credentials, slammed the back door in a cloud of dust. A big white van had drawn up opposite the feed centre. The driver was leaning on his elbow and looking at me. 'Cristóbal – *por dónde andas?*' growled a deep, well-modulated voice.

'Paco... it's you!' I responded, recognising the figure at the wheel. 'You're looking good, and I see you've joined the bearded men.' *Por dónde andas?* – literally 'Where do you walk?' – is a hard one to answer, though I suspect it's a rhetorical greeting, and I have always responded to it as such. I crossed the street and took Paco's hand. His face burst into a great smile beneath the new beard.

'*Qué dice el hombre?*' he said.

Now, *Qué dice el hombre?* – 'What does the man say?' – is an even more abstruse sort of a greeting in my opinion than *por dónde andas?* I mean, what is the man supposed to say in reply to that? I'm always a little flummoxed by these formulaic Spanish greetings, fearing that despite years of residence I still don't quite pass muster in this most basic communication.

'Great to see you, Paco,' I offered. 'It's been a long time, and apart from the fungal growth you look well. And how about Consuelo and Paz?'

'We're all well, by the grace of God. But I've had a thought, Cristóbal, and here is my thought: do you not think it a good idea that we should go again to the hills of the Contraviesa and enjoy the beauty of the almond blossom?'

'Hell yes, Paco. I was thinking of ringing you to suggest it, because it's already fading on the lower hills...'

'There's still time: if we go higher we've still got a couple of weeks.'

Paco is my only country Spanish friend who would suggest such a thing. Other country people I know are not unaware of the beauty of nature and the countryside around them; they just live and work amongst it, rather than taking active steps to seek it out. The idea of walking into the hills to find the most spectacular grove of blossoming almonds would no more occur to them than it would occur to a commuter to hop off a train a stop early simply to admire the station. 'I'll give you a ring next week, then, and we'll make a date,' I said, and Paco slipped the van into gear and rolled round the corner.

Paco Sanchez is remarkable in lots of ways. He was born into a farming family in Torvizcón, where he lives to this day. His father made his living from growing vegetables, and as a child Paco would always be with him in the *huerto*, watching and learning. At eighteen he pulled together enough money to buy a team of mules, with which he scraped a desperately hard living ploughing the steep hills around the village.

There was some wild gene in his make-up, though, that made Paco a Communist, a seeker and a traveller, and with Consuelo, his bride from the village, he left home to seek his fortune in Switzerland. They worked as farm labourers, wherever they could find a job, and saved pretty much every Swiss franc they earned. The scheme was conceived to return to Spain with enough money to buy a patch of land – for Paco's father had been a *jornalero*, a day worker with little land of his own. After several years the couple came back to Torvizcón with the funds to buy a house in the village, a fertile plot of alluvial silt down in the river, a small grove of olives and a whole hillside of almond trees up on the Contraviesa. In those days nobody wanted to buy property in the countryside, let alone farm it, so it was cheap.

They lost no time in making the land pay, and within a very few years were running a thriving business. Paco had been fired up with new notions from his time in Switzerland and was probably the first man in the Alpujarras to espouse the cause of organic agriculture, which contributed even more to his neighbours' conviction that he was a dangerous radical. At the time this was flying in the face of the wind, as all his contemporaries were embracing the racy modern chemical way of farming. Paco told me that he was doing nothing new; he was simply putting into practice all that he had learned from his father. In those days, everybody had farmed organically – nobody could afford the new chemicals and artificial fertilisers – so results were achieved by dint of skill, observation and a grinding round of work.

Paco and Consuelo were good at what they did, and had the imagination and confidence to look beyond the local market to sell their produce. They discovered an organic food outlet in Germany and started gearing their output to its tastes. They produced *pan de higo* (fig bread), almonds and jams and conserves of every sort of fruit; they pickled peppers and capers and dried tomatoes in the sun, as well as apricots, persimmons and loquats. Preserved olives they sold by the bucket, and olive oil and even the odd crate of Paco's home-made wine – which, if the truth be told, was a bit of a hit-and-miss affair. Every month or so a van would come down from the organic co-operative in Germany and return laden with the delicious products of Paco and Consuelo's industry. On the proceeds, they bought a big white van of their own and, not without misgivings, exchanged the team of mules for a small bulldozer.

But one of the effects of Paco's wild gene, and avid reading on ecological matters, was to make him a little radical and even puritanical in his aims. The business of shipping the delights of the Alpujarras all the way to Hamburg for the benefit of its well-heeled denizens didn't seem quite right to him. So he decided to set up a local co-operative in order to bring together the increasing number of organic growers and consumers in the Alpujarras.

I don't know how Paco had the energy, after long hot days spent labouring amongst his fruit and vegetables and then driving around the Alpujarras to distribute boxes of produce, but somehow he managed to convene a meeting of interested parties. As I had written a book, it was felt I would 'lend weight' to the proceedings, so I was nominated to be *vocal*, or spokesperson, with special responsibility for co-ordinating the livestock sector. I was, in fact, the only member with any livestock, beyond the odd chicken, which meant that I had to co-ordinate myself. This was not as easy as you'd think, due to my tendency to fall asleep once the first item on the agenda was called and to doze quietly all the way through to 'any other business' – the inevitable result of a combination of hot night air, alcohol and the drone of voices arguing interminably over fine procedural points. At the first meeting I jerked awake to discover my vote was required to establish the name of the group. Paco had suggested 'Alcaparra', meaning 'caper', which struck me as a fine name for an agricultural co-operative. There wasn't much competition so *Alcaparra* it was, and I was able to return to my slumbers.

The co-operative leased a small shop in town, which soon became a gathering point for the local alternative community. On sale were honeys and tofu and natural cosmetics made from avocado pears and other unlikely ingredients, but mostly mountains of rather unprepossessing vegetables. When it was *habas* (broad beans) season the shop would be crammed from floor to ceiling with *habas*. But of course everybody had their own *habas*, so nobody wanted to buy them. It was the same with artichokes – there's only so many things you can do with an artichoke – and not much more promising for tomatoes, peppers, aubergines and beans. As for oranges or lemons, they were a complete waste of time, as everybody had trees of their own.

In order to breathe some life into the livestock sector, I stuck up in the shop what I considered to be humorous posters, advertising succulent locally produced lamb. The response was, to say the least, poor, because ninety-nine per cent of the membership was vegetarian – and if they weren't that, then they were vegan, or were fasting.

Unsurprisingly I began to feel redundant at meetings and little by little my attendance dropped off. Paco, who had been voted president by unanimous consent, was so efficient and seemed so good at maintaining order among the co-op's more anarchic elements that I felt sure I wouldn't be missed. But before long, I heard of bitter disputes erupting about what constituted organic produce – did you have to grow it yourself or could you do things like import herbs and spices from India? Paco thought the group shouldn't be too puritanical, but he was out-voted by the organo-fundamentalists and eventually expelled. And the co-operative he had so painstakingly set up slid down the tubes.

●

A revival of the Almond Blossom Appreciation Society, as Paco had dubbed our previous year's outing, would be just the thing to rise above such setbacks. I consulted Ana about the possibility of being given a free day to go walking in the mountains with my friend. There was an element of suspicion in the look she gave me. I fear that women in general are unable to rid themselves of the notion that, when men go off on a jaunt together, they inevitably descend to boozing and licentiousness. I reminded her of how the previous year Paco and I had returned from our Almond Blossom Appreciation having imbibed nothing but water all day. I don't think we even had anything to eat. Such was the purity of our motives.

'Hmm?' mused Ana sceptically. 'Then why are you making such a point of asking me? It smacks of a guilty conscience.' Which just goes to show how undervalued consideration and transparency can be.

Undeterred, I drove Chloë to school the next day, which gave me an early start. An Almond Blossom Appreciation expedition is a thing to be taken seriously, not an excuse to linger in bed till the middle hours of the morning. As I headed over the Seven-Eye Bridge and turned east towards Torvizcón, I gazed up at the three great snow-cloaked peaks of the Sierra Nevada. The early morning sun, just rising over the bulk of the Contraviesa, illuminated the high east-facing slopes with a pale tinge of rose. Before long I swung round the bend into the Rambla de Torvizcón and saw the village lurking in its cleft down by the dry river. When the slopes above it are arrayed in almond blossom and the blue smoke from the village fires curls upwards into the bright winter sky, that's the time to see Torvizcón. In the heat of summer, with the life and the colour baked out of the hills around, you'd best stay on the road and keep on going towards the Eastern Alpujarras.

I parked in the square and headed up the hill towards Paco's house. It's a stiff climb because Torvizcón is a steep village and Paco and Consuelo live at the top. I was panting hard by the time I got to the steep alley with its diagonal ridges to give a purchase to passing mules.

'*Hola,* Paco!' I called as I rounded the corner.

'*Qué dice el hombre?*' came Paco's voice from the roof.

'What are you doing up there, man? We're supposed to be off on a walk.'

'I'm just finishing off these few tiles...'

I looked up at what he was doing, then moved around a bit and, shading my eyes with my hand, looked some more.

'You've got that all wrong, Paco. That's not how you put tiles on.' I was rather pleased with the way I'd rattled off this traditional Alpujarran way of greeting, rubbishing a man's efforts. My command of the idiom was improving.

Paco looked down at me from his vantage point with what I took to be a withering look, though I couldn't see his face as it was silhouetted against the sky. 'Cristóbal, every single man in this village has passed by my roof and said exactly what you've just said. Now I expect that sort of conservatism from my stick-in-the-mud Alpujarreño neighbours, but I thought you, as a *guiri*, knew a thing or two about the wider world.'

'Apparently not, then, Paco. Perhaps you could illuminate my darkness with an explanation. Also who is this pig and why is it rubbing against your railings?' A sleek pink pig – a Large White, as it happened – with a red collar and a bell hung about its neck, had just slunk into view.

'That', said Paco, climbing down his ladder, 'is the Public Pig and it has come for its breakfast.' He pulled its tail in a friendly way. 'It's communally owned by the people of Torvizcón and fed at the public expense until the *fiesta* of San Antón...'

'And what happens then?'

'*Hombre,* then it gets raffled off and whoever wins it gets to eat it,' he responded, before yelling, at the top of his voice, 'Paz!' (pronounced as a Yorkshireman would say 'path') to summon his daughter from inside the house. 'Your pig's here,' he shouted.

'*Voy*,' came the reply – 'coming'. The pig started to get frisky at the sound of Paz's voice, and began hopping from foot to foot jingling its bell.

'As for the tiles…' continued Paco. 'We were in Galicia in the autumn and I noticed that in some villages they have this singular way of laying them so that they look good and drain better. But I fear it may take a thousand years before the *tontos* of this village accept that it's actually an improvement. I sometimes wonder if the evolution of ideas actually works at a slower pace in the Alpujarras than elsewhere on the planet, And I also think, Cristóbal, that perhaps you have been living here too long.'

Before I could offer a considered reply to this suggestion, Paz came through the door, dressed in regulation school uniform of baggy jeans, tight T-shirt and hooded top. She was carrying a bowl of slops and leftovers. The Public Pig nearly turned itself inside out with delight. Paz placed the bowl on the ground and the pig launched itself upon the gruesome-looking fare, its face suffused with ecstasy.

'*Hola*, Paz,' I said. '*Qué tal?*' I wasn't going to trouble an eighteen-year-old with *Por dónde andas?* or *Qué dice el hombre?*

'Things are fine,' she said, fiddling with a troublesome lock of her long hair. 'Though the exams are a bit of a pain right now.'

'What are you studying these days?' – the typical old man's question.

'I'm specialising in Classics... Ooh and I've got to run – I've got a Latin exam today and my lift to school is about to leave...'

'Best of luck, then I'm sure you'll do fine – and so will your pig...'

'It's not my pig, Cristóbal, it's the Public Pig; but I think it likes me a lot.' And she bent to scratch it behind the ear while the pig looked at her thoughtfully.

I was looking at Paz thoughtfully, too, surprised to the point of speechlessness by her gestures and voice. It wasn't that there was anything unusual about them; in fact the opposite. She sounded exactly like my own daughter. The style of delivery, the intonations, the body language and gestures – they were exactly the same. If I were to shut my eyes it could almost be Chloë. Of course they were both products of the same school, the Órgiva bear-pit, but they weren't close friends or even part of the same gang; after all, Paz is eighteen and Chloë fourteen. It was humbling to reflect how the influence we have as parents is as nothing compared with the power of the peer group. I pondered this fact a little sadly, as I waited for Paco to finish cleaning his tools. Eventually he emerged, pulling on a light jacket.

'*Vamos al campo,*' he said. 'Let's head for the hills.'

●

We walked together down the *rambla* – the flash-riverbed – out towards the Cádiar river and the Almegijar bridge, stepping up the pace a little to warm ourselves in the cool of the morning. Parked on the bridge was a big vintage motorbike and, standing beside it, a boyish grin playing behind his moustache and spectacles, was its owner. 'José, *qué alegría* – what happiness, what are you doing here?' I called.

'Oh, I forgot to tell you,' said Paco. 'I invited José Pela to come along with us.'

'*Hola*, Cristóbal. *Qué dice el hombre?*' – we repeated all the conventions. But I was genuinely delighted to see José, who is the teacher at the primary school in Torvizcón. He had came down to the Alpujarras from Santander in the north almost twenty years ago, with his beautiful raven-haired wife, Mara, and they had a son not long after Chloë was born. I had first met him at the inaugural meeting of the *Amigos del Río Guadalfeo*, a campaign group set up to stop the dam being built in the Guadalfeo River, and we had remained good friends.

José had never learned to drive a car. His beloved motor-bike was a much more suitable form of transport for getting to the little school far up in the folds of the *rambla*, where he used to teach, and he was quite content to leave the driving to Mara. Then, one morning six years ago, on the quiet road above Puerto Jubiley, Mara's Land-Rover jumped the crash barrier and rolled over the edge. Nobody knows quite how this could have happened but José was left alone with their six-year-old son, Aretx. They had been a very close family, and the two were left utterly desolate.

When José moved to the school at Torvizcón it was a foregone conclusion that he and Paco would become friends. They both shared a restless curiosity about the world and its ways and, although José had a rather different approach – his unassuming manner and knack of drawing other people out made him a sensitive and popular teacher – he thoroughly enjoyed Paco's more passionate and extrovert ways. I like them both immensely and often think what a fine, albeit tiny, *tertulia* we would make. The *tertulia* is a peculiarly Spanish phenomenon where a group of friends will gather regularly to discuss a topic – be it politics, religion, music, poetry, literature, art or whatever. Although inevitably one drinks, as most *tertulias* gather in bars, it is the talk that is the thing. I had always wanted to be invited to join a proper long-established *tertulia* – Madrid has some that go back generations – but I don't think Órgiva has such a thing... or at any rate I haven't been asked to join it. I'm happy, though, to make do with Paco and José. They are opinionated, pleasingly radical and unstoppably loquacious, and our Almond Blossom Appreciation Society is, for me, about as good as a *tertulia* could ever be.

'Last time I passed this way the path was somewhere here,' said José, beating at some brambles with a stick. 'But it's got so overgrown. Nobody uses these paths any more.' Nonetheless, after a bit of thrashing about, we found the cobbled old mule-path and began the long climb up to the village of Almegíjar. Paco and José immediately launched into a torrent of animated conversation. As for me, I have always thought it unwise to talk too much when climbing steep hills, so I kept quiet and just slogged on.

It was not yet 9.30, but it was already hotting up and we soon stopped to take off our jackets and look at the view below us. 'José is finally getting his act together and finding himself a new woman,' confided Paco, wiping the sweat from his face with a spotted handkerchief. 'He's been on his own for long enough. I keep telling him it's doing him no good. Eh, José?'

'I suppose not,' replied José, struggling to get his breath. 'But sometimes I wonder.'

'You can't have doubts, man! You've got hordes of women lining up,' said Paco with a grin. 'They send him poetry,' he added, turning to me.

'Tell me more, José. What's your secret?'

'It's the Internet,' said Paco. 'That's the way things are done nowadays. José has put himself on offer on the Internet.'

'I posted a notice a few weeks ago,' said José a little shyly. 'And... well... I got an awful lot of replies. I'm not sure quite what to do about it.'

'It seems they're all poets, José's women – and they're all desperate to marry him.'

'Have you actually met any of these people?' I asked.

José kicked a stone off the path and scratched his ear. 'No, not yet,' he said, 'but I'm going to have to do something about it soon... You know, meet up with one of them.'

'Would that be the medical researcher from Sevilla you're thinking of?' asked Paco, who seemed well informed on the subject. 'She wrote him pages and pages of barely disguised erotic verse. I think she could be the one, José, no?'

'Hmm, I mustn't be too hasty, you know. It could all be a terrible mistake.'

'Don't be a fool, man. You've got to try them all,' said Paco with a salacious smirk. 'Although it's romantic love with a view to marriage that José's after. He's not just some cheap cyber-Lothario like you or me...'

I was quite surprised by Paco's irreverence when talking about what I reckoned must be really a rather sensitive subject for José, and tried to make my own comments more sympathetic. 'Well, I think it's a wonderful idea,' I enthused earnestly, 'and I hope it works out for you. I'd certainly do it in your position...'

'So would I,' said Paco. 'In fact, I'm thinking of doing it even though I'm not in José's position. The thought of all that poetry makes my eyes water...'

'I can't see Consuelo getting terribly excited about it,' I said.

'It's amazing,' said José, 'All those people out there on the Internet, just desperate to get together with somebody. It's been like an avalanche, it really has.'

We were all quiet for a while, thinking our various thoughts on the theme.

By now we had reached the terraces just beneath the village. The path here was one of those beautiful ancient ways, with broad steps of cobbled white river-stones. 'Here's our first almond grove,' I said. 'Let's stop and contemplate it for a bit.'

If ever I find myself doubting the pleasure of living somewhere as abstrusely remote as the Alpujarras, I think of moments like these. The pale stones of the track were interlaced with bright-green spring grass and in the corners were clumps of luminous yellow oxalis – the *pica-pica* that children love to pick and eat for the sweet vinegary taste of its stalks. Above the *pica-pica* were stone walls, harbouring a population of tiny lizards darting from sunshine to shade. And overhanging the walls were the blossoming almond trees.

Now, an almond flower is quite the loveliest thing ever seen. There's only the subtlest of scents, but, with the exquisite beauty of the pale pink petals, clouds of them against the burned black of the trunk, you hardly need a scent. And through the mist of petals, which hum with great blue *abejorros* or carpenter bees, you see the bright blue of the sky. It makes your heart droop with pleasure like a heavily laden branch.

We stood, the three of us, in this perfect place, drenched in warm winter sunshine. I sat down on a stone and squinted against the sun at the view.

'Here, Cristóbal, drink…' Paco nudged me with his *bota*.

A *bota* is a leather wine bottle and an essential accessory for any self-respecting rural Spaniard. It's shaped the way you'd think a goat's stomach would be shaped, and made of soft brown goat hide with a waterproof lining of pine resin tar. In the plastic cap is a pinhole, just enough for a needle-thin stream of wine to pass.

I was pleased with this opportunity to display my credentials, because I reckoned that Paco and José were looking forward to a snigger at my expense. But the truth is – even though I say it myself – long practice has made me pretty slick in this esoteric country skill.

The first thing to remember is that it's quite unacceptable to put the spout in your mouth and suck it – which on the surface seems the obvious thing to do. The Spanish tend to be delicate about sharing bottles of water or wine with the sort of person who wraps their lips around the spout to drink. They fear the backwash and floaters.

The technique for drinking from a *bota* is to tilt your head back, open your mouth and raise the bag about a hand's breadth from your lips. Then you squeeze it enough to eject an accurate stream of wine into the back of your mouth, while you slowly move it away from you until your arms are straight. This aerates the wine and allows a little sunlight to enter as the fine stream arcs, glittering through the air. It's essential to maintain a steady pressure, to allow for wind deflection and to swallow constantly with your mouth open – a physical refinement not everyone can master. All this is second nature to a man who knows the *bota*, but it's endlessly amusing to watch beginners as they spray wine deep into their nostrils, in their eyes, all down their fronts and, on the odd occcasion when they do manage to get a squirt into their mouth, to see them hacking and coughing and incontinently blurting the wine up and out.

I thought it a little early in the proceedings to be starting on the wine, but entered into the spirit of the thing nonetheless and took the proffered *bota*. Paco and José watched with barely disguised disappointment as I took a long pull. The wine, the rough Alpujarran country variety known as *costa*, burned as it splashed onto the back of my palate, vapourising and filling my mouth with hot, tar-scented mist.

I rocked forward and lowered the *bota* to finish, with barely a drop dribbling down my front.

'Uggh, *costa*,' I said, grimacing, and wiping my mouth on my forearm. 'I mean, you can drink the stuff but you can never really like it. Can you?'

'What nonsense, *tonto*,' said Paco sharply. 'Of course you can enjoy *costa*, and the one you're drinking is perfectly good.' And, as if to illustrate the point, he lifted the *bota* from my unworthy hands and took a long, satisfying pull.

'You must understand, Cristóbal,' José explained, 'that you can't approach *costa* like those fancy Catalan wines you favour. You have to bear in mind the fierce conditions up there in the Contraviesa, the hardship and the pain of caring for those old vines by hand.'

'That's the truth,' interjected Paco, 'but you've become too *delicado* to notice. Consorting with all those literary folks has shrivelled your balls – you no longer know the meaning of physical work.'

Paco had touched a nerve here: having spent nearly thirty years of my life making a living from manual labour of one sort or another, I found it hard to think of writing as a proper job. Somehow, earning money from sitting at a table with a book and a pen, doesn't feel quite... well, honest. In an attempt to defend myself I told them about the appalling *costas* I'd drunk on my shearing jobs, and suggested that most of these wines had industrial alcohol added to the vat.

My fellow members of the Society winced at the very idea. 'You've been prejudiced by your too narrow experience, my friend,' José chided me. 'Trust us. We'll get you some decent *costa* before the day is out, and see if we can't change your mind.' And with that he raised the *bota* again and took another few mouthfuls. This talk of fine wine was making him thirsty.

We continued along the cobbled way to the village of Notáez, whose pretty patios and little squares were displaying the signs of an early spring – lemon trees were bursting into bud, bougainvillea draped itself across the stone walls and succulents burst exuberantly over the edge of their pots. Passing through the village we struck up the hill towards Cástaras. As we walked we talked of the demise of local agriculture, and of the *caminos*, the mule tracks built in the times of the Romans or the Moors and only now falling into disrepair.

The *camino* that we were following wound among the village's few remaining cultivated terraces, some so tiny as to be barely worth the effort. A terrace might contain a single orange tree, surrounded by a dozen lovingly tended *haba* plants, a clump or two of poppies and a few feathery wild fennel in the corner by the rocks. In places streams of water cascaded over stone walls to spread across a tiny paddy field of deep green alfalfa, or along the furrows of a potato patch. We stopped and admired the beauty of the painstaking work.

'Do you know what a *vergel* is?' asked Paco.

'*Claro,*' said José.

'No, I mean Cristóbal, *tonto*. Of course *you* know!'

'What is a *vergel*, then?' I asked.

'It's one of those old words that come from the Arabic,' Paco explained. 'Of course it is, it still sounds like Arabic and it means "garden" but with just a hint of art and a bigger hint of paradise. Anyway, these are *vergeles*, and by the time Chloë, Paz and Aretx have children they'll all be gone, and with them the beauty and richness of these villages will be lost for good.'

Paco loves agriculture with a passion; he's the sort of man who can be moved to tears by the sight of a well-made dung heap. To walk in the Alpujarras with him is a revelation. He will describe the different agricultural styles of men or villages as if they were painters or composers, each with his own distinctive signature.

From the endangered *vergeles* of Notáez we passed by means of an ascending zigzag path into wide open country with rolling hills of almond groves, teetering on the brink of the great gulf of air that separated us from the long range of the Contraviesa. This was what we had come to see. For an hour or more we walked beneath a luminous cloud of blossom amongst the twisted black trunks of the trees. Larks sang invisible from high in the air above their nests, a cock crowed from a distant *cortijo* and the breeze sighed gently amongst the fronds of broom.

Apart from an occasional 'ooh' or 'ay', we didn't say much. There wasn't much to say. To feast upon the beauty of the flowering almonds was the reason for our expedition. There seemed little point in telling one another over and again how impressed we were. Glutted with the loveliness of it all, we smiled inanely at one another now and then or watched with pleasure as José shook his head and whistled quietly to himself, or Paco, with a sprig of lavender behind his ear, caught some falling petals and pasted them to the sweat of his forehead. I suppose the air, too, was filled with the delicate scent of almond blossom, but I've never been able to smell it myself. Paco and José both swore that if you cut a branch of almond blossom and bring it into the house, it fills the room with a scent of marzipan and honey.

'In Cástaras we'll stop for sustenance... accompanied by the fine wines of the Contraviesa,' announced José importantly. 'Cástaras is just around the corner.' But Cástaras was not round the corner, nor the next one. When finally we caught sight of the village it was time to sit down together and take another pull at the *bota*.

Cástaras is the last village of the western Alpujarras – or the first, depending on where you're coming from. Over the watershed begins the different landscape of the east, with its cinnabar mines and parched and deeply eroded hills.

As a counterpoint to the change, Cástaras is as lush as an Andalucian village can be. It's set high on an impregnable rock in a forest of giant poplars, watered by the steep river whose sound fills the valley as it cascades from the towering cliffs above. Until a few years ago the place fell into almost complete abandonment as the population left in search of an easier, less isolated life. But new inhabitants have been trickling in, and little by little the pretty village is coming back to life.

We threaded our way through the narrow streets and came out in the main square, where a couple of plastic tables from the *posada* had been placed out in the sun. Both were occupied by couples engaged in gnawing on what looked like crusty rolls filled with omelette – *bocadillo de tortilla*. We decided to sit inside and drew up three stools to the bar. A tall thin youth with a mane of black hair emerged from behind a curtain, wiping his hands on a rather questionable-looking black cloth. He looked at us enquiringly.

'Give us some wine,' ordered Paco, 'and we'll drink while we think what we're going to eat.'

Three small tumblers appeared, to be filled with a deep red wine from a jug that stood beneath the bar. For a *tapa* came a dish of home-cured olives – little black and purple *arbequinas*. They were delicious... it boded well. We drank a little wine and started to think about what we would like to eat.

'Right,' said Paco turning to me. 'What do you make of the wine?' I took a few little sips then held it up to the light.

'Mmm,' I mused. 'I rather like it. It's fruity and full-bodied and interesting with no sourness, and it's a lovely deep red, as opposed to most *costas*, which are more...

brown.' I hadn't really a clue what to say. It tasted like a hundred other *costas*; but I knew all those words in both languages and they seemed not inappropriate.

Paco and José were both now looking at me with what I thought was a pitying sort of a look.

'This is a foul wine, Cristóbal,' said Paco.

'Foul is too strong a word,' said José. 'It's not that bad, but it might have been a little better a few months ago. You've got to drink these wines young; they only get worse with time.'

Paco sniffed the wine disdainfully. 'Unless I'm mistaken,' he said, 'this one's from Los Garcías de Verdevique. They usually do much better than this. I suspect it's been in that *jarra* too long.'

He called into the kitchen: 'Some more wine when you've a moment, but make it a different one this time.' Out came the youth, wiping his hands on his cloth. He fished about for a minute beneath the counter, then came up with another *jarra*. Oddly enough he didn't offer to change our glasses, but refilled them with the new wine.

'So, what have you got for us to eat?' asked Paco.

'I can do you a *bocadillo de tortilla* if you don't mind waiting a bit.'

We masticated this information.

'What else have you got?' asked Paco.

'Nothing else, just *bocadillo de tortilla*,' came the practised reply.

We consulted one another, considering for a while the ramifications of this extensive menu. None of us particularly fancied *bocadillo de tortilla*. The youth stood patiently by, chewing slowly. 'Well then, what's it going to be?' he asked pleasantly as he refilled the tiny glasses.

'Hmm,' mumbled José. 'It's not an easy choice... but I reckon we'll be having three *bocadillos de tortilla*...'

'Right,' he said. 'Three *bocadillos de tortilla*.' And he wrote it down on a notepad and disappeared through the curtain.

The three of us were left alone in the bar. From a tinny loudspeaker came a radio programme of jazz and flamenco. We addressed ourselves once more to draining our glasses. This one was a more *costa*-like *costa*, pinkish brown and viscous. We all sipped and sat back. It really didn't seem bad this time, but I decided not to commit myself; I would wait for the experts to pronounce their verdict. As I watched them they seemed suddenly to be suffused with pleasure, to swell a little with the bloom of well-being that a good wine brings you.

'Now, this one's a better wine, Cristóbal,' announced José. 'Can you not perceive the difference? That last one, though rich and ruby red as you say, caked the mouth with a layer like pig fat does and would therefore be useless to accompany a meal...'

'Whereas this delicious little wine,' continued Paco, 'fills your mouth with a blossoming vapour as it warms to your body temperature. It prepares the palate for the pleasure of food just as it prepares the soul for the pleasures of love.'

José and I both put down our glasses and stared hard at Paco, who was watching out for the youth to order a refill. 'Paco,' said José, 'I should never have let you see those letters. I'm afraid the poetry's gone clean to your head.'

●

Later, in the heat of the afternoon, we got lost on the hill; the path vanished, and after crashing ineffectually about in the scrub for a time, we found ourselves beside an *espartalón*, a patch of esparto grass that looked like a reedy marsh, stranded on the dry hill. Esparto – *Stipa tenacissima* – is one of the defining plants of the Mediterranean. It grows abundantly in the wilder parts of Andalucía higher than a thousand metres above sea level. It's a tough, wiry grass, coarse and virtually unbreakable – you can even tie knots with it. It was traditionally one of the great resources of the rural poor, used for making shoes, ropes, mats, baskets – anything that is now made with plastic or rubber.

We sat on a rock for a while and tried to get our bearings, while Paco absent-mindedly began plaiting some strands of grass. 'Have you ever met Agustín?' he asked.

'Which Agustín? I know at least four Agustines.'

'Agustín Góngora, the old man who has the esparto museum in Torvizcón.'

'Ah, no. But I've been wanting to meet him and see his museum for years.'

'Then let's go and see the old *comunista* right now,' said Paco, jumping to his feet and heading off down towards the river.

My enthusiasm was genuine. I had been intrigued by Agustín Góngora for years, ever since filling up the car with petrol in Torvizcón. Some years ago a certain Pepe Vílchez, a native of the village, had a big win on the National Lottery and with the spoils he decided to indulge his oldest and dearest fantasy, and built a colossal petrol station by the bridge at the bottom of the village. The crowning glory of this Herodean work was a niche set into the wall by the Coca-Cola vending machine, wherein was displayed an esparto statue of a mule accompanied by a couple of officers of the Guardia Civil. They wore the unmistakable patent leather tricorn hats and belts and were properly hung with holsters and guns. But that aside, they were buck naked – and stupendously endowed – with every feature exquisitely fashioned from esparto. This deliciously irreverent tableau, I was told, was an original Góngora. It was there for years, but (sad to relate) the last time I went there it had disappeared.

We passed through the tangled back streets of Torvizcón until we reached a large house with a broad vine-shaded terrace. I remarked on the crowd milling around, chattering and enjoying the warm evening air.

'That's not a crowd,' said Paco. 'That's Agustín's family.'

We negotiated the throng of squabbling babies and children, mothers, fathers and aunts, until we came to the man himself, a brown-skinned, white-haired ancient, the undisputed king of this lively court. Paco embraced him warmly.

'*Hola*, Agustín. I've brought a couple of friends to see you.'

Agustín rose and shook our hands, studying us with his quick smiling eyes. '*Encantado*,' he said. 'I expect you'll be wanting to see the museum.' And, so saying, he led the way round the back of the house and unlocked a low green door. 'There was talk of installing my museum in some grander building down in the town,' he told us. 'But I prefer to keep it up here so the family can enjoy it and I can exercise some control over how it's run.'

The museum was a typical Alpujarran house, a maze of small rooms with whitewashed walls and low beam and cane ceilings, also whitewashed. It was populated by a fantastic array of improbable characters and creatures. I walked from room to room, spellbound by what I saw. People had told me that Agustín had an extraordinary talent, but I had no idea that he was this good. And the man was just the same, his sparkle and wicked wit undiminished by his eighty years or more, giving us a running commentary as we passed among his fabulous creations.

The singer Lola Flores was there, demurely clad, as was Miguel Ríos, the Granada rocker. A hoity-toity school-mistress sat sidesaddle on muleback, going home for the holidays, while a voluptuous poultry-maid stood naked amid a hilarious gaggle of esparto chickens. There were local characters and satirical political figures, most of them semi-naked and all artfully and wittily crafted from esparto grass.

'Now what do you think this is?' the artist asked with a wicked grin, waving a couple of unfathomable creations at us. 'Not the first glimmer of an idea...' I ventured.

'It's a bra,' he snorted. 'And these are esparto knickers. It's all that's left of my lingerie line. I've been working on this for ten years now, but most of the more interesting creations are in Madrid. They're going to get models to wear them on a catwalk for a TV show. The producer rang me the other day and complained that the knickers were too big and kept falling down, so I'm making some esparto braces to keep them up.'

I wondered aloud if I ought to buy a set for the wife. Paco shook his head. 'Do you really want to go home stinking of *costa* and bearing a pair of esparto knickers?' he asked. Perhaps not. A stunt like that could bring the reputation of the Almond Blossom Appreciation Society into serious disrepute.

THE WAVE OF COLD

I N 2004 IT RAINED IN JUNE. Two hours of torrential
downpour made rivers in the dust and the hot pine
trees steamed, filling the air with heady scent. Then it
stopped, and we knew that it wouldn't rain again till
autumn. September came in hot and dry and, though there
were some tantalisingly cloudy days towards the end of the
month, not a drop of rain fell. And the same in October.
If it doesn't rain in October people start to scratch their
heads and worry: this is the time when most of the year's
rain tends to fall, not gently like the spring showers, but in
great bursts that wash away mountain tracks and flood the
river-beds and *acequia* channels. The lack of rain that year
became a talking point, as old sayings were dusted off and
bandied about. The Spanish, who are much given to pithy
and often meaningless rhymes, have a doom-laden saying
for just about any weather condition in any season. The air

that autumn was thick with gloomy predictions in doggerel, but still there was no rain.

So there was no grass, either. The baked earth of summer stayed the same, whereas normally one of the beauties of autumn is the film of fine green grass that spreads like a low-lying mist across the parched land. In November the coolness turned to cold, and the days were filled with a beautiful clear autumn light. Some clouds gathered around the tops of the Sierra Nevada and in the morning we woke to see a sprinkling of new snow on the peaks. But that was all; no rain fell in November. It doesn't rain a lot in December anyway, so by Christmas there was a tangible feeling of concern. And the incipient drought was not just confined to Andalucía; the whole of Spain was affected, including dank Galicia in the north. Reservoirs throughout the country were low, and in the mountains the springs began to dwindle as the aquifers that fed them dropped to critical levels.

By Boxing Day the Indian Ocean had erupted, taking three hundred thousand lives in a monstrous welling of waters, and leaving millions in destitution and misery. It seemed foolish and distasteful to complain of anything after a cataclysm like that, but here in Andalucía we had our own climate disaster. Rolling down from the north and intensifying fiercely as it crept over the heights of the sierras came what the Spanish call the *ola de frío* – the wave of cold. To the north of the mountains, in Guadix, the temperature sank that first night to eighteen degrees below zero, freezing the life from all but the hardiest shrubs and trees. As the mass of icy air came down off the mountains and moved south, it warmed a little but not enough to save the crops in fields and greenhouses from Málaga to Almería.

Well-established avocado trees hung limp and brown; the bananas, mangoes and papayas that had thrived on the semi-tropical coast shivered and died. In the greenhouses, the tomatoes, peppers, aubergines and beans – after tourism, the economic engine of this region – turned to mush. Tens of thousands of small farmers saw their hopes of a harvest crushed and their future in ruins.

We got off lightly. We woke that first morning with our water system frozen solid; this is normally such a mild climate that nobody bothers to bury their pipes. I got up before dawn – Chloë has to be on the school bus at eight o'clock – and put the kettle on. The cats, a good indicator of temperature, were lying in a heap in the warm ashes of the fire; the dogs, curled up with their noses up their arses, didn't even move as I came down. Outside, the stars glittered bright in the icy air and the moon shone with a terrible pallor over the white valley. On dark winter schooldays, I light candles for Chloë as she eats her toast and honey. It's a little thing, and foolish perhaps, but candlelight lends warmth to the dark of early morning. That morning, I left Ana in bed conserving some warmth, grabbed some brush and kindling and built a blazing fire. Then, to warm us all from within, I made a pot of thick, hot porridge.

As Chloë and I headed down the track I could see the sheep huddled together and steaming in the deep straw of the stable. Normally they sleep scattered about beneath the stars, in the yard. Reaching the fields down by the river we saw the scarecrow, immobile with his wooden gun, staring across a glittering field of alfalfa, each of the thousands of plants white with crystals of frost. At the mouth of the irrigation pipe was a small glass mountain of icicles. We had never seen anything like it before.

Halfway across the river, Chloë cried out, 'Look, Dad! There's ice forming on the edge of the water!' I couldn't see it, being too busy steering out of the ford, but on the way back I pulled up on the hill leading down to the river, and got out to look. I stepped onto the muddy hummock that goes down to the water and promptly crashed down onto my back as my feet slipped away from under me on the ice.

I shot down the bank until I was in the water up to my knees, and howled curses as the bone-gnawing cold washed into my shoes and up my trousers. I struggled up, half-winded, onto one elbow. To my right there came a groan and, seemingly in slow motion, the car, with the driver's door open, slid slowly into the river and headed across to the middle. The handbrake had got frozen and hadn't engaged properly. The river was about to pour in through the open door, so I staggered to my feet and plunged in pursuit of the car, hauled myself in and slammed the door. With my legs and feet numb I drove on up to the house and crawled back into bed with my sleeping wife. This is something really nice to do: get up, get really cold, then go back to bed and enjoy the wonder of the warmth of a human body. Your partner won't like it a bit, but it's only fair if you're the poor schmuck who has had to get up and get the family ship underway.

Later, Manolo turned up wearing a black fur Red Army cap with a red star badge on it that Bernardo had bought for him on one of his periodic visits to the world outside the Alpujarras. He came bearing a frozen branch of *retama*. The sprinkler had been playing on it in the night, and as it froze hard the fronds had become more and more thickly encrusted with ice until it looked like a great glass chandelier.

'Look how beautiful it is,' he said with a great smile of delight.

●

This was an entirely different sort of winter from any we had known in our time in the mountains. And even the old folks, whose constant refrain is 'This is the way it used to be back in the old days', had seen nothing like it. The temperature on the north side of the Sierra Nevada stayed below fifteen degrees for weeks, causing thousands of hectares of olives to freeze and die. The whole harvest was lost. There was snow on the south coast, and even across the Mediterranean: the population of Algiers, most of whom had never seen snow, woke up one morning to find their seaside city cloaked in white.

On that day, there was a heavy snowfall in the Sierra Nevada, which gave a little hope for water later in the year, and for the first time the snow reached the hills around our farm. I took the dogs for a walk and ten minutes up the track we were walking in a thin crust, which soon became a deep white blanket. The branches of the mountain shrubs drooped low and heavy with the weight of frozen snow, giving the landscape a surreal look; these Mediterranean plants were not conceived to bear snow. Soon it was knee-deep. The dogs had never seen snow and were wild with excitement, Bumble ploughing through it like a bulldozer, while Big leapt along in her footprints like a porpoise.

As I walked through this unfamiliar, glittering landscape, my thoughts turned to the high southern slopes of the Sierra Nevada. I had an urge to climb as far as I could into that new and untouched landscape and ski beneath the peaks and the startling blue sky, with only the swish of my skis breaking the muffled silence. Unfortunately I was hindered by two serious problems. Firstly, I hadn't a clue how you got up there when the trails are covered with snow, and secondly I was a very rusty skier and not at all sure I could be trusted on my own. I put the case to my two friends, Jesús and Fernando, who run Nevadensis, a small company that arranges mountain-guiding for the Sierra Nevada.

'You can come with us,' they said. 'We're taking the mountain club from the university up there next week. We're both going, and Gerardo will be leading us. You remember Gerardo?'

I did. Gerardo, who had led an ice-climbing weekend I once went on, was the Sierra Nevada's equivalent of Sherpa Tenzing. In spite of being nearly as old as me, he was the fittest and hardest mountain man I had ever met. He was utterly indefatigable, and expected the same from everyone else. In a sudden rush of casual machismo, I put my deposit on the counter.

Ana was appalled when I told her. 'You must be bonkers,' she said, looking pityingly at me, 'at your age and condition.'

I was about to remonstrate about the injustice of the remark when Château, our fat black cat who lives on the kitchen work-surface and only ever raises himself to eat or hawk up a fur-ball into the cutlery tray, suddenly leapt through the door and shot up the jacaranda tree. It was a thing he had never done before (or since), so we watched him agape. The cat looked pretty nippy on the lower part of the trunk, but as he gained the topmost fork his enormous inertia began to overcome his momentum. He teetered for a moment, scrabbling for a grip, and then fell clean out of the tree with a great thump, knocking the wind out of himself. 'There,' said Ana picking up her astounded cat and stroking it. 'Let that be a warning to you: you're just too old and unfit for that kind of stunt.'

This needled me, so off I went.

The Nevadensis group consisted entirely of the university's mountain club members, except for myself and a bloke called Paco, who was about the same age and level of fitness as me. We headed up the mountain to a refuge, then spent the afternoon practising the sort of skiing we were going to use to slide up from there – on through the snow towards the ominously-named Pico de los Machos.

The exercise involved fixing sealskins – well, not actually sealskins, but a fur-fabric substitute – to the bottoms of our skis, to enable us to 'ski' uphill. With varying degrees of success we attached the skins and, in a long straggly line, slithered off uphill. Once we had climbed high enough, we clamped our heels into the bindings and zoomed down, then turned round and clambered back up again. Of course, it all seemed pretty futile in the way that skiing does, but it was a lot of fun going down – and going up gave a sense it was doing you some good.

After we had climbed and zoomed a few more times, we returned to the refuge to gather heaps of pine logs from the forest to warm the place up. As the sun slipped behind the peaks, the temperature dropped like a stone, so we all tumbled in and slammed the door to keep out the bitter cold. Then, to kill the hours of darkness and help forget the cold, we had a party. It was a fairly static sort of a party, admittedly, as the refuge was tiny and there was no room to move – and in any case nobody fancied straying too far from the fire, which had been cunningly sited so that it heated only one corner of the room. But it was a talking, laughing and drinking party, with pasta and sausages, a lot of noise and a fair bit of booze.

Deep into the festivity I crept outside to take a leak, shutting the door carefully behind me. The sound of conviviality vanished as I stepped towards the trees, my feet squeaking and crunching on the frozen snow. The night was clear and moonless and the pines stood motionless beneath the frozen burden of snow. Returning to the hut, I noticed a figure standing in the clearing between the wood and the hut. It was Rafa, a student of astrophysics, and he was looking at the stars, which, it has to be said, were quite dazzling. I'm used to seeing some pretty bright stars at El Valero, where there is very little light pollution to obscure their shine, but these had a clarity all their own; they seemed to pierce the sky and hurtle towards you in the most vertiginous manner. 'Do you know your way about the heavens, Cristóbal?' Rafa asked. It seemed a surprisingly intimate question.

'Well, I know the Plough... and the Pole Star... and the one that looks like a squared-off question mark,' I said hesitantly.

'That would be Orion's belt.'

'And isn't that one Sirius?'

'Actually no, that's a satellite. See, it's moving just discernibly. You need to go just a bit further on for Sirius,' and Rafa helpfully manoeuvred my arm. 'Interesting, isn't it,' he continued, 'that the ancients could see pictures abstracted in these constellations? It's an ability we seem to have lost.'

It was indeed interesting but it was also ten below zero, with the beginning of a nasty wind whipping towards us, so I cut short the conjectures and returned to the warmth of the hut. The party ebbed and flowed for another couple of hours until there was nothing left to drink and the fire died down and the cold started to bite and we disposed ourselves around the hut in a grunting heap of sleeping bags, ski-boots and woolly hats.

It's hell getting out of a sleeping bag on an icy morning in an unheated hut, and I couldn't help wondering why people ever come up as high as this. As I stepped outside into the blinding whiteness, I could see all the way down to where I lived. It looked warm down there, where there were oranges and lemons and even a banana tree. Here were only pines and snow and a couple of half-frozen choughs coughing in the woods.

We made some hot drinks somehow, and then set out. In a long line we slid up through the pinewoods and out onto the bare slopes above the tree line. Gerardo, silver-haired and with an impressive beer gut, led the way, grinding relentlessly up the hill. He was, bar Paco and I, the oldest member of the expedition, the rest of the party being in their late twenties, yet he was by a long head the fittest man there, and he showed no mercy. Up we slogged, and up and up with no suggestion of a halt.

As the bulk of the party hung limp, their muscles screaming, mouths open, gasping great lungfuls of icy air, Gerardo ground on effortlessly upwards – slip, slither, pole... The man was inhuman. Flesh and blood could not keep up this pace. Some of the party wept, some begged, a couple simply stopped and stayed behind. But Gerardo powered on up towards the peak.

His reason for this unsympathetic attitude, avowedly, is not to humiliate or physically wreck his followers, but to challenge them, to knock them into shape and to get them up with a minimum of fuss to where they can start skiing, or ice-climbing or whatever. If you dropped back you had to catch up, and if you were lucky enough to catch up at one of the very few rest stops, then as soon as you crawled in, panting and on your last legs, the front group, who had already rested for two minutes and were now impatient to be on their way, would move off.

This torment went on all morning, with Gerardo climbing relentlessly away at the front; those in the middle head down, doggedly following him; and several knots of disconsolates grumbling and puffing at the back. It was bright from the snow in spite of the greyness of the day, and bitter cold, though the heat we generated with the effort of climbing forced us to remove our outer clothes. 'Maybe we should stop and eat our sandwiches here,' someone suggested.

'No,' said Gerardo. 'Better to push on to the top; then we can eat our lunch looking over the other side.' We were high up now; we could see the valleys and chains of mountains below us swathed in cloud, but it was still an hour's steep slog to get to the top. The awesome Gerardo turned and headed in a series of steep zigzags up towards the peak.

When we finally reached the Pico de los Machos I felt too ill from the exertion – and perhaps the altitude of some 3,005 metres – even to think about eating. It was also too cold to hang about much, so we poked our heads up over the peak into the vicious wind to take a look at the lesser peaks and swirling cloudscape below, and then, clamping our heels into the skiing position, we turned to the descent. That was the moment when I realised my foolishness. I hadn't skied on slopes like this for perhaps twenty-five years, and I hadn't exactly been an ace back then. I found myself looking down a vast, broken plain of snow, steeply inclined. It seemed to go on down for ever until the slope itself was lost to view in a boiling sea of cloud impossibly far below. Now, I'm not a nervous person at all, but my legs and knees, which were already quivering from the muscular exertion of the climb, began at that point to quake, literally, with fear. Nearly everybody had already set off, and were little more than dots far below by the time I had steeled my courage sufficiently to launch myself down the slope.

I reckoned no harm could come to me if I just kept it slow, but within seconds I was rocketing down at break-neck speed. The slope was ice with the odd rock sticking through, and here and there swirls of fine powdery snow. I couldn't get a grip on that ice. By turning uphill I managed to stop. I panted and looked in terror at the awful expanse of slope that still remained. A hundred metres below I saw Paco, who looked to be in a similar predicament. I stumped inexpertly round and slithered off fast on the other tack. I slowed and, almost losing my balance, managed another turn. Then I hit hard ice. My lower ski slipped away, I leaned over, flailing my arms, and fell with a heavy crump onto the hard-packed snow. Aah, bliss. I was unharmed and could sit and rest here for a minute, take respite from that awful downhill rush.

But there came a time when I knew I had to bite the bullet. Off I went, and got in a couple of goodish turns, but then, hitting a great sheet of ice, I hurtled down faster and faster until I was completely out of control. My eyes filled with tears of cold; the world raced past in a blurred vision of white... faster and faster until suddenly I was airborne, feet and skis somewhere up over my head. An almighty blow and I was half-buried in cold soft snow... Ah, the peace; ah, the softness... But something was wrong. I did what I could to pick myself up, and only half of me responded. My left side no longer worked; the arm didn't react to the commands I was sending it. It hung limp and heavy at my side. I sat up and rocked to and fro in the snow, clutching my injured arm and groaning. Dislocated shoulder... that's what it had to be.

What the hell was I to do now? There was pain, a huge aching pain, but it seemed lessened by the fear of the abnormal state of my body and concern about my situation. Further down the hill I saw Paco again. He too was sitting in the snow, clutching his upper body and rocking to and fro. Way down below I saw three figures detach themselves from the main group and move back up the hill towards us. Somehow I managed to haul myself to my feet. My skis had come off with the fall, and tucking them beneath my right arm, and with the right arm holding the left arm in place, I started trudging downhill. The jolt of each step was a shock of pain. I had the feeling that my arm was only held on by skin, and I was desperate to protect it so that it shouldn't break that skin and fall off altogether. After a painfully long time I reached Paco. He was in a bad way, pale and drawn, groaning piteously. He couldn't speak. I stood for a bit looking at him and wondering what to do.

Finally Gerardo arrived with Jesús and Fernando. They unclipped their skis and fussed around us. Jesús tried to manipulate my arm back into its socket, but after I had yelled and cursed at him, and the arm showed no signs of going back in, he gave up. 'I'm sure there's supposed to be a way of straightening it out... bending it at a right-angle and popping it back into its socket,' he said. 'But it doesn't seem to work on you.'

Paco was in too much pain to put up with such horseplay. A decision was made to call a helicopter.

'I don't want a helicopter,' I protested. 'I can walk out on my own.' I was worried that, having not taken out any insurance, it would tip us into serious debt.

'No you can't,' they assured me. 'With a thing like this, the sooner you get to hospital and get it back in, the better.'

So they rang the helicopter with a mobile phone, which, by some miracle, had coverage. They gave careful directions as to just where on the mountain we would be found, and we sat down to wait. Paco, pale and drawn with pain, was moaning all the while. His injury was much worse than mine; I could at least keep a sense of what was going on around me.

After twenty minutes or so we heard the sound of the helicopter. It drew closer, and then faded again and disappeared altogether. Jesús's phone rang. He gave some more directions. The sound of the helicopter appeared again, increased a little, and then moved away. More instructions and yet more. Paco groaned loudly. I started to shiver. Suddenly we caught sight of the helicopter ferreting about among the ravines and valleys below us. Those of us with whole bodies leapt up and down and waved jackets. At last the machine veered and headed up towards us.

It turned and hovered two metres above the ground, fifty metres away from us. Two big men in the uniform of the Guardia Civil Mountain Rescue Service jumped down, crouched and ran across the snow towards us. They assessed our wounds, telling us that the machine was unable to land on such a steep slope, so we'd have to get into it at the hover. The two Guardia helped poor Paco across and, with an unceremonious shove, heaved him into the back of the cockpit. It was then that I realised that they had sent us a four-man helicopter – with four men in it, for there were two pilots. How the hell were we all going to fit on board?

The bigger of the two Guardia grabbed the runner, heaved himself into the cockpit, and sat on top of Paco. I could hear the poor man's shrieks above the sound of the roaring engine. I grasped the runner with my good arm and tried to pull myself into the cabin, but I hadn't the strength. The other Guardia, meanwhile, got his shoulder under my butt and, with a great heave and grunt, boosted me over the rim of the cockpit door, where I tumbled helplessly into the cabin, landing with an agonising thump. I screamed at the impact... but found that my arm had suddenly, magically, re-attached itself to my shoulder. The pain had disappeared, too. I wiggled the arm this way and that. It was a little stiff, but it worked. The Guardia had, entirely by accident, relocated it.

I grinned like a lunatic as my rescuer squeezed in behind me. And then, with a lot of grunting and wriggling, so that everyone was sitting on at least one other person, we set off across the mountains towards Granada. I watched, euphoric at the sudden absence of pain, and thrilled as the snowy peaks slid beneath the machine and the world fell away in folds of blue to the gorges and valleys of the Sierra.

Poor Paco, squashed beneath the enormous policeman, was in too much agony to take in anything at all, but for me, well, these vistas and the miraculous release from pain seemed almost worth the trauma.

In a very short time we found ourselves in the hospital in Granada. The doctor took one look at Paco, grabbed his arm, twisted it and pushed. Paco's eyes nearly burst from his face. 'God, it's gone! The pain's gone!' he cried.

They trussed us up like a pair of oven-ready chickens and told us to take it easy for a bit, which we felt inclined to do anyway. Then we signed a form and showed our Social Security cards. 'How much are we going to owe for the helicopter?' I asked a little nervously.

'*Nada*,' said the nurse. 'It's free. All mountain rescue is paid for by the Junta de Andalucía.' I was deeply impressed.

●

Early in the New Year I drove to Granada for a hospital check-up. My shoulder had felt extremely sore in the run-up to Christmas, and was made worse by the need to chop olive and almond logs for the fire. Olive is wonderful and burns like oak, with a slight cedar-like scent, but almond is the best of all and burns with the heat of coal. We were thankful for both as the temperature continued to drop. By the end of December we had lost almost all our young orange trees, the new Valencia Lates that we'd painstakingly planted and nurtured simply drooped and turned black amongst the glittering fields of frozen alfalfa.

Arriving in the city I parked the car by the river and, cuddling my arm, walked up the main thoroughfare towards the centre. A dense throng of people, many clad in the furs and Loden coats which are the preferred winter attire of the Granada bourgeoisie, was surging along beneath the great plane trees of the Paseo del Salón. The nearer I got to the centre, the thicker the crowd grew, and I shrank back instinctively to the side of the pavement to protect my bad arm from the jostling. Something was going on, but what?

As I was swept round the corner of Reyes Católicos into the Plaza del Carmén, I realised: it was the Día de la Toma, an annual celebration that recalls the handing over of the keys of the city to Isabela and Ferdinand in 1492 by Boabdil, the last Moorish king of Granada. This commemoration also provides a convenient excuse for Granada's ultra-Right to get onto the streets and try and drum up a bit of support for their repellent ideas. Dotted amongst the well-heeled and tightly packed *Granadinos* were groups of young men and women in black outfits waving Spanish flags and jabbing the air with placards scrawled with racist slogans. Stalls erected round the edges of the square were decked with anti-immigrant posters and leaflets, while a few steps away from where I was standing a pale, clammy-faced young man thrust his arm out in a Nazi salute and stood interminably to attention.

I have to admit that the atmosphere was not particularly threatening; rather than any incipient violence, there was a sense of anticipation, as if something really exciting was about to happen. And then there was a ripple in the crowd, and the event was upon us: the military band had arrived. I peered around the leather jacket in front of me to catch a glimpse, and to my surprise – as the Right are supposed to be good at this sort of thing – found one of the sloppiest, most inept marching bands imaginable slouching dully past.

No sooner had they raised their tubas and euphoniums for the first inharmonious blasts than the upper doors of the town hall burst open like a cuckoo clock and a host of dignitaries staggered from their cocktails out into the freezing cold on the balconies. A howl of approbation rose from the eager crowd as a small, dark, top-hatted man on the centre balcony began to wave a huge Spanish flag emblazoned with the heraldic arms of Granada.

'Y GRANADA?' shouted the top hat.

'QUÉ?' howled the horrible host.

'Y GRANADA?' he repeated.

'QUÉ?' came the rejoinder.

'Y GRANADA?' one last time.

'QUÉ-É-É?' they roared back.

It was all very baffling – 'And Granada?' 'What?' was the limit of the exchange – but this was the climax all right, and, as the band strolled off out of the square, the ranks of the Right headed for the bars. Puzzled and rather dispirited, I continued on my way to the hospital.

SUMMONED BY BELLS

WE HAD ALREADY EXPERIENCED a severe drought during our time at El Valero, but the dry spring and summer that followed the *ola de frío* seemed harder and more disoncerting. People talked of little else: of how reservoirs throughout Andalucía had sunk to desperate levels, and mountain springs that had never run dry in living memory were reduced to the feeblest of drips. In the *vega* between our valley and Órgiva, farmers had ceased to irrigate as the river dried up and the *acequias* with it, and in Granada province there were towns that had been rationed to a few hours of water a week. Yet still the sprinklers played all night long on the golf courses of the coastal strip.

Summer, and a drought-stricken summer in particular, brings with it the prospect of bush fires. Many of the aromatic plants that cover the hills of Andalucía (the lavenders, thymes, artemisia, rosemary and cistus) are rich in combustible oils, and at the slightest spark will burst into flames... and for centuries past they have been allowed to do so, as the shepherds who graze the wilder terrain fire the scrub in order to rejuvenate their grazing grounds. There are those who would have it that fire is a part of the natural cycle; it enriches the poor earth with potash from its ashes and allows the countless seeds that lie dormant beneath the soil some light and space to germinate.

But these days bush fires – even bonfires – are tightly controlled throughout Andalucía, and prohibited in the summer months, for the damage they have caused in recent years has been immense. It doesn't matter a hoot about the loss of fast-growing scrub, but when forest is burnt, it is an altogether different matter. For a tree to survive in the harsh conditions of the mountains of Andalucía is little short of a miracle – and, given the susceptibility of the land to erosion, and the dearth of forestry, every single tree needs to be protected.

It's a rare year when we don't see a fire from the farm. First you smell the smoke on the hot air, then cast around until eventually you catch a blue-brown haze shimmering above a distant hill or at night the sky glowing red above black mountains. Then the helicopters arrive. A faint chopping becomes a roaring that echoes across the mountains and fills the valleys, as the machine races overhead dangling a great orange bottle containing a thousand kilos of water. Right into the heart of the fire the pilot flies, seeking to drop his load at the very root, then back to the reservoir to refill. For a big fire a further helicopter will turn up, and there's a powerful biplane, too, that comes to help out. Then, if things start to get really out of hand, they send in a couple of twin-engined flying boats and a huge four-engined aircraft.

The noise of all this echoing amongst the mountains sounds almost apocalyptic, and there is an undeniable drama to this spectacle of men and their amazing machines pitted against the fire, to say nothing of the poor bloody infantry – those who fight on the ground amongst the flames, with brooms and buckets. The risk to these men is appalling: that summer, eleven of them were killed in a fire to the north, near Guadalajara, when the wind turned and drove the flames amongst them. So the sight of a fire, which at night has a kind of terrible beauty as it illuminates the mountains, fills everyone with despair, and with anger against the perpetrators. For it has to be said that the majority of bush fires are started intentionally, for insurance payouts, politics, even in vengeance upon neighbours, as well as to improve grazing.

And there is also the constant threat that a barbecue or bonfire will throw out a stray spark. This happened to me some years back, and nearly frightened me out of my wits.

●

It was in April, a month that is sufficiently close to winter not to have to worry too much about fires – and, in my defence, it was a year or two before the controls were imposed. I was tidying up a corner of the farm down by the Cádiar River; sometimes the chaos that is the natural order of things in the countryside gets to me and I feel compelled to try and impose some sort of order. I made a heap of dry canes and bits of old fig – you can't use fig as firewood as it gives off no heat; just a pungent, headache-inducing smoke – and set light to it. It was only a small heap and I reckoned that I had been pretty careful about siting my bonfire, but even so, as it caught, the faintest zephyr began to ruffle the leaves of the canes. Almost before I knew it the flames moved into the long grass, spread, set light to a bush and licked at the stems of the canebrake. The zephyr became a breeze and the flames became a fire.

Panic seized me: I could see things would be out of control within seconds. I searched wildly about for something to carry water with, and spotted a bucket dangling from a branch. Thanking Providence, I grabbed it and leapt down the bank to the river, scooped some water, raced back and hurled it at the fire. Then, without even stopping to see if it had done any good, dived back down to the river. Like a madman, I leapt to and fro with my bucket, stumbling and panting, in a frenzy of terror lest the fire consume my farm.

I was fortunate, for within a few minutes a lucky bucket of water doused the root of the fire and the flames were reduced to wisps of smoke and a sodden sludge of ashes. But the memory – the panic, the smoke – remains sharp and clear.

One of the more distressing manifestations of drought is the hardship that livestock suffer. It's a popular belief that sheep and goats will eat anything, which holds true when they're desperately hungry, but like any other organism they have their preferred foods, and will only move on to the less agreeable stuff when these are used up.

Last year, as the dry summer advanced, grazing grew desperately scarce, to the extent that I started thinking about feeding my flock with alfalfa, in spite of the fact that it was all we had to see them through the coming winter. It's an almost fundamental folly, though, to feed your reserves before it's absolutely necessary, and I hung on, pushing the flock to forage high up the mountain in search of every last edible scrap.

Domingo, with a flock several times the size of mine, didn't have the option of feeding them; it would have been far too expensive. So I was surprised, and impressed, to see them maintaining their good condition. This Domingo achieved by devoting himself singlemindedly to his flock, drawing on a deep fund of skill and knowledge. He would be up at first light every day, leading the sheep off to ever more distant pastures where he knew some scant reserve of moisture might provide a little grazing, where the tortuous orientation of a hillside protected its slope from the sun's harsh rays, or where he had noticed a stand of plants that would nourish his poor charges for an hour or so.

On through the long, hot days of summer, Domingo sweltered and toiled at the head of his great tripping mass of sheep, making his way over the hillside on his nameless bay horse and accompanied by the stalwart Chica. It was amazing to see how well the young collie, born and bred in the misty bogs of the Low Countries, coped with the fierce heat, and I began to suspect Domingo of taking special care to find her water and shade. For the flock he cut branches of eucalyptus and poplar, or felled whole canebrakes in the river so they could browse on the unappetising fibrous leaves. He took them to places no shepherd had ever been, high on the horrible southern flanks of Campuzano, among the crags and the pines, where they gorged upon unfamiliar high-growing plants: juniper, cotton lavender and the pink rock rose *Cistus albidus* – plants they would never normally see in their usual grazing grounds, let alone eat.

If they ranged too far to get home, Domingo would sleep on the hard ground beneath the stars, surrounded by his woolly companions. He carried a mobile phone with him so he could let Antonia know where he was, in case she should worry. The sheep, as I said, looked as good and fat as I had ever seen them, but it was the most exhausting regime.

The old men shook their heads bleakly as one dry week followed another and prophesied worse times on the way. That's what a drought does: it brings on uncertainty, fear and depression, even in these fortunate lands where we are sheltered from the reality of crop failure and subsequent hunger or starvation.

And still it didn't rain. I took a party of walkers up into the high mountain meadows only to find that none of the flowers were blooming, and where a thick cover of grass and grazing plants should have been forming there was only dust and stones, populated by thousands of the little Sierra Nevada beetles.

I thought of my shepherd friend, Antonio Rodríguez, who grazes his flock on these high pastures. For him things would be even harder than for Domingo, whose flock inhabited a world far beneath the high mountain grazing. For up here the intensity of the sun and the icy winds had withered all but the toughest and spikiest plants – grazing that the most famished sheep would find hard to stomach.

It was a depressing thought, especially as Antonio had only recently managed to rebuild his flock after the results of a blood test for brucellosis had forced him to slaughter nearly two-thirds of his animals. But that's the way it is with shepherding: occasionally there's a windfall of one sort or another, but mostly the shepherd lives at the whim of cruel and heedless Nature.

Down at El Valero, by some amazing mechanism of nature, rosemary and anthyllis flowered, but there was almost nothing else for the sheep to eat, and little by little they started to get restless. We hoped desperately that they wouldn't remember just how good the grazing was on the other side of the river, though I had a nagging fear that once the water level was low enough they'd be off, following some embedded memory, to lay waste our neighbours' vegetable gardens and fruit trees. Sheep, as I've often said, are obtuse creatures, but when times are hard they can turn into raiders of audacity and cunning.

I shouldn't have been worried about the welfare of our neighbours' vegetables, however, for our sheep's designs turned out to be targeted much closer to home. It was four in the morning, on yet another hot, hot night and I was fast asleep. I was so deeply asleep, in fact, that when the sound of bells dimly percolated into the murk of my consciousness, I assumed it was a dream and rolled over. Later, as the edge of light sliding down the shutters became sharper, the sound came again and this time the dogs began to bark.

I leapt from the bed and rushed outside. There were sheep everywhere, frenetically devouring the plants that grow round the house. The dogs shot through the door barking; the sheep panicked, and rocketed as one down the steps. With Big and Bumble at my heel, I hurtled buck naked – no time to bother with clothes – in pursuit. The flock thundered through the vegetable patch, out by the pool and hurled themselves over the stone wall, down to that part of the farm that belongs to them.

I turned and looked at what had previously been the lovingly tended fruits of Ana's labours. It was hardly a catastrophe on the scale of earthquakes and hurricanes, almost farcical in fact ('SHEEP RAVAGE VEGETABLE PATCH'). But it put me in shock, this orgy of herbivorous gluttony that had just taken place. The sheep had been eating Ana's organic fruit and vegetables, and the flowers that were planted around them, all night long. The only things that had survived were the courgettes, which, it would seem, are abhorrent to sheep. The rest was just a miserable mess of trampled and half-masticated plants, spattered here and there with glistening *cagarrutas*, sheep turds.

I stood there in the first light of day, still wearing nothing but my boots, slack-jawed and appalled by the damage, and wondering how the hell I was going to break the news to Ana. But Ana was already there, stooping amongst the remains of her raspberries. She had followed me down, and as she looked about her I could hear that she was sobbing. I put my arms around her. I couldn't think of anything to say. What *would* you say?

There was little she could say, either, though I worried at once as the words trickled out: 'I can't put this right... I can't do it all over again... All that work and... and there's nothing left...' This was so unlike Ana – the stoic among us who always kept going, who always saw the funny side.

What was exercising me immediately, though, was to establish where the wretched sheep had got in, and to fix things so that it wouldn't happen again. The whole lamentable episode had, I was bitterly aware, been my fault: I was the one who had delayed feeding the alfalfa to the sheep, and I was the one responsible for the fencing. I examined the boundary minutely, looking for tracks in the dust, or wool on the thorns, but the fencing was all intact. I couldn't make it out. There was one possibility though. We had built a high stone wall to support the terraced garden that surrounds the pool. The entrance to this terrace was contrived according to a drawing I had seen of the fortified entrance to the crusader castle of Crac des Chevaliers in Syria, which was conceived to discourage attacking armies, who would find themselves hemmed in amongst stone walls with defenders pouring boiling oil and other substances inimical to their well-being upon their heads. I figured this ought to scotch any incursions planned by mere sheep into that part of the farm we had designated as our garden.

I crouched down and scanned this piece of formidable medieval military architecture for tell tale signs. *Cagarrutas*... there were *cagarrutas* all the way up the steps. They must have been nervous. They couldn't have got through the wooden gate, but a patch of heavily scuffed earth at the top of the wall attested to the fact that they had walked up the steps and then leapt the remaining wall. Fifty sheep – that's two hundred scrabbly little hooves... The evidence wasn't hard to see.

Later that morning, Manolo turned up; I found him crouched down among the remains of the vegetable patch. He turned and looked at me as he heard me enter. There was a diplomatic edge to his usual grin of greeting. 'The sheep been here, then?' he said, perhaps a little unnecessarily.

'The buggers jumped up the wall. They've been here all night. They've had the lot. A bad business...'

'A bad business,' repeated Manolo, tossing a bunch of ravaged radishes onto the compost heap. 'But not as bad as all that – a lot of this ought to come back. Maybe not those cabbages, but you don't like cabbages anyway; you told me so yourself.'

'No... You're right. None of us do. I don't know why Ana plants them. We usually end up giving them to the sheep anyway.'

'Well, there you go, then,' said Manolo matter-of-factly, 'and the tomatoes and garlic will be fine, the sheep didn't manage to break through onto the triangle patch.' I hadn't thought to check but this was a huge relief to hear. 'Give me a couple of hours and I'll have this all sorted out, and in a month you won't even remember the sheep were here,' he promised.

A COUPLE OF PRIMATES

A S ANA RESTORED HER EQUANIMITY and the integrity of her vegetable patch by spending the cool of the day clearing beds, I would head down to the fields to cut bundles of fresh alfalfa for the sheep. This is one of my very favourite jobs. I used to cut the crop with a Grim Reaper-style scythe, but Manolo so ridiculed my scythe work that I've come round to his traditional Alpujarran way – down on my knees with the *hoz* (pronounced 'oth') or sickle. It's slow work, and a little tedious, but it does groom the land in a most appealing way. The cut part of the field is left mown like a lawn, while the face of the tall, uncut alfalfa curls away like steep green cliffs and headlands. And the kneeling also puts you in touch with the insect world, that population supposed to dwarf human numbers by several million to one.

The technique is to kneel on one knee, grasp a handful of alfalfa with your left hand and sever it at the base with the sickle, repeating the process over and over again until you have a huge green bundle to hoist on your shoulders. I like to haul it straight up to the stable, where the sheep fall ecstatically upon it – there's nothing sheep like more than alfalfa.

I remember when I was young and of a more contemplative cast of mind, I would lie on the edge of a pond, looking through the shadow of my head into the depths of the water. At first I'd see nothing, but little by little, as my eyes became accustomed to the scale of this microscopic universe, I'd begin to see the teeming population of improbable animalcules – like some tiny version of the Serengeti. Hosts of infinitesimal creatures, flippered and legged and feelered and finned, perhaps even with tiny tooth and claw, but more probably armed with suckers and cilia and palps and invasive ovipositors. Daphne there were, and hydra, and *paramecia* (if that's the correct plural of *paramecium*); also water fleas and pond skaters and beetles, spiders and boatmen.

Well, it's a similar thing with the alfalfa field: after a while I get bored with the repetitiveness of the work, lay down my sickle and hunker down to see what's going on at ground level. The alfalfa becomes a towering rainforest and slowly, in the dark of its depths, the jungle population is revealed. Creatures that are metallic green and scarlet and yellow scurry about like a spill of coloured beads in constant motion. Infinitesimal spiders, pale like ghosts, cast slender lianas and lines from the forest canopy to the floor, and spin webs for the capture of creatures so tiny as to be beyond human imagination. Beetles of every persuasion scuttle to and fro with peculiar purpose, and everywhere are columns of ants, engaged in their unfathomable tasks. More sinister are the hairy black caterpillars, giants wriggling through the green penumbra; Manolo tells me these huge beasts can reach plague proportions and devour whole crops of alfalfa, though, touch wood, that has never happened to us.

Higher in the canopy are the ladybirds, thousands of them, all welcome allies in the battle against the *piojos* – aphids – in the orange trees. And fluttering above the canopy are clouds of small blue butterflies; they look as if the alfalfa flowers themselves, which are a similar blue, have taken wing and come to life.

●

It was lucky that, in order to fit in with Ana's astrological plans, our tomatoes had been moved to the sheep-proof triangle patch by the alfalfa, for a summer without tomatoes would be unthinkable. Above all else, tomatoes are the basis for gazpacho and, in common with most of the population of Andalucía, we make and eat gazpacho almost every day from July till September.

People are passionate about the way to make true gazpacho, or their own version of it: there are those who abhor, for example, the use of a cucumber; others who insist upon the juice of a lemon rather than vinegar. I add a fistful of basil and mint and leave the peppers out – and Domingo, who, it has to be said makes a good and gutsy gazpacho, tells me that the secret is to add a dash of honey. Now, part of the beauty of gazpacho – for us, at any rate – is the fact that in summer we can usually gather all the ingredients, apart from the honey, fresh from the garden. This lends the dish an extra sanctimonious appeal.

Using honey from our own hives would, doubtless, be an even greater pleasure, and well-intentioned people have for years suggested we keep bees. And maybe we should, but then these same folk also counsel us to keep goats and make our own cheese, plough with our own mules, slaughter pigs for the pork and sausages, make our own wine and yoghurt and jams, and plait our own esparto grass into ropes and baskets. No thanks, we reply: we want more free time rather than less.

It's curious how enthusiastic friends can be about ideas that would fill our lives with more work and drudgery; things they wouldn't dream of doing themselves, but that seem to them just the thing to keep us from succumbing to boredom in our rural idyll. I have to admit, though, that we do feel a little tempted by bees; it would seem like the right thing to do for the farm. Bees are somehow fundamental to existence – why, Albert Einstein himself reckoned that if the bees went humanity would soon follow. But our farm is thick with wild bees anyway, and sometimes the humming from the eucalyptus or the blossoming oranges rivals even the sound of the rivers.

So for the present we leave beekeeping to the beekeepers. And besides, the whole business of keeping bees is fraught with difficulties. There's the crop plane that sprays the valley with dimethoate, which is fatal to bees, and then there are the inevitable diseases which take their toll, not to mention the depredations of the *abejarucos*, the bee-eaters. The valley swarms with these beautiful birds. They live in the holes in the rocks above our neighbour's farm, La Herradura, and swoop down across the road as you drive past, winging their way out high across the valley. This gives you the opportunity to watch them from above as they twist and turn and hover and stall. And as the sun catches them they shine with all the colours of the most florid parrots you could imagine. The *abejarucos* are the most spectacularly exotic creatures that live here, and they fill us with wonder and delight. Of course the beekeepers take a different view, because bee-eaters do eat an awful lot of bees.

Chloë has become party to Domingo's affectation of putting honey in the gazpacho, and to humour her I usually add a spoonful or two. But that month our supplies ran out, and on a whim I decided to walk up to collect supplies from Juan Díaz, our favoured beekeeper, who lives high on Carrasco, the lush spring-watered hill that bounds the valley on its western side. I could have taken the car I suppose, but it wouldn't have been the same; there was a certain romance in the idea of slogging up a hill on a hot summer day to fetch a pot of honey.

By the time I reached the little grove of walnut trees below Juan Díaz's *cortijo*, my shirt was sticking to my skin and the cotton rag with which I wipe the sweat from my brow was limp and sodden. The sun hung motion-less directly overhead, burning my nose and ears, and the super-heated air lay still and heavy. I stopped beneath the shade of a tree and looked out across the gulf of still air to Campuzano, the waterless hill on our own side of the valley. It had been eighteen months now without a drop of rain and the scrub-covered slopes were dull with that yellowish pallor of dying vegetation.

Approaching the house, I passed an open-cast rubbish dump, the universal element of a traditional Alpujarran farm, and called out to announce my presence. The Díaz house is, like many in the Alpujarras, built on a *camino* or mule track, so in following the way you pass right through its porch. Receiving no reply, I ducked under the overhanging vine and passed through to where the track continued on the other side.

There, holding a tin bucket, stood Juan's wife, Encarna, a strong, bright-eyed sixty-year-old, who was wearing, in spite of the heat, an apron over an old floral printed dress, over a pair of woollen trousers.

'*Hola, vecino,*' she cried – Hallo, neighbour. 'And what brings you up this way?'

'*Hola,* Encarna… *Qué tal?*'

She wiped her hands on the apron and shook my hand. 'Hot,' she said – the Spanish talk about the weather just as much as the British – 'Hot, and still no rain. It's all going to ruin… but what can we do? We must just put up with what we're given, no?'

This particular philosophical discourse is an almost formulaic greeting, and doesn't really require an answer.

Juan was apparently seeing to his bees in the little poplar copse just up the slope behind the house. 'Go and find him,' she urged. 'He loves to show people the hives.'

'Okay, I will', I answered and walked apprehensively off in the direction she indicated.

Juan Díaz, a tall, thin man whose grey hair and aquiline nose were hidden under a large veil, was leaning over a wooden box in the spindly shade of the poplars, engaged in one of those arcane tasks that beekeepers do. Half of him was obscured by a cloud of smoke and bees. He saw me and nodded his head discreetly in greeting. 'Come on over and take a look, Cristóbal, but gently,' he intoned.

'Not bloody likely, Juan. It's alright for you – you're veiled.'

'So you're nervous of the little bee, then?'

Spanish bees tend to be aggressive, so I don't feel in the least feeble declining to poke around them without a veil. I watched from a safe distance as Juan broke the propolis seal of a hive and lifted its lid. The murmuring of the bees rose a little in pitch and the hundreds of bees that obscured his person turned into thousands. They crawled all over him, scores of them moving on his bare hands. He seemed perfectly calm, moving with a measured delicacy. Actually I thought it unlikely that a bee could get its sting into Juan's hands anyway, given the cracked-leather texture of his work-hardened skin. He had told me that he cauterised the deep fissures that followed the folds of his hands and fingers by filling them with gunpowder – yes, gunpowder from a shotgun cartridge – and setting light to it. Juan Díaz was hard.

'What are you doing there, Juan?' I called in a manner calculated not to aerate bees. He was silent for a while as he performed a particularly tricky part of the operation. Eventually he said: 'I'm looking for the queen. I think she may have escaped into the upper part of the hive. But I'll leave it for now. It can take a long time to find a lost queen.'

He gently put back the lid and exchanged his veil for a battered straw hat proclaiming his affiliation to the 'Caja Rural' – the Country Bank – and came forward to shake my hand. Then he led me to the small store at the back of the house where he kept his honey. Most of the year's crop was still settling in a big plastic tub. On the surface was a thick crust of pollen, dead bees, flakes of wax and general detritus from the hive.

'This,' said Juan, dipping his finger and licking it, 'is the best stuff of all. But the honey-buying public prefer it without the dead bees.' He fetched me out one of the few remaining jars of the previous year's honey, and took off the lid for me to approve. The honey was dark and thick like malt, and gave off a heady scent of orange and almond blossom, mountain herbs and that mysterious essence of the bee.

Juan had some watering to see to before we could stop for a drink, so picking up his mattock he strode towards his terrace of maize. I followed him into the forest of tall stems, laced with rivulets of running water, as he gave here a chop, there a poke with his mattock, adjusting the flow across the stony earth. It was cool and lush, a dim green penumbra of respite from the dust and glare outside. The plants, thick with leaf, towered way above our heads, and each was hung with several fat cobs of corn. I couldn't help wondering where all the water was coming from, as there was not this much water at the moment in the whole *acequia*. 'I have a tank now,' he explained, with a noticeable glint of pride. 'Come, I'll show it to you.'

As we walked, he asked me about the high pastures which he'd heard were very dry. 'There's nothing there, not a stitch of grazing,' I told him and then voiced my worries about Antonio Rodríguez, whose sheep grazed the land up there. 'It must be desperate for him,' I said, 'trying to keep this new flock of sheep alive. I don't know how he manages... And being all on his own, too, it must weigh hard on him.'

I had got to know Antonio a decade ago, when I spent five days and nights with him helping to take his sheep down from the mountains to the coast at Almuñecar – a transhumance, as it is called, now virtually extinct in Spain. Even then it was hard going, crossing not just hillsides but dual carriageways. Antonio is the gentlest of souls, a man whose heart brims with goodness and generosity, and at forty-five he longs for a wife and children. Vain hope, because local girls don't want anything to do with the life of a shepherd; it's just too damn hard.

'But he's not on his own,' said Juan, looking at me in surprise. 'For all his troubles, Antonio is happy as can be; he's absolutely head over heels in love with his little daughter. She'll be coming on for two by now.'

'Daughter? I didn't even know he had a woman...' I burbled.

'Yes, he's been married three years now. His wife is Moroccan from the High Atlas; she's no stranger to the hard life – she loves it up there. You couldn't find a happier family.'

This, I thought to myself, is about the best news I've heard all year. It seemed so unexpected and yet so right. And then, emerging again into the sunlight, Juan led me up a steep path, at the top of which we found ourselves looking into an enormous circular concrete tank. He turned to me for my reaction.

I considered the construction in silence for a moment, then, as its enormity registered, exclaimed: '*Hombre!* That is one hell of a tank, Juan. Must be half a million litres.'

'Six hundred thousand,' he said proudly. 'It cost five pesetas a litre to construct. Three million, I ended up paying.' Spain uses the euro now, but sums of this magnitude are still calculated in pesetas – and this, £15,000 near enough, was an enormous sum of money for a subsistence farmer to spend.

Juan showed me the outlet, where a small river was gushing from the tap and flowing down a channel to course among the maize. It was an impressive set-up, and the maize looked good and healthy, but it also seemed a huge amount of effort. Surely, I suggested, it would work out cheaper and easier to dispense with the crop altogether and buy in grain from the feed centre.

'That's true, Cristóbal, but you never know what you're getting in those sacks,' he replied thoughtfully. 'It probably comes from America and therefore it's probably genetically modified, and I don't think we're ready for that in the Alpujarras yet. I keep my own seed from year to year. Also there's more to a crop of maize than the grain: there's the leaf for forage for the mule, and the stalks for bedding, and once we've taken the grain from the cobs, the *panochas* make good fuel for the fire. And besides...' – he paused a moment for emphasis – 'I like my field of maize. It's green and cool in the summer. A *cortijo* is not a proper *cortijo* without a summer crop of maize.'

So that was it: it was as much an aesthetic, even an existential decision, a simple matter of keeping the pigs, mule and poultry happy. In my heart I applauded it. 'But what about the wild boar?' I asked. Everybody knows that if you grow maize or potatoes, you're certain to have your crop destroyed by the *jabali*. There's nothing in this world they like better than those succulent tubers and sweet cobs.

'I've installed an electric fence,' he explained. 'They're terrified of electricity. I've grown corn here five years now with not a whisper of trouble.'

This was the first time I had heard of anybody using an electric fence in the Alpujarras. Juan was embracing modernity, the pragmatic approach, with his concrete tank and his electric fence, while hanging on tenaciously to the traditional ways. Juan and Encarna work ferociously hard all the hours of the day and every day of the week except for Thursday mornings, when they walk down to the road and hitch a lift into town to go to market. And they work like this to sustain their traditional, self-sufficient way of life, almost as if it were an end in itself.

I looked at the low whitewashed house with its thick stone walls, the hens scratching about in the dust, the magnificent vine drooping with fat green grapes, the geraniums bursting exuberantly from old pots and tins, and was reminded of the simple unselfconscious beauty that I had first loved about the Alpujarras. It's true that it isn't to everybody's taste – the poverty and apparent shabbiness put some people off – but there is an integrity to this beauty that has to be sifted from the rubbish and the thorns and dust. Moving to the edge of the terrace I looked down across the valley at our own farm, and wondered if we too had managed to preserve its intrinsic charm.

'Cristóbal, why so thoughtful?' asked Encarna, who was standing behind me wiping her hands on her apron. 'Come on in. I have a special treat for you,' she announced.

We ducked our heads and entered the little kitchen. Juan began busying himself tying up a string of bright red peppers, while Encarna stepped around her rough wooden table to the freezer humming away in the corner. Freezer... I did a double take. A freezer is the one convenience we lack and cannot have; our solar power system is just not up to it. Yet a freezer would make our lives very much easier.

It's easy to forget that Juan and Encarna, living up here on Carrasco, have proper electricity.

'You'll find this is the best way to enjoy honey,' she said, and laid an ornate carton of ice cream on the table.

'I don't believe it?' I cried incredulously. 'How on earth did you get ice cream all the way up here without it melting?' To be honest, though, it was the incongruousness of finding ice cream at all in this bastion of bucolic orthodoxy that most surprised me.

'In a cool box with extra ice packs,' Encarna answered simply. 'Our granddaughter brought it up on her motorbike a few days ago as a surprise. She said it was her favourite flavour. It's called... Oh, I don't know what it's called... some foreign name.'

'Tiramisú,' I read. And, relishing my amazement, she plopped a spoonful into the bowl and covered it with a dollop of honey mixed with almonds. Bliss! Sheer bliss!

●

The next day, while driving into town, I found myself musing over Juan's concrete tank. Spending such a large amount to water a few trees and some maize made no economic sense at all, and yet Juan and Encarna knew exactly what they were doing. They had invested their savings so that they could live the traditional life they had chosen on the farm they loved.

Wasn't that what we were trying to do at El Valero? We similarly had to pay for the privilege of living on our own *cortijo*. If we were to sell all our oranges, our olives, almonds and lamb... even in the best of years it would not square the accounts. In terms of money, labour and time, our mountain farm, like Juan's, is an anachronism. But it's a hell of a nice anachronism. We chose the farm for its simple functioning beauty and it would never be enough just to sit there and admire it – or even write about it, for that matter. We need to go on taking some active part in our landscape, ploughing its soil, planting its orchards, tending its trees. That's how we keep a sense of who we are.

Fortunately Ana feels much the same, and Chloë, who has lived her whole life here, won't even hear talk of living anywhere else, although of course within a very few years she may be off to university or making her way in the world. My hope is that she'll always have El Valero to come back to, should she need to recharge her batteries or find the solace of home.

Chloë, however, was far less impressed by my philosophical maunderings than by the surprise of having ice cream served up on our very own *tinao*. I had managed to acquire a cool bag and to fill it with enough frozen ice packs and insulation to get a tub home more or less intact. It was fruits of the forest with mascarpone flavour – an almost unimaginable luxury.

Evening crept towards night, the heat lay limpid upon us, and one bowl led to another and then another. Before long the whole lot had disappeared and we were left looking at the box and feeling just the tiniest bit uncomfortable.

We savoured the vanishing treat in a bemused silence, broken only by the flapping of hundreds of moths around the bare bulb above the table, the insane screaming of hot cicadas, the booping of an owl in the riverbed, and the occasional quiet roll of abdominal thunder. It's the heat that does it to you; it saps the strength, weighs down the limbs and drugs the mind. As a prolonged heatwave gets underway, you find yourself not just slurring your words, but slurring your ideas. Your attitude takes a bashing too, and you get sloppy. You can only read the simplest stuff and even maintaining a lively conversation becomes an impossible task.

The fabulous ice cream was gone, and all that was left was the tub. I had the lid and was considering it carefully, while Ana paid similar attention to the box. We ran them round in our hands, considered the top and the sides and the bottom. I noted, wordlessly, how neatly the lid with its recessed rim would fit on the box. All in all, the thing seemed like a very marvel of ingenuity and design. The texture of it was firm, yet flexible, and there was an agreeable transparency to the plastic. I looked at Ana and she looked back at me, and in our look there was a wordless corroboration, each of the other's thoughts (you get this sort of thing when you've been living together for a long time). Together, we were marvelling at this simple, utilitarian object of perfection and – in its way – its ineffable loveliness.

Gradually we became aware that our daughter was watching us in amazement.

'Look at the pair of you. You're like a couple of primates,' she spluttered. 'It's only an ice cream tub, for heaven's sake!'

Ana and I looked up at each other, lid and box in hand, and then at Chloë; and in one of those rare moments of perfect synchronicity all three of us exploded into laughter.

And then what happened?

CHRIS STEWART BRINGS EVENTS UP TO DATE

Ten years on from the publication of Driving Over Lemons, **Chris Stewart** talks about life at El Valero, what's changed in his valley, how the success of the books has affected him and his neighbours, and whether he ever regrets leaving Genesis.

Chris, the first thing everyone always wants to know is – are you still living on the farm, at El Valero?

It's funny how often people ask that. They tend to say: 'Are you still living on that dump of a farm you describe in the books, or have you moved to some marble-clad villa in Marbella?'

Clearly those people have not read the books! Either that or I have failed absolutely to get the message across. The answer is a crystal-clear yes. After twenty years, we still greatly enjoy living here, and the only way we are leaving is in a box – and not even then, as a matter of fact, as both Ana and I would like to be buried beneath an orange tree on the farm.

Mind you, I do sometimes wonder if we could have stayed at El Valero without the books and the royalties we earn from them. A lot of farmers, and especially organic farmers, find they simply can't get by without some other source of income. It was pretty fortunate that our source turned out to be writing books.

Do you still feel the same way about the farm as when you moved here?

I had just turned forty when we bought El Valero; Ana was a few years younger. Looking back, it was a good age for a move. We could manage the constant round of work and still have energy left to look about us and make improvements. I can't imagine starting out on some of those schemes today – fencing off the hillside for the sheep, for example, was an absolute killer of a task.

Curiously, during the first years I grew convinced that the one thing we needed to put everything in order was a tractor – as if it was a universal panacea that would sweep away the drudgery of farm work. I remember thinking, when I was offered a contract for Driving Over Lemons, 'Maybe, I'll be able to buy that tractor.'

And when I got my first royalty cheque, I did buy a tractor – a ropey old model which had reached the end of its useful life in Sussex. It was a vehicle that should have been put out to rust rather than shipped to Spain, especially to a farm like ours. I drove it for a few weeks but found it completely terrifying, wobbling and tipping on the tiniest of inclines. Which is the way a hell of a lot of farmers go, with a tractor tipping on top of them. So I've kept a pretty wide berth from it ever since.

Did the success of Driving Over Lemons have any immediate impact, beyond buying tractors?

It gave us freedom from daily worries about money – that's a very welcome thing. It was a relief to no longer be pitied by friends or family, who thought we had been daft to sink all our money into a subsistence farm. And I no longer had to tear myself away from the farm to go shearing in the gloom of the Swedish winter, or do the rounds so much in Andalucia. Not that I regret all those shearing expeditions in the high mountains. They gave me an insight into a vanishing way of life, a ready source of stories, and a lot of local friends. We would have had a very different experience of Spain if we hadn't needed to go out and find paid work.

The book also carried some sense of vindication of the crazy decision we had taken when we upped sticks and moved here. Even my mother, who had always hoped I would live in a nice Queen Anne house in the south of England, volunteered that she now almost understood what it was that we saw in the place.

Just how tough was it in the early days?

I'm not sure we stopped to think about it. We weren't exactly hand-to-mouth, as the shearing brought in enough for us to get by on, given that we had the fruits of the farm. We always

Driving over the river, with Chloë aged about five. The farm really is on the wrong side of the river – and we still have to ford it to get across.

had fresh orange juice, olives, wonderful vegetables, and an occasional leg of lamb. But we were, I suppose, pretty close to the breadline, which I think did us good. It would be foolish to extol the virtues of poverty, but you can learn a lot from a few years of straitened circumstances. For us, it bound us as a family and rooted us on the farm. We had to make things work because that was how we fed ourselves.

Were you prepared for the book's success?

Every publisher makes it their first task to tell an author, once they have commissioned their book, that they won't make a bean out of it. And mine were the same: 'Don't give up the day job,' they said. Not that there was any choice about that. If you're a farmer, you can't. I had no inkling that my whole life was going to turn around and the writing would become the thing that I do.

Although your books are sold as 'Travel', you actually stay at home!

That's right. I hardly move from the farm from one chapter to the next in Driving Over Lemons, though the orbit extends to Seville and back to Britain in A Parrot in the Pepper Tree, and there's a chapter in Morocco in the third book, The Almond Blossom Appreciation Society.

But the main things I write about are the kind of everyday things that happen to all of us, in our different ways. Children growing up and leaving home to become students, as has just happened to us with Chloë. And all the peculiarities of life – the snarl-ups and delights – which are perhaps odder for us because of the remoteness of where we live.

Of course, in Spain, where I have recently been published, they really can't put my books under travel, so they put them under 'Self-Help', along with books on the spiritual path and harvesting your inner energy. Strange bedfellows.

You've become a bestseller in Spain over the past couple of years. Have your neighbours now read the books?

When Driving Over Lemons was published, Domingo – my nearest neighbour and the book's true hero – got his partner Antonia to translate and read it to him… but only the bits in which he appeared. Later, when it came out in Spanish, he read a chapter every night

before going to sleep. Of course, he never mentioned this to me, though he told Antonia that he enjoyed the book.

But the funny thing about Domingo is that he is not Domingo at all – he has a quite different name. For many months, as I was writing the book, I would tell him that I was writing a book in which he appeared as a major character. Would it be okay to use his name or would he rather I change it? 'Me da igual,' he would say in his typically Alpujarran way; 'It's all the same to me.' I was pleased because I felt I had created an affectionate portrait of a good friend, and it felt right to use his real name.

Well, I asked him again and again, just to make sure, and each time received the same assurance. And then, at the last possible moment, he came up to the house, very animated, and said: 'Cristóbal, I've been talking to somebody who knows about these things and he tells me that I could get into a lot of trouble as a result of this book – legal problems and family problems and God knows what else. So I want my name changed.'

I could see that somebody in a bar had been spreading a bit of mala leche – 'bad milk' – as the

Lemons and Parrots in Spanish

Spanish put it. I was a bit sorry about it, but he was adamant, so I set about changing the names of all his relatives and his farm, and so on. Of course, anybody local reading the book would still know exactly who Domingo was, but he didn't seem to mind that. As far as he was concerned, as long as the character was called a different name, it wasn't officially him.

Then, as time marched on, my-friend-aka-Domingo, inspired and encouraged by Antonia (who, of course, isn't called Antonia), took up sculpture and started making a bit of a name for himself by creating the most dazzling bronze figures of animals. By this time Lemons was selling like hot buns. And so he decided to go for an alias – and to my great delight chose to call himself, for artistic purposes, Domingo.

What about your other neighbours? What was the reaction like from them?

There was a bit of everything. One woman in Orgiva complained very publicly that I had not painted an accurate picture of the people of the town, 'because we don't eat chickens' heads'. Apparently *everything else was fine: it was just the culinary stuff that stuck in her throat, so to speak. Well, having comprehensively researched the subject of chicken head cuisine, I can say authoritatively that some Orgiveños do and some of them don't. I know this because I've had the pleasure of sharing the odd chicken's head myself.*

The locals in general began to register the success of the book because people started to turn up clutching copies. This gave a bit of a boost to the drooping Orgiva economy, which made me popular with the café owners. Antonio Galindo, who owns the bakery, a café, two bars and a discoteca, embraced me publicly in the high street and said I had turned his fortunes around. So that felt good. And not long after, I was honoured to be the recipient of the Manzanilla Prize for Services to 'Convivencia y Turismo' (which loosely translates as 'harmony between cultures and tourism'). This singular honour was manifested in the form of a tin sculpture of a manzanilla (camomile) plant – what the Spanish often call a pongo (as in the phrase 'Dónde demonios lo pongo?', which means 'Where the devil do I put this?').

News of the award got into the national paper, El Pais, where it was seen by an anthropology professor, who then published a scathing letter stating that I had contributed more to the dilution and demise of Spanish culture than any other single person. That shook me a bit, and a few days later I was stopped on the road into town by Rafael, who farms olives, oranges and vegetables in Tijola, our nearest village. 'I have just read your book, Cristóbal,' he boomed. I hung my head to await the worst. 'You are the greatest writer of the Alpujarra,' he intoned. 'You are...', he paused searching for a very particular epithet, 'a Rambo of the mind'.

It's the nicest critical review I've ever had.

So is it the people, as much as the farm, that keep you in Andalucía?

Without a doubt. We've been made incredibly welcome here. And the Spanish rural way of life suits us. But the land has got into our blood, too. When you spend twenty-odd years building and gardening and planting trees on a plot of land, you develop a connection that runs deeper than the normal sense of 'home'. All those repetitive chores of tilling, sowing and harvesting exert a subtle influence that affects the essence of who you are. And if you believe that you are what you eat, then we've become Andaluz through and through, since for two decades now we have turned the earth and pulled up vegetables, picked fruit from the trees on the terraces we've tended, collected and eaten the eggs from the chickens whose care is the first imperative of every day, and eaten the sheep that graze amongst the wild plants that grow on the hills around the house.

And there's the water, too. Nearly eighty percent of us, give or take a few bottles of wine, is made up from the water from our very own spring – I've wondered a little what we look like inside, given the amount of limescale at the bottom of our kettle. But I feel sure this place has seeped into us. We've been formed by all the little griefs and agonies, and triumphs and delights, that have peppered our lives since we moved here.

So how could you ever leave a place like this? How could you sell it? How could you put up with estate agents tramping around it with notebooks and snooty clients pointing out loudly how sub-standard and ill-conceived everything is? El Valero was never a buying and selling property. We didn't buy it as an investment; we bought it as a home. Which is lucky because it may well be the only property in Spain worth less than it cost twenty years before... and I'm glad because I've never wanted to sell the place anyway.

What do you think Spaniards in general see in the books? You'd think the humour is peculiarly English.

I thought so, too, and the books weren't published here for some years. But it turns out that the Spaniards find just the same bits funny as the British. They enjoy the way the rural Spanish are portrayed. I've had all sorts of people coming up, some of whom I didn't know could even read, wanting to tell me the bits they find funny. That said, the urban Spaniards think that we are completely bonkers. Our farm – and the Alpujarras – is very far from the spotless way that most modern Spaniards like to live.

Translation's a funny thing, though. I was interviewed by two young Taiwanese journalists, who explained to me what a humorous book the Chinese had found Driving Over Lemons. Out of curiosity I asked them if they could translate the title. I know a bit of Chinese and it struck me as peculiarly long. They scratched their heads, then said Sheep's Cheese and Guitar Heaven: a Ridiculous Drama of Andalucia.

What did Chloë think about the books?

Well, she was mystified by the English title! I have a vivid memory of her worried face when she first heard us discussing it. 'Driving Over Lemons – an Octopus in Andalucia... what on earth does that mean?' I think she was about seven at the time. So ever since then I have been the 'Octopus in Andalucia'.

She once said she would much rather I wrote novels: to her, my books are really just diary pieces and too familiar to be interesting. But secretly I think she gets quite a kick out of my success. A few months ago, she went to open a bank account in Granada, and as she handed across her ID card, the woman behind the counter exclaimed, 'Ay, Chloë Stewart... you must be the girl in the book! Ay, how I loved the book.' It's no bad thing to be known at the bank.

Do you think Chlöe – or Ana – might write her own version of life at El Valero one day?

No. Ana has not the remotest desire to write, although she types with style and wit. (And has just reminded me that she might still go into competition with a plot for a 'body-stripper book'). It's hard to say with Chloë; I hope that we've given her a childhood that could give her something to write about. But right now she's a university student – and has flown the nest. She shares a flat in Granada and, as you might expect, has euphorically embraced urban life. Nothing is more likely to induce an enthusiasm for all things urban than a country childhood.

So now there's just Ana and me again on the farm, rattling like peas in a drum. This has been a tough rite of passage, and nobody tells you about it. You spend eighteen years living your life around, and for, your offspring in the most unimaginably close and intimate way... and then they're gone. There's nobody to wake in the morning and make sandwiches and breakfast for before heading off to the school bus.

Of course, we get a lot of pleasure from Chloë's happiness in her new life, and we're proud of her independence and her making her way in the world. But it's an odd stage, nonetheless.

What is the menagerie cast these days? You've got the sheep, and chickens...

It's the same old crew really, with occasional losses due to 'natural wastage', which of course is where I'm headed myself. The top of the pecking order is the wife, my favourite member of the menagerie, along with Chloë – who still, I think, sees this as her home. Then there's there the unspeakable parrot, Porca, Ana's lieutenant and familiar, who arrived by chance to make his home with us about nine years ago. This creature is one of the villains of my second book, A Parrot in the Pepper Tree.

The parrot dominates the five cats, who range far and wide on the farm, feasting abundantly on rats. Then there are two dogs: Big, a hairy terrier we found abandoned by the road, and Bumble, an enormous and amiable mongrel, whose function is to monopolise the space before the fire and bark at intruders. And since we're so remote and there are few visitors, he and Big keep in practice by barking all night long at the boar and foxes and other nocturnal creatures. Which makes it hard to sleep.

The dozen or so chickens earn their keep by providing us, as you might expect, with eggs. And we've got a colony of fan-tailed doves, which are on the increase again after a winter when a pair of Bonelli's eagles reduced their number from around a hundred to just seven. They are more cautious now and don't go outside much. Paco, my pigeon-fancier friend and telephone engineer, is going to get me some stock from Busquistar, up in the high Alpujarra. Apparently those pigeons know how to deal with eagles, because the crags and valleys up there are thick with them.

And finally there's the sheep, and there always will be the sheep, for I cannot imagine the dull silence of the farm without the bongling of the bells and the bleating of lambs. They provide us with the most delicious meat and, take it from me, eating home-grown lamb is one of the best treats of country life. The flock keeps the grass beneath the orange and olive trees neatly trimmed like a lush lawn. And then they range far and wide on the hills above the house, grazing on the woody aromatic plants that grow there: rosemary, thyme, broom, anthyllis, wild asparagus. At night they return to the stable, and there they copiously deposit the little heaps of beads and berries that, trodden into the straw, make the rich dung which goes to nourish the fruit and vegetables and, at one remove, us. The whole, wonderful circular ecological system.

It sounds like farming is still a passion, even if you've become more of a writer than a farmer.

I've loved farming since I discovered it at twenty-one, but if truth be told I'm not very good at it. Maybe it is a vocational gift, like medicine or music, neither of which I'm particularly good at, either. I long for the model farm, but under my care weeds seem to get the upper hand, the livestock seize every chance to destroy the plants, and every agricultural villain seems to be stalking me – mosaic virus, red spider, scale insect, aphids, blossom-end rot. You name it.

Orange trees and sheep – the mainstay of the El Valero eco-system

So it is lucky that, in terms of making a living, I've gravitated to becoming a writer. Albeit a writer who spends a lot more time farming than writing. If you've spent your life doing physical work it's hard to take entirely seriously the idea of sitting down for a day's work at a computer. I still do a bit of shearing, too, which is something I am quite good at – and which nobody else around here can do, except my-friend-aka-Domingo. So at least there's something that enables me to hold my head up in an agricultural way.

I made a living out of shearing for thirty years, but it's hard when you hit your fifities, and now I only do a few days a year – my own sheep, Domingo's, and one or two other jobs in the village. I dread these shearing days because I know what a physical effort it's going to be. But when I actually get down and stuck in, it's like dancing a dance you knew and loved long ago. Also, I get to see my handiwork year-round, idling on the hillsides, happily scratching themselves.

And it means that people still know me around the town as the Englishman who shears sheep. I know most of the farmers and they'll come and holler into my ear in bars. So I've got two different kinds of local identities. The sheep man and the book man.

You originally had a peasant farm with no running water, no electricity, no phone for miles around. Are things now very different?

We still rely on solar power, but more and better – enough, in fact, to run a freezer, which is a boon. Meantime, our house becomes ever more ecological. We've just installed 'green roofs' – a flat roof, lined and covered with soil and drought-resistant plants and grasses – by means of which insulation we have managed to raise the winter temperature in our bedroom to a comfortable six degrees. And we've got a solar water heating system that I'm currently working on.

If it weren't for the great thug of a four-wheel drive parked on the track, our carbon footprint would be virtually nothing at all. That has become of the utmost importance to us... and, at the risk of sounding sanctimonious, so it should be to all of us.

You care a great deal about environmental issues. Do you think your views have become more trenchant since moving to Spain?

—

I'm not so sure about that. I was a pretty trenchant ecologist long before I moved to Spain. But one of the amazing things about writing a successful book is that people suddenly start to listen to what you have to say. This is rather gratifying, as you may imagine, but it's not that you are saying anything different. It's just that you no longer have to raise your voice to be heard. I think it's the duty of anybody who finds themselves with access to the public ear to use that platform to expound ideas for reducing the sum total of human damage and misery.

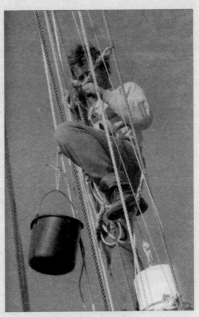

Up the mast during an epic trip across the Atlantic, told in Chris's new book, Three Ways to Capsize a Boat

The building of a dam casts a shadow over both *Driving Over Lemons* and its sequel, *A Parrot in the Pepper Tree*. How did that work out?

—

Well, as you can see, we're not underwater yet. By great good luck, the authorities ended up building a dam much lower than their original plan, so unless they knock it down and start again the water level will never affect our farm. It is a sediment trap rather than a reservoir, so it's filling up at a great rate with rich alluvial silt, which is wonderful for spreading on the land. It's beautiful, too, the way the river meanders amongst the banks of mud, and there's an aquatic ecosystem developing there, with ducks and herons and legions of frogs.

Talking of water, in your latest book, *Three Ways to Capsize a Boat*, you leave the land altogether to recall some epic and extremely funny seafaring adventures.

I'm glad you enjoyed it. Yes, Capsize is a book that I had to get out of my system. It seems odd, but I found myself writing snippets of it throughout the last ten years, maybe even longer. It was as if my mind was fixating on the sea. In buying El Valero I had to make a choice between the mountains and the coast. It's curious how being born and raised in inland Sussex I should come to see these two types of landscape – neither of them prominent around Horsham – as somehow fundamental to my wellbeing.

I chose the mountains, and have lived in them very contentedly for twenty years, but I do have a yearning for the sea, which comes from my early thirties when I had a brief life-changing encounter. It all started when I talked my way into a job skippering a yacht in Greece – without knowing how

to sail. So I had to learn, and one thing led to another and I ended up crewing across the North Atlantic. It marked me for life. Writing about it was fun. I didn't have any notes, because back in those days I didn't have the remotest intention of becoming a writer, but many of the experiences I had were so vivid that they all came flooding back. It was a great pleasure, too, thinking myself back to the sea, reliving it in a sense.

The trouble is that it has opened that old wound, and I am now to be found at any hour of the day or night lost in a reverie, staring at pictures of wooden sailing boats and wondering if I ever might own one.

My plan, a new gauntlet that I am throwing down for myself, is to sail around the world before I finally slip away. Not with all the ballyhoo and fol de rol of round-the-world racing and record-breaking. I'm not that sort. For me it's a matter of ambling slowly around it and wondering at all the terrible, immeasurable beauty of it. Ana indulges these crazed notions with diplomacy and tolerance. I have suggested that she may be permitted a pot of basil on the stern rail in lieu of a farm and garden – and, I suppose, having the beastly parrot along would be most appropriate.

It sounds like you were pretty smitten with the Greek islands, too. You enthusiastically describe sailing to Spetses, before embarking on your Atlantic adventures.

There's a whole lot to be said for Greece: it has the mountains and the sea in the most glorious combination, as well as the gorgeous influence of Byzantium and the Levant. And its great advantage over Spain

is that the Greeks have so far not destroyed the beauty of their coasts and islands. If they do, the old gods will never forgive them.

I could have happily lived in Greece, with its sea and mountains, and the olives and oranges and the Mediterranean climate to go with it. But I always had a romance about Spain, its language, music and culture, and the great cities of Sevilla, Granada and Córdoba. So I have no terrible regrets.

One final question that you are always being asked is your role in Genesis. You were in the

Even the Spanish seem obsessed with Genesis – and my schoolboy career as their drummer. I'm on the right here, pouting next to Peter Gabriel.

original band. Can you tell us more about this?

I wrote about this a bit in A Parrot in the Pepper Tree, where I confess that I was never a very good drummer. The other members of the band very sensibly threw me out when I was just seventeen, having played on just two not very good songs on the first album. So I narrowly missed rock stardom. Actually, with me on board I fear that they would have got nowhere – and, once Phil Collins took my place, they did rather well for themselves, for which I'm delighted.

Our paths cross from time to time, and I'm always surprised by how they've managed to surf the vicissitudes of celebrity life and come through unscathed. I get the vaguest sense of it even here in Spain, where Genesis have a huge following. I emerged one day from an interview in a recording studio in Madrid to find no fewer than four young recording engineers lined up to shake the hand of a founder member of the great band.

If you could do it all over again, would you still have thrust a wad of notes into Pedro's hands and bought El Valero?

Without a moment's hesitation. And, if I'd known things were going to turn out the way they did, I'd have given him double the asking price. If I'd had the money, of course, which I didn't. I don't think there's anything better you can do in the middle of your life than to pick it up and shake it around a bit. Do something different, live somewhere different, talk another language. All that keeps your destiny on the move and keeps your brain from becoming addled. So there you have it – maybe the Spanish are right and Driving Over Lemons really is a self-help book.